STUDY GUIDE AND UNIT MASTERY PROGRAM
by John G. Carlson and Rita L. Atkinson to accompany

Introduction to
PSYCHOLOGY

TENTH EDITION

Rita L. Atkinson
Richard C. Atkinson
Edward E. Smith
Daryl J. Bem

HARCOURT BRACE JOVANOVICH, PUBLISHERS

San Diego   New York   Chicago   Austin   Washington, D. C.
London   Sydney   Tokyo   Toronto

Printed in the United States of America

ISBN: 0-15-543693-7

To the Instructor

The *Study Guide* is designed to assist students in mastering the content of the introductory course in Psychology whether the course is taught by conventional lecture methods or by unit mastery methods. For students who are in a unit mastery taught course, a separate introduction is available prior to the first chapter in the *Study Guide*. For instructors using a unit mastery approach, a detailed introduction, rationale, and suggested methods are included in the related *Instructor's Guide*.

In our preparation of the *Study Guide*, consideration was given to three major difficulties students often encounter: First, they may be uncertain about what to learn from each chapter--how to distinguish crucial material from less important details. Second, they may fail to recognize notable figures in the field or to learn the meanings of specific psychological terms and concepts. Third, they may have no satisfactory way of knowing how well they have mastered the material until after an examination (which often is too late).

The four or five sections of each chapter in this *Study Guide* have been designed to help students in each of these areas. The first section is a list of learning objectives to help students focus on what they should learn from the chapter. Next in most chapters is a section containing important names and contributions of selected individuals identifed in the chapter. Following is a section asking for the important terms and details in the chapter. Students should be able to provide brief identifications for each of these. Items missed then become an object for further study. (A key is provided at the end of each chapter.) The next section, dealing with more complex ideas and concepts, leads students through the text chapter by highlighting conceptual material, theories, research, and major conclusions, but excluding Critical Discussions. You may wish to focus on the latter in class. (There are two levels of questions on ideas and concepts: On one level, about 60 percent of the items refer to "basic ideas and concepts." These are asterisked and designed to draw attention to the chapter's most essential points. On the other level, the remaining 40 percent of the items refer to important but less essential ideas and concepts. In a conventionally-taught course, it is left for you to decide the level of detail to which you would like your students to attend and to inform them at the start of the term. In a unit-mastery taught course, however, the quizzes that are furnished with the program assume that students have dealt with *all* of the ideas and concepts items.) Finally, two multiple-choice sample quizzes (and answer keys) provide students with an opportunity to practice taking exams and, at the same time, help point out their areas of weakness.

To All Students:
How to Use this Guide

The *Study Guide* is designed to help you in several ways: It tells you what you should learn from each chapter; it introduces the names, terms, and concepts you will encounter in the text; and it provides examination questions that will enable you to determine just how much you have learned. Note that the pages of the *Guide* are perforated to allow you to tear out selected sections for ease of use with your text.

Each chapter in the *Study Guide* parallels one in the text, and there are four or five sections for each chapter. The first section lists the Learning Objectives--the fundamental ideas and facts you should learn from the chapter. After you have looked over the Objectives, take the time to read and enjoy the text chapter your instructor has assigned. That way you will have the opportunity to gain perspectives on the area of psychology presented in *Introduction to Psychology* before you become involved in the details of preparation for further learning and examinations. You may want to refer back to each objective after you have covered the appropriate section in the text. Or you may prefer to complete the chapter and then see if you have mastered all the objectives. In any event, the learning objectives cover the important ideas in each chapter; they include topics you will probably be expected to know on examinations.

From the Names section and from the Vocabulary and Details section of the chapters you will acquire an acquaintance with the key figures, important terms, and specific facts presented in the text. (Answer keys are at the back of each chapter in the *Study Guide*.) Although these items are meant to be completed after you read the text and before more in-depth studying, they also may be profitably used later as a review before examinations. There is probably not sufficient room in the blank space within every item to allow you to write the answers. Our intention is that you will attempt to answer each item on a separate piece of paper or in the margin of your *Study Guide*. That way, you can cover the answers and use these items for self-review before examinations, making the attempt to state each answer before looking at the correct response. The list of terms and concepts may seem long for some chapters, but if you learn them all you will have a good grasp of the material that is likely to appear on examinations. It is a good idea to complete these sections of your *Study Guide* before turning to the Ideas and Concepts section because many of the terms are used in the context of questions in that section.

A word of warning: The Vocabulary and Details items cannot serve as a substitute for the text chapters. They do not treat all the ideas presented in the text.

It is from the Ideas and Concepts section of each chapter that you will gain insight into theories and conceptual material in psychology, categories or outlines of text information, methods and results of experiments, and

v

relationships or distinctions between fine points. (You will also encounter additional terms that are best defined in the context of conceptual material--these are generally italicized terms and printed in boldface type when they are especially notable.) There are two levels of Ideas and Concepts items. The ones that are marked with an asterisk (about 60 percent of the items) are the basic or main points; the remaining items deal with less essential material. It is for your instructor to decide the level of comprehension he or she expects in the course, determining whether you use some or all Ideas and Concepts items.

It is *not* intended that you write out every answer to the Ideas and Concepts questions, although you may occasionally find tables or blanks convenient to complete in the *Study Guide*. To write out every answer would be a very time-consuming and probably unnecessary task. Rather, it will be to your advantage to prepare for examinations by marking your text in some way--say, with a highlighter or by underlining--the portions that are covered by these items. (Note that the Ideas and Concepts items do not cover the Critical Discussions. It is left to your instructor to decide whether to include this material in class discussions or examinations.)

Finally, turn to the Sample Quiz sections of the *Study Guide* and answer all the questions on the first quiz. Check your answers against the answer key. For questions on which you made an error go back to the text and review the appropriate material. Then turn to the second quiz for further self-evaluation of your mastery of the chapter.

To summarize, there are four or five sections in each chapter of the *Study Guide:* Learning Objectives, Names (in some chapters), Vocabulary and Details, Ideas and Concepts, and Sample Quizzes. First look over the learning objectives, read the chapter, and then proceed to the names, vocabulary, and concepts, and finally to the quizzes. These sections are designed to help you gain perspective, identify the names and special terms in psychology, to understand the conceptual material in the text, and to allow you to evaluate your learning. Remember, however, that the *Study Guide* is designed as a supplement, not a substitute, for the text. Used properly, the *Study Guide* will enhance your comprehension of the text.

vi

To The Unit Mastery Student

ASSUMPTIONS OF LEARNING

A wise man once likened students to three products of nature: a stone, a sponge, and a spark. Learners who are like "stones" tend to resist learning; new ideas and knowledge tend to "bounce off" and leave no impact. "Sponge" learners soak up knowledge readily, yet retain it passively in its original form. "Spark" learners, however, *actively* pursue knowledge, applying themselves in the process of learning and transforming the knowledge they acquire through ongoing dialogue and interaction with the knowledge source. Active learning reaps maximum rewards and benefits for students, and it is the process emphasized in your *Study Guide*.

In accordance with suggestions made by Carl Rogers, a well-known psychologist whose views are discussed in your text, several assumptions underlie the active learning model used in this *Guide*:

1. **Significant learning takes place when the subject matter is seen to have relevance for one's own purposes.** In other words, a person learns best those things which he or she perceives are involved in maintaining or enhancing themselves. To the degree that you are interested in and committed to the study of psychology--the useful science of the individual--you will come to know well a body of knowledge about the subject.

2. **Learning can proceed more rapidly in a supportive environment.** In an environment where personal security is assured and there is little or no threat, differentiation of information can take place, partial meanings can be explored and put together in a variety of ways, and understanding will develop. As you will see, the process used in the *Unit Mastery Program* allows you to explore material in a more predictable environment with fewer sources of anxiety and worry.

3. **Learning is facilitated when students direct the learning process.** When you choose your own directions, decide your own course of action, determine your own rate of study and learning, and benefit from the consequences of these choices, then significant learning is maximized. This form of participative learning is much more effective and rewarding than is passive, externally directed learning.

4. **Significant learning is acquired through doing.** The process utilized in this *Study Guide* is action-oriented. You will participate through reading, thinking, writing, answering questions, correcting, and reviewing. This is *not* a passive process; rather it is a behavioral and experiential process in which learning is sparked.

This *Unit Mastery Program* is designed to help you become a master in the art of active learning, to develop such "cognitive" skills as conceptualization, memorization, analysis, comparison, and synthesis. The program will also help you by providing a mechanism for consistent, ongoing feedback. Feedback, as a learning tool, is important in letting you know immediately if you are on the right track. Consider feedback to be a "cue" to tell you that you are on course, or that you need to go back and review the material again, rather than just a way of determining if you have the "right answer." In other words, think of feedback as part of the learning process, rather than an end in itself.

Finally, beyond training in the "active" approach to learning, this *Guide* is intended to help you explore the fascinating world of psychology, to gain insight as to how psychology is part and parcel of your everyday life, and to afford you a glimpse of how psychological principles impact on your daily interactions with others.

THE UNIT MASTERY METHOD

Objectives of the Program

Unit mastery learning is a positive alternative to traditional methods of college instruction. The very name implies a shift in the concept of instruction--from mere learning to "mastery" learning. This notion means that instruction is segmented into meaningful "units," each of which are studied until a high rate of competency, or "mastery," is achieved. Mastery learning also implies that you can retake examinations on material until you have mastered the information. You move on in the program when you have achieved mastery over the current unit.

Some of the other characteristics and benefits of the mastery learning approach are these:

1. **Objectives of the course are clearly outlined and the criteria for mastery are clearly defined.** Your final grade is self-selected, in the form of the number of units you complete by the end of the semester. You know in advance what you need to do for a particular grade, and you know where you are going and how you are doing as you progress through the term.

2. **Feedback is a fundamental part of the program.** In the *Unit Mastery Program* you are given timely and specific feedback on your performance. After you have taken a quiz, the course staff will most likely grade your work immediately. This can be an important reward for having completed a chapter. Additionally, the grader will have text references available for each quiz question, and can refer

you to the relevant sections of the text so you can look back for information and clarification. Review after a quiz is a key part of the mastery learning process. This "look back" can help you determine what material you missed, misunderstood, or did not grasp entirely. An advantage of doing this immediately is that you have the chance to consult with the teaching staff right then and there, while questions are still fresh in your mind.

3. **You select the pace of learning and you determine the rate of progress you wish to make.** You are tested on a certain amount of material when you decide that you are ready, so that external pressures are kept to a minimum. However, it is important for you to remember that while you have a tremendous amount of freedom in this program, you also carry the major responsibility for learning. It is your job to pace yourself so that you can complete the course on time.

4. **Frequent personal contact with teaching staff is built into the program.** In contrast to some traditional college instruction, there are frequent opportunities for interpersonal contact with your instructor and teaching staff in the *Unit Mastery Program.* When you take quizzes, there is greater availability of instructional staff to assist you with immediate feedback and individualized help if you need it. Some of the course assistants may be former students who have completed a unit mastery course. They can provide both knowledge and emotional support, having been through the program themselves.

Concerns and Cautions

In the *Unit Mastery Program,* there are a number of quizzes for each chapter. Each quiz covers somewhat different aspects of each chapter of the text. For this reason, you should not anticipate that you can pass a second quiz on the chapter by merely reviewing the errors you made on the first quiz. You may need to restudy the entire chapter or selected portions before taking another quiz. There may be times when you find that you miss the mastery criterion for several quizzes in a row. While this can be disheartening, try to keep in mind that **all** students, even the most well-prepared ones, may have difficulty from time to time. It is best if you do not try to compete with or compare your performance to that of friends or classmates. Rather, find a pace and level of comfort that works for you while still allowing

viii

you to attain the goal you have set for yourself. Making mistakes is part of the learning process, not a mark of failure.

A caution: Procrastination is a major barrier for students who are enrolled in courses using mastery learning methods. Because exam schedules are not pre-fixed and announced, they are determined by you, according to your level of readiness. This approach demands a level of maturity, planning, and self-discipline from you that may be new and unfamiliar. While you enjoy great personal freedom in this approach, you also must assume a great deal of personal responsibility for the outcomes. It is not a good idea to wait several weeks before taking your first quiz, nor is it wise to take two or three quizzes in a row, and then wait several weeks to start again. Putting off studying and test-taking until the last few weeks of the semester can have serious results in terms of your course grade, in addition to the emotional stress and anxiety you will feel when you realize that you cannot "catch up" after all. One strategy that is recommended is to plan to study a fixed period of time each week. If for some reason you are unable to meet your goal for any one week, then extra study time should be scheduled for the week following. This will help keep you on track and up to date.

Some Outcomes for You

By now you may be wondering about your ability to fulfill the requirements for a course using the unit mastery approach. However, there are a number of positive outcomes for the student who studies conscientiously and completes the assigned units.

1. You know what is expected of you. The goals and criteria for course completion and grades are stated up front. You are in a position of certainty at all times, so concern about "How am I doing?" and performance anxiety should be at a minimum.

2. Unit mastery instruction allows you to self-pace your tests. This approach helps you schedule your exams when you feel most prepared and allows you to pace your quizzes to fit into what else may be going on in your life--for instance, other course exams, social obligations, or illness. This experience can serve to help you become more effective in your studying in general, with the result that you may find yourself acquiring better study habits across all your coursework.

3. The ongoing testing and immediate feedback creates a reward schedule that contributes to a sense of success and confidence. Because the opportunity to retake quizzes and obtain help from the staff are built into the program, test-taking anxiety and fear of failure should be greatly reduced as you make your way through the course. Moreover, as you progress through the assigned chapters, you will experience a systematic improvement in your studying and test-taking skills. The actual process of working through material using the unit mastery approach has benefits beyond mere practice and repetition.

4. A sense of "self-efficacy" develops as you work through the *Unit Mastery Program*. As you progress through the term, you begin to experience a sense of personal control and competence that is a direct result of your own actions, decisions, and performance. You will learn more and you will know you are learning more. Perhaps this sense of personal "mastery" over your own educational environment is the most powerful outcome of the *Unit Mastery Program*.

BEGINNING THE PROCESS

The initial or introductory study of any discipline requires a two-pronged approach to knowledge: the first is the study of basic vocabulary and the basic facts of the field, as well as knowing the major contributors to the subject matter. The second focus of knowledge is the study of the more complex ideas and concepts of the field, the pulling together of larger units of information that have meaning beyond the individual facts and specifics. These two components, basic "vocabulary and details" and "ideas and concepts," form the main structure for the design of this *Guide*. Careful study and attention to *both* components will reap maximum rewards for you as you learn about the field of psychology.

Mastering Vocabulary and Details

What are they? The Vocabulary and Details section includes terms and language specific to the field and basic facts of the discipline. (Prior to this section, the names of major researchers and theorists who have contributed to the field may also be called for, depending on the focus of the particular chapter.)

When and how do I fill out this section of the guide? For most students, the best time to go through the guide is right after reading the entire chapter. However, the *Study Guide* is segmented into subsections corresponding to the text, so you can read your text and complete portions of the *Guide* at the same time, rather than attempting all of the questions at once, depending on your preference.

Complete each blank before going on to the next one. (As noted in *To all Students,* it may be best to write your answers on a separate sheet of paper or in the margin of the *Guide.*) It is important that you do the items in order because one item may contain material that assumes you have answered a previous item. If you cannot think of the answer, or if you discover later that your answer does not match the one in the key, go back to the page of your text that is referred to in the item. After you have completed your answers, refer to the key at the end of each chapter to check your answers against the correct ones. While it is important to answer items correctly the first time through, **the critical thing is that you understand the items when you are finished with the process.** Merely finding the right answer in the key and filling in the correct blank of the guide is a much less effective way to develop your understanding of the material.

Why should I fill out this section of the guide? Working through the Vocabulary and Details section of the *Study Guide* systematically and completely will help you identify areas of strength and weakness, thereby helping you target terms and details needing more study. Moreover, approximately one-half of your chapter quiz items will be drawn from the Vocabulary and Details items.

Mastering Ideas and Concepts

What are they? Concepts are abstract ideas that help to generalize specific units of information. As discussed in your text, ideas and concepts are important for you to know because they are the melding of many bits of information into a larger whole, which has meaning of its own. This larger unit of knowledge helps us understand and grasp meanings that go beyond concrete, specific knowledge, and helps us see patterns in everyday life.

When and how do I fill out this section of the guide? It is probably a good idea to complete this section of the guide after you have done the Vocabulary and Details portion. A strong foundation of basic knowledge will help you work through this section of the guide; building on that knowledge will assist you in completing this section of the guide.

The items that are found in this section may require you that you answer essay questions, fill in charts and tables, or complete diagrams. Some items will ask you to remember explicit information from the chapter, while others will call for higher order thinking processes such as comparing and contrasting ideas, generating new examples of a particular concept, or integrating new material with information you already have. Because you are being asked to analyze and synthesize material, rather than merely to recall information, there is no answer key for this section of the guide. However, text page numbers are given for reference to the section of the chapter where related material is presented. Refer to these text pages for feedback regarding your answers.

Why should I fill out this section of the guide? The main point of this section is to provide you with a mechanism for organizing material into a coherent whole, while at the same time relating the parts of the whole to each other. This process helps new information "fit into" a meaningful framework. You will learn in your text that this is an important aspect of long-term memory. Approximately one-half of the Unit Quiz items will be taken from the Ideas and Concepts section of the guide, including items without asterisks.

Sample Quizzes

As discussed earlier, self-evaluation in a "safe" environment is a major component of the active learning process. Sample quizzes are provided in the *Study Guide* for you to test your mastery of the material you have read. Two Sample Quizzes are provided for each chapter. Taking the time to go through these quizzes and checking your answers with the key at the end of the chapter gives you the opportunity to assess your level of knowledge immediately after working through the *Study Guide* sections, and gives you a chance to determine how much material you have retained over time. These quizzes also help you assess your readiness level for taking the Unit Quizzes in class.

Contents

Each chapter in this *Guide* consists of Learning Objectives, Vocabulary and Details, Ideas and Concepts, two Sample Quizzes, and an answer Key. Some chapters contain important Names.

Nature of Psychology

Learning Objectives

1. Be able to name and define the five perspectives in psychology described in the text. Know what characterizes each, and how each approach differs from the other four.

2. Be familiar with the historical roots of the biological, behavioral, and cognitive perspectives and the way in which contemporary versions of these approaches differ from earlier ones.

3. Know what distinguishes the experimental method from other methods of scientific observation. Be able to define, and to differentiate between, an independent variable and a dependent variable.

4. Know what is involved in the designing of an experiment. Be able to define, and to differentiate between, an experimental group and a control group.

5. Understand the use of measurement in experimental design, including the use of sample means and tests of the significance of a difference between means.

6. Know when correlation is an alternative to experimentation and understand its advantages and disadvantages.

7. Know the meaning of differences in the size and the arithmetic sign of a coefficient of correlation. Be able to show, with an example, why correlation does not establish cause-and-effect relationships.

8. Be familiar with direct, survey, and case-history methods of observation. Understand when and why each is used and the advantages and disadvantages of each.

9. Be familiar with the different fields of specialization within psychology.

10. Be familiar with the new field of cognitive science and the disciplines that are relevant to this area of research.

Names

1. The view that behavior should be the sole subject matter of psychology was maintained in the early 1900s by the American psychologist _____. (10)

2. At about the same time, the European physician _____ was developing the psychoanalytic conception of human behavior that blended unconscious cognitive processes with biologically-based instincts. (12)

Vocabulary and Details

SCOPE OF PSYCHOLOGY

1. Psychology can be defined as the _____. (6)

PERSPECTIVES IN PSYCHOLOGY

1. The nineteenth century "cognitive" perspective made use of data obtained through an individual's observation and recording of his or her own perceptions, thoughts, and feelings, in the method called _____. (9)

2. The _____ perspective in psychology seeks to specify the _____ (electrical and chemical) processes that underlie behavior and mental processes. (9)

3. By contrast, the _____ approach in psychology studies the activities of an organism that can be directly _____. (10)

4. The position taken by the behavioral perspective, termed _____, gave rise to the study of eliciting stimuli, responses, and rewards and punishers for behavior; the offspring of this approach is called _____ psychology, or _____ for short. (11)

5. The _____ perspective in psychology is concerned with _____, such as, perceiving, remembering, reasoning, decision making, and problem solving. (11)

6. In the _____ approach, the basic assumption is that much human behavior is caused or motivated by _____ processes, that is, by beliefs, fears, and desires of which a person is unaware. (12-13)

7. The _____ perspective focuses on subjective experience--the individual's personal view of events, that is, his or her _____. (13)

8. Some phenomenological theories are said to be _____ in the sense that they emphasize qualities that are unique to humans (as opposed to animals), including the drive toward _____. (13)

9. Reducing psychological concepts to biological ones is the kind of explanation called _____. (14)

METHODS OF PSYCHOLOGY

1. The term "scientific," as used in the definition of psychology above, means that the research methods of psychology are _____--that is, they do not favor one theory

2   Chapter 1

or hypothesis over another--and they are _____, in that they allow for repetition of observations and results. (15)

2. In the prototypical scientific method, called the _____ method, the researcher (a) carefully introduces _____ of variables (conditions), and (b) takes measurements to discover _____. (16)

3. A _____ is defined as something that can vary or occur with different values. (16)

4. The _____ is manipulated by the experimenter independently of what a subject does, whereas the _____ is a measure of the subject's behavior; we say that the latter is a _____ (dependent upon) the former. (16)

5. The term _____ refers to the procedure used in collecting data. (17)

6. An experimental design might consist of a single independent variable that is present for some subjects, in the _____, and absent for other subjects, in the _____. (18)

7. Alternatively, an experimental design may involve the manipulation of several independent variables at the same time; this type of experiment is termed _____. (18)

8. _____ means a procedure for assigning numbers to different levels, amounts, or sizes of a variable. (18)

9. The discipline that deals with sampling data from a population and drawing inferences about the population from the sample is called _____. (18)

10. The most common statistic is the _____, the arithmetic average of a set of values. (18)

11. When the experimental method is not practical, the _____ may be applied to determine whether some variable that is not under experimental control is associated or _____ with another variable. (19)

12. The statistic that is used in the correlational method is the _____, symbolized by the letter _____, defined as an estimate of the degree to which two variables are related. (19)

13. A correlation coefficient is a number between _____ and _____. No relation is indicated by _____; as the absolute value of r goes from 0 to 1, the strength of the relation _____ (increases/decreases); a perfect relation is indicated by _____. (19)

14. If r is preceded by a + sign, the variables are said to be _____ (positively/negatively) related; if r is preceded by a - sign, the variables are _____ (positively/negatively) related. (19-20)

15. We may carefully record human or animal behavior as it occurs naturally in the observational method termed _____. (21)

16. In another (indirect) observational method, termed the _____, psychologists may use questionnaires or interviews. (22)

17. In yet a third type of observational method, indirect observations may be made of individuals, groups, or institutions by obtaining biographies, or _____, for scientific use. (22-23)

PROFESSIONS IN PSYCHOLOGY

1. The use of experimental methods to study how organisms react, perceive, learn, remember, and are motivated characterizes the field of _____. (23)

2. Within experimental psychology, the study of animals in order to compare the behavior of different species is termed _____. (23)

3. The field of _____ is concerned with the application of psychological principles to the diagnosis and treatment of emotional and behavioral disorders. (24)

4. The term _____ was introduced in the 1970s to describe those areas of research in psychology that a) are concerned with _____, such as perceiving, remembering, and problem solving, and b) overlap with other disciplines that have interests in these processes. (26)

5. A branch of computer science that is concerned with developing computers that act intelligently and computer programs that simulate human thought processes is called _____. (26)

Ideas and Concepts

SCOPE OF PSYCHOLOGY

* 1. For each of the representative problems in psychology in the table below, indicate a major experimental result or phenomenon and, if possible, its significance. Be sure you can define the related terms noted in italics. (6-7)

Problem	Results or Phenomenon	Significance
Living with a divided brain (*split-brain*)		
Conditioned fear		
Childhood amnesia		
Obesity and *anorexia*		
Expression of aggression		

PERSPECTIVES IN PSYCHOLOGY

* 1. List the five perspectives by which a topic in psychology can be described. Be able to apply three of them to a common example, such as crossing the street or reading a study guide. (7-8)

* 2. a) To what period of history and to what individuals can the roots of cognitive psychology be traced? With what did their questions deal? (Be able to give some examples.) (8)

* b) Outline some historical highpoints of the biological perspective in psychology citing an important figure. (8)

* c) When was scientific psychology born, and what was its fundamental idea? (8)

*Basic ideas and concepts

3. a) In what major respect did the nineteenth-century biological perspective differ from the modern one? (9)

b) On what did the nineteenth-century cognitive approach focus and how was data obtained? (9)

c) Was introspection an effective method? Explain. (9)

* 4. a) In principle, to what do all psychological events correspond? (9)

b) For each of the following topics, indicate a main contribution of the biological perspective to its understanding. (9-10)

—the split-brain phenomenon:

—learning (use the term *neurons* in your answer):

—memory (use the term *hippocampus* in your answer):

—motivation and emotion:

* 5. What is one reason why a strictly biological approach to psychology would be inadequate? (10)

* 6. a) What were John Watson's criticisms of introspection as a method for psychology and what did he propose as an alternative? (10-11)

b) Apply the behavioral approach to each of the following sample problem areas. (11)

—fear (use the term *conditioning* in your answer):

—obesity:

—aggression:

* 7. a) Discuss the role that mental processes play in the behavioral perspective. (11)

b) How many psychologists still profess to be "strict behaviorists"? (11)

* 8. How does the modern cognitive approach differ from its nineteenth-century version? Cite two assumptions of today's cognitive perspective. (11-12)

* 9. a) In what respects was the development of the modern cognitive approach a reaction to S-R psychology? (12)

b) Relate the "telephone switchboard" and "computer" metaphors to the behavioral and cognitive perspectives in psychology. (12)

6   Chapter 1

c) Again, as you did with the other perspectives, apply the cognitive approach to the sample problems that follow. (12)

—fear:

—childhood amnesia:

—obesity:

—aggression:

* 10. a) In Freud's psychoanalytic conception, what is the origin of impulses for human actions? What does society attempt to do with such impulses and what are the main results? (13)

*   b) Did Freud view the causes of actions to be our rational reasons for what we do? Explain citing man's two basic instincts and indicate the view of human nature that this approach supports. (13)

        c) Do most psychologists accept Freud's view of the unconscious? On what would they agree? (13)

        d) Apply the psychoanalytic approach to these sample problem areas. (13)

—childhood amnesia:

—obesity:

—aggression:

* 11. a) In part, why did the phenomenological approach develop and what aspects of other perspectives in psychology did it reject? (13)

*   b) In what respects do the goals of phenomenologically-oriented psychologists differ from those of other psychologists? (13)

        c) Discuss the view of the *free will* versus *determinism* issue taken by phenomenological psychologists. (13)

*   d) Explain what is meant by the "tendency toward growth and self-actualization" that provides a major motivational force in humanistic theories. (13-14)

  12. a) Indicate the various associations and alignments of the field of humanistic psychology. (14)

        b) Discuss the pros and cons of the position of some humanistic psychologists that psychology should not be a science at all. (14)

  15. a) In what sense is the biological perspective at a different level than other perspectives? (14)

*   b) How does the biological perspective "make contact" with the more psychological perspectives? Cite an example and use the term *reductionism* in your answer. (14)

*   c) What is your authors' answer to the question, "Is psychology just something to do until the biologists get around to figuring everything out"? Give two reasons why or why not. (14-15)

    d) When are the various perspectives in psychology compatible and when are they competitive? (15)

METHODS OF PSYCHOLOGY

* 1.   a) What distinguishes the experimental method from other methods of scientific observation? Give an example. (16)

      b) In this example, indicate the *independent* and *dependent variables*, respectively. (16)

* 2.   Using the experiment in your text that investigated the effects of marijuana on memory as a prototype, can you design a study to investigate the relationship between amount of caffeine consumed while studying and later performance on a mid-term examination? What would be the independent variable? What could serve as the dependent variable? What sorts of variables should be controlled? (16-17)

  3. Why are most controlled experiments conducted in laboratories? Be able to cite examples. (17)

  4. What kind of a general statement can be made when the effects of a single independent variable are observed in a controlled experimental design? Give some illustrations. (17-18)

* 5.   a) Why are numbers assigned to variables? That is, why does measurement play such a fundamental role in the scientific method? (18)

      b) What must be done when experiments make measurements on a sample of subjects rather than on just one subject? How is this accomplished? (18)

*   c) Describe what happens when the difference between the means of two samples is large. What happens if it is small? Use the terms *significance of a difference* and *statistically significant* in your answer. (18)

*   d) What does it mean when a statistical test indicates that a difference is significant? If a difference is not significant, then what may it be due to? (18-19)

* 6.   Look at Figure 1-7 describing scores on two tests of hypnotizability in your text and be able to answer the following questions. (19-20)

      a) Why are the tallies "scattered" to some degree rather than in a straight line? What is r for these data? In your authors' words, what does a correlation coefficient of this magnitude mean?

8   Chapter 1

b) What would it have meant if the tallies had all fallen in a straight line? What would the value of r have been?

c) Are these variables positively or negatively related? How do you know? (Can you visualize the approximate scatter pattern of the tallies if the direction of the relationship were opposite?)

d) In psychological research, what does it mean when the absolute value of a correlation coefficient is:

—.60 or higher?

—.20 to .60?

—0 to .20?

* 7. a) Indicate one common use of the correlation method. (20)

   b) What can be done with the variation in scores on two tests? Cite an example. (20-21)

* c) Why are tests important in psychology? (21)

* 8. When two variables are correlated (even highly), does this necessarily mean that there is a cause-and-effect relation between them? Explain using an example in your answer. (21)

* 9. a) When do we use the method of direct observation in psychology? (21)

   b) What is one risk when making observations of natural behaviors? Cite an example. (21)

   c) Are laboratories ever used when making direct observations? Give an example and indicate the three types of data that were gathered in this instance. (21-22)

10. a) What specific kinds of observations have been made with survey methods? Which of these are probably the most familiar? (22)

* b) List four features of an adequate survey. (22)

* 11. a) How are most case histories prepared and why is this method necessary? (23)

   b) Cite a risk in the use of retrospective methods of data gathering. (23)

PROFESSIONS IN PSYCHOLOGY

* 1. For each of the fields of psychology in the table below be able to properly identify the types and activities of psychologists in the profession. (23-25)

Field of Psychology	Psychologists: Types	Psychologists: Activities
Biological		
Experimental		
Developmental, Social & personality		
Clinical & counseling		
School & educational		
Industrial & engineering		(Use the term *person-machine interface*)
Other		(Use the term *evaluation research*)

2. What proportion of psychologists work in colleges and universities? Look at Table 1-1. What field employs the largest percentage of psychologists? (23)

* 3. a) List three main objectives of the new field of cognitive science. (26)

   b) Be able to recognize some of the disciplines that are relevant to cognitive science. (26)

10   Chapter 1

c) Discuss two beliefs of the field of cognitive science. (26)

d) Why do your authors feel that the emergence of cognitive science is an important milestone in the history of science? (26)

Sample Quiz 1.1

1. "The scientific study of behavior and mental processes" is the definition offered in your text for: a) psychology; b) neurobiology; c) behaviorism; d) cognitive science.

2. Introspection refers to: a) the study of eliciting stimuli, responses, and rewards; b) self-observation of one's own perceptions, thoughts, and feelings; c) biological assessment of functions that underlie behavior and mental processes; d) the study of the unconscious.

3. In a strict behavioral approach, mental processes: a) are conceptualized as metaphors for interpreting observable behavior; b) can be used as explanations for behavior only if observed through careful introspection; c) are viewed as primarily unconscious in nature; d) are not considered at all.

4. The cognitive perspective assumes that: a) we can study mental processes by focusing on behaviors; b) we can study mental processes best by way of the method of introspection; c) only by studying mental processes can we understand what organisms do; d) both a and c.

5. In the psychoanalytic approach, behavior is said to be mainly caused by: a) the drive toward self-actualization; b) neurobiological processes; c) unconscious processes; d) eliciting stimuli.

6. Reductionism refers to: a) the search inward to discover one's maximum potential; b) the dominant research method employed by nineteenth-century cognitive psychologists; c) a form of explanation, where psychological concepts are interpreted in terms of biological ones; d) the process whereby forbidden impulses are driven into the unconscious according to psychoanalytic theory.

7. Numbers are assigned to variables: a) to make them appear scientifically respectable; b) so that they may be added and subtracted from one another; c) to facilitate precise communication; d) none of the above; variables are always expressed qualititatively rather than quantitatively.

8. If there were no relationship at all between two variables, a correlation coefficient of _____ would be obtained when the correlational method was applied: a) +1.0; b) -1.0; c) +.50; d) 0.0.

9. The survey method is characterized by: a) the employment of questionnaires and interviews to collect data; b) the development of biographies of individuals, groups, or institutions for scientific use; c) the assumption that the best metaphor for human thought processes is the electronic computer; d) the use of direct observational methods to study behavior.

10. Physiological psychologists are to biological psychology as comparative psychologists are to: a) experimental psychology; b) industrial and engineering

psychology; c) school and educational psychology; d) clinical and counseling psychology.

Sample Quiz 1.2

1. Which of the following has *not* been a finding of psychological research? a) Virtually no one remembers events occurring prior to the age of three. b) Prior deprivation of food leads to later overeating when food is abundant. c) Aggression usually can be controlled by allowing individuals to express aggressive feelings either directly or vicariously. d) Under certain circumstances the right half of the brain might not know what the left side of the body is doing.

2. The view that behavior should be the only subject matter of psychology was proposed by: a) Sigmund Freud; b) John Watson; c) Aristotle; d) Hippocrates.

3. S-R psychology is an approach taken within the _____ perspective: a) cognitive; b) phenomenological; c) biological; d) behavioral.

4. In Freud's view, the impulses for human action are originally derived from: a) our natural tendency to actualize our potential; b) immediate subjective experience; c) innate instincts; d) the conflict between society's rules and the individual's conscious desires.

5. When psychological concepts are translated in terms of biological concepts, we speak of: a) phenomenology; b) reductionism; c) cognitive psychology; d) behaviorism.

6. The point of view of your authors concerning the importance of psychological explanation is that: a) it is important only until biologists can provide more concrete explanations of behavior; b) psychological concepts can help guide biological researchers; c) psychological concepts can never be reduced to biological ones under any circumstances; d) both a and b.

7. Of the following terms, which best characterizes the experimental method: a) survey; b) correlation; c) case history; d) control.

8. The field that is concerned with the application of psychological principles in the treatment of disorders is: a) clinical psychology; b) experimental psychology; c) introspectionism; d) cognitive science.

9. Personality psychologists: a) are interested in human development; b) are experts in learning and teaching; c) focus on differences and unique qualities among individuals; d) typically work in institutions that deal with emotional and behavioral problems.

10. Artificial intelligence is a branch of: a) clinical psychology; b) personality psychology; c) educational psychology; d) computer science.

Key, Chapter 1

Names

1. John Watson
2. Sigmund Freud

9. a, 22
10. a, 23

Vocabulary and Details

1. scientific study of behavior and mental processes

1. introspection
2. biological; neurobiological
3. behavioral; observed
4. behaviorism; stimulus-response; S-R psychology
5. cognitive; mental processes
6. psychoanalytic; unconscious
7. phenomenological; phenomenology
8. humanistic; self-actualization
9. reductionism

1. unbiased; objective
2. experimental; control; relations among variables
3. variable
4. independent variable; dependent variable; function of
5. experimental design
6. experimental group; control group
7. multivariate
8. measurement
9. statistics
10. mean
11. correlational method; correlated
12. coefficient of correlation; r
13. 0; 1; 0; increases; 1
14. positively; negatively
15. direct observation
16. survey method
17. case histories

1. experimental psychology
2. comparative psychology
3. clinical psychology
4. cognitive science; cognitive processes
5. artificial intelligence

Sample Quiz 1.1

1. a, 6
2. b, 9
3. d, 11
4. d, 11-12
5. c, 12-13
6. c, 14
7. c, 18
8. d, 19

Sample Quiz 1.2

1. c, 6-7
2. b, 10
3. d, 11
4. c, 13
5. b, 14
6. b, 14-15
7. d, 16
8. a, 24
9. c, 24
10. d, 26

Biological Basis of Psychology

Learning Objectives

1. Be able to identify the major components of a neuron. Know the functions of sensory neurons, motor neurons, and interneurons and the difference between neurons and nerves. Understand the process of axonal conduction.

2. Be able to identify the main features of a synapse and to describe synaptic transmission. Understand the role of neurotransmitters and the difference between excitatory and inhibitory synapses.

3. Be able to name and to diagram the relationships among the major components of the nervous system. Be able to explain the functioning of a spinal reflex.

4. Know what structures comprise each of the three concentric layers of the human brain. Be able to describe, in general, the functions of these structurres.

5. Be able to define and describe the cerebral cortex. Be able to describe its major areas and know approximately where each is located.

6. Be familiar with the right/left differences typically found in humans. Know what functions are usually controlled by each of the two hemispheres.

7. Be able to describe, in general, the differing structures and functions of the two divisions of the autonomic nervous system.

8. Be familiar with the major endocrine glands and their hormones. Understand the interrelationships between the endocrine system and the autonomic nervous system.

9. Be able to define and differentiate between genes and chromosomes. Understand what is meant by dominant, recessive, and sex-linked genes. Be familiar with the several chromosomal-abnormality syndromes discussed in the text.

10. Understand the multiple contributions to human traits, including polygenic transmission and environmental interaction. Be familiar with the use of selective breeding and twin studies.

15

Names

1. The Nobel Prize winner who is known in part for his pioneering research on effects of the split-brain operation is _____. (52)

Vocabulary and Details

COMPONENTS OF THE NERVOUS SYSTEM

1. The basic unit of the nervous system is a specialized cell called a _____. (33)

2. Neural impulses are received by the neuron on its _____ and on a number of short branches that project from the cell body called _____. (34)

3. Neural impulses are transmitted from the neuron to other neurons, muscles, or glands, by way of a slender tubelike extension called an _____. (34)

4. At the end of the axon are fine collaterals that end in small swellings called _____ which _____ (do/do not) touch the neuron they will stimulate. (34)

5. This junction between two neurons is termed a _____; the gap between the synaptic terminal and the dendrites of the receiving neuron is called the _____. (34)

6. Transmission across the synaptic gap is made possible by a chemical called a _____ that is stimulated by arrival of a neural impulse at the synapse. (34)

7. A _____ is a group of specialized cells in the sense organs, muscles, skin, and joints that detect physical or chemical changes due to stimulation and translate these into neural impulses. (34)

8. In turn, these events are transmitted *to* the central nervous system (the brain or spinal cord) by the first of three types of neurons, termed the _____. (34)

9. *In* the central nervous system (plus in the eyes), the second type of neurons, the _____, receive signals from the sensory neurons and transmit them either to other interneurons or to neurons leading out. (35)

10. *From* the central nervous system, the third type of neurons, the _____, transmit outgoing signals to the _____, that is, the muscles and glands. (34)

11. A _____ is a bundle of elongated axons that may contain both sensory and motor neurons. (35)

12. Besides the neurons, another type of cells in the nervous system are called _____; these are specialized for "glueing" or holding the neurons in place and for other functions (rather than for reception or transmission of impulses). (35)

13. In the electrochemical process of neural transmission, or _____, electrically charged atoms and molecules, called _____, cross the membrane that holds together the protoplasm of the neuron. (35)

14. In particular, positively charged sodium ions, abbreviated _____, enter the cell in the process called _____, during which the inside of the cell membrane becomes _____ (more/less) negative that it was when at rest. (35)

15. The process of depolarization repeating itself successively along an axon's length, is termed the _____. (35)

16. The _____ is a thin fatty sheath, in segments separated by gaps, that insulates the axons of most neurons; the sheath allows nerve impulses to jump from one gap to the next, thereby _____ (increasing/decreasing) the speed of axonal conduction. (36)

17. In accordance with the _____ of action, a neuron discharges at a constant level when stimulation from multiple synapses reach a specific _____. (36)

18. When a nerve impulse travels down an axon, it stimulates small spherical or irregularly shaped structures in the synaptic terminal termed the _____ that, in turn, discharge neurotransmitters. (36)

19. One neurotransmitter that is normally excitatory is _____ (abbreviated _____), particularly prevalent in the portion of the brain important in _____, called the hippocampus, and also in neural transmission to the cells of skeletal muscles. (38)

20. Another neurotransmitter, _____, (abbreviated _____), produced mainly by neurons in the brain stem, causes _____ (stimulating/depressing) psychological and mood effects ("arousal"). (39)

21. A third neurotransmitter, _____, has an _____ (inhibitory, stimulating) effect on muscle movement and also may be involved in the _____ (tranquilizing/stimulating) effects of certain drugs used to treat anxiety. (39)

22. In the brain structure, the hippocampus, a receptor molecule called _____, may play a role in _____ storage. (40)

ORGANIZATION OF THE NERVOUS SYSTEM

1. All of the neurons in the brain and spinal cord comprise the _____. (40)

2. The _____ consists of the nerves connecting the central nervous system to the other parts of the body. (40)

3. The peripheral nervous system is in two divisions, one of which, the _____ transmits information to and from the muscles (as well as sensations from the skin and joints). (40)

4. The other part of the peripheral nervous system, the _____, consists of neurons running to and from the internal organs. (40)

5. Most of the nerve fibers connecting various parts of the body to the brain are gathered together to form the _____, that contains three types of neurons: _____, _____, and _____. (41)

STRUCTURE OF THE BRAIN

1. The brain may be described as consisting of three concentric layers: the _____, that includes most of the brain stem, the _____, closely interconnected with the hypothalamus and having some control over both this structure and the brain stem, and the _____. (41-43)

2. The normal level of functioning characteristic of the healthy organism is called _____. (42)

CEREBRAL HEMISPHERES

1. The outer layer of the cerebrum termed the _____, or simply _____, is _____ (more/less) highly developed in humans than other animals. (46)

2. The primary anatomical division of the cerebrum is into two roughly symmetrical _____, referred to simply (in accordance with the side of the body) as the _____ and _____, separated by a deep longitudinal "fissure." (46)

3. Specific areas of the cortex are involved in reception of information from the _____ systems and control of movements of the body, or _____ responses. The remaining largest, _____ areas are concerned with memory, thought, and language. (47)

ASYMMETRIES IN THE BRAIN

1. _____ is the area of the frontal lobe of the left hemisphere just above the lateral fissure that is important in the production of speech in most people. (50)

2. The broad band of nerve fibers connecting the two hemispheres that allows the immediate transmission of information between them is termed the _____. (51)

3. The procedure sometimes performed on epileptics that involves severing the corpus callosum, leaving the two hemispheres functionally separate, is termed the _____ operation. (52)

4. In some research with split-brain patients, investigators have taken advantage of the fact that when the eyes are fixated straight ahead, images to the left of the fixation point (the left visual field) go through both eyes to the _____ (right/left) hemisphere; whereas images in the right visual field, go to the _____ (right/left) hemisphere. (52)

AUTONOMIC NERVOUS SYSTEM

1. The portion of the peripheral nervous system that controls the _____ and _____ is called the *autonomic nervous system* because its activities are _____ or self-regulating. (56)

2. The autonomic nervous system is itself in two parts that are often antagonistic--the _____ division tends to activate the internal organs as a unit during times of _____; the _____ division tends to affect internal organs individually during times of _____. (56, 58)

ENDOCRINE SYSTEM

1. The _____ consists of a number of glands throughout the body that indirectly controls cells by way of chemicals, called _____, that are secreted into the bloodstream. (58)

2. One endocrine gland, the _____, located below the hypothalamus in the brain, is sometimes called the "master gland" because it produces many different hormones that have a variety of functions and that influence other glands. (58)

3. One hormone produced by the pituitary gland is _____ (abbreviated _____), the body's main stress hormone. (58)

4. In turn, ACTH acts upon the _____, (located at the top of the kidneys), which play an important role in mood, arousal, and coping with stress. (59)

5. The adrenals secrete one hormone called _____ (also known as _____), and a second hormone called _____ (also known as _____), both of which are important in the activities of the sympathetic nervous system (and other glands) during times of emergency and stress. (59)

GENETIC INFLUENCES ON BEHAVIOR

1. The field of _____ (or _____) combines the methods of genetics and psychology to study the inheritance of behavioral characteristics. (60)

2. Hereditary units are carried from parents to offspring by structures called _____ found in most body cells; at conception _____ (how many?) of these units are contributed each by the human mother and the father, for a total of _____, that are duplicated in the cells. (60)

3. Each chromosome is composed of hereditary units called _____ made up of a segment of _____ that actually carries the genetic information. (60)

4. A gene is said to be _____ when it determines the form of the trait it specifies in a gene pair with either a dominant or a recessive gene; a _____ gene determines the form of a trait only in a gene pair with another recessive gene. (61)

5. The disorder _____, a genetically caused deterioration of the nervous system accompanied by behavioral and cognitive problems, results from a single _____ (dominant/recessive) gene transmitted from each parent. (61)

6. The disease _____ is caused by a single _____ (dominant/recessive) gene and involves deterioration of certain areas of the brain accompanied by a loss of memory and mental ability beginning around age 30 or 40. (61)

7. A person's sex is determined by the _____ pair of chromosomes distinguished by their appearance; the male pair contains the chromosomes represented by the symbol _____, while the female pair contains the chromosomes represented by the symbol _____. (62)

8. Because it is the 23rd chromosome pair that determines a number of genetic disorders owing to abnormal or recessive genes, such problems are called _____. (62)

Biological Basis of Psychology   19

9. To say that most human characteristics are determined by many genes is to say that they are _____. (63)

10. Two humans who develop from a single fertilized egg (or _____) are called _____, or said to be _____. (64)

11. Twins who develop from different egg cells are called _____, or said to be _____. (64-65).

Ideas and Concepts

1. a) Biologically speaking, upon what does behavior depend and what systems are involved? How might these systems function in, say, stopping a car at a red light? (Use the term *feedback* in your answer.) (33)

   b) Cite some aspects of behavior and mental functioning that can be understood better in terms of underlying biological processes. (33)

COMPONENTS OF THE NERVOUS SYSTEM

* 1. Be able to identify the parts of the neuron below using appropriate terms from the key to the related items in your *Vocabulary and Details* section. (34)

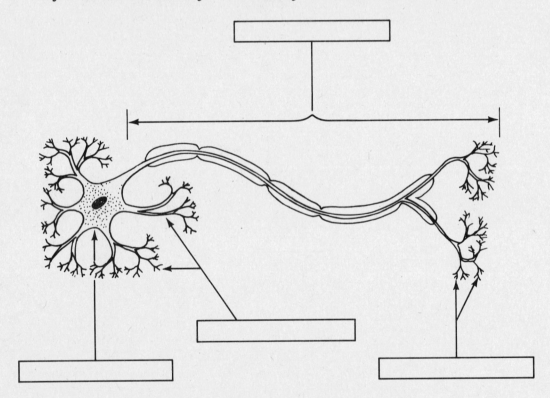

2. a) Are all neurons alike in terms of size and shape? Explain. (34)

   b) Are there just a few neurons and glial cells? Give some estimates. (35)

*Basic ideas and concepts

20   Chapter 2

* 3. a) Compare the speed of neural transmission with the speed of electricity. What analogy do your authors use to describe axonal conduction? (35)

* b) Keeping this analogy in mind, describe in detail the process of axonal conduction using the terms *electrochemical, ions, Na+, cell membrane permeability,* and *depolarization* . (35)

* c) Does the nerve impulse diminish in strength during transmission? Why or why not? (35)

* 4. In detail, why does depolarization occur, and what does it mean to say that the cell membrane acts as a "highly selective filter"? Use the terms *ion channels* and *ion pumps* in your response. (35-36).

5. a) What is the relationship between phylogenetic level and presence of the myelin sheath? (36)

b) As one indication of its significance, what may result from degeneration of areas of the myelin sheath and what is this disease called? (36)

* 6. a) Why is the synaptic junction between neurons so important? (36)

* b) Describe the all-or-none process of discharge of a neuron. (36)

c) In the usual case, when neurotransmitters are involved in neural transmission, how does the process work? Use the terms *synaptic vesicles, neurotransmitter* and *receptor molecules,* and *lock-and-key action* in your discussion. (36-37)

7. Must a neuron receive impulses from only one or a few synapses? What determines when the neuron will fire? (37)

* 8. a) Why must the effects of a neurotransmitter be very brief? (37)

* b) Detail two ways in which this brevity is achieved. (37)

9. How many different neurotransmitters are known to date? Is a given neurotransmitter always excitatory or inhibitory? Explain. (37)

10. a) What is Alzheimer's disease? Discuss the role of ACh in this disorder. (38)

b) Describe the mechanism by which ACh may be involved in certain instances of muscle paralysis. (38)

* 11. In terms of effects on the neurotransmitter, NE, how do the drugs *cocaine* and *amphetamines* produce their stimulating effects? How does the drug *lithium* depress a person's mood level? (39)

* 12. In terms of the neurotransmitter *dopamine*, explain the symptoms of the disorders of schizophrenia and Parkinson's disease. (39)

13. Explain in detail how the NMDA receptor differs from others and how it might play a role in determining how memories are stored. Use the terms *long-term potentiation* and *glutanate* . (40)

ORGANIZATION OF THE NERVOUS SYSTEM

* 1. Be able to fill in the blanks in the diagram below to show the overall organization of the nervous system. (40)

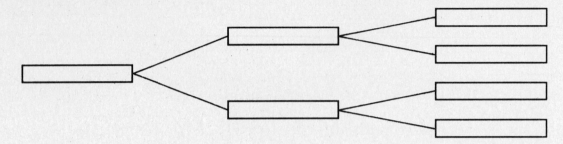

* 2. Discuss the functions of the somatic and autonomic nervous systems. (40)

* 3. a) Describe the sequence of events in the knee jerk reflex and its function. (41)

   b) Is the brain necessary in this sequence or is the spinal cord sufficient? Explain what role the brain may serve. (41)

   c) What structures comprise the simplest reflex? Most reflexes? (41)

STRUCTURE OF THE BRAIN

* 1. For each of the structures of the central core in the table below, indicate major functions. (42-43)

Structure   Functions

Structure	Functions
brain stem and medulla	
cerebellum	
thalamus	
hypothalamus	(Include the term *homeostasis*)
reticular system	

*   2. In the diagram below, identify the location of each of the brain structures listed in the preceding table. (See also Figures 2-6 and 2-7.) (42)

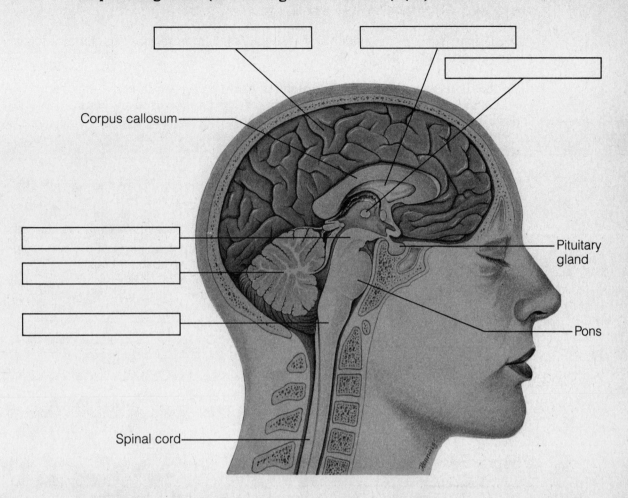

Corpus callosum

Pituitary gland

Pons

Spinal cord

3. What happens to the major nerve tracts that come up through the brain stem when they reach the medulla? (42)

4. a) Indicate the role played by the hypothalamus during stress with respect to homeostasis. (42)

   b) What two things may happen when the hypothalamus is given electrical stimulation? (42)

*   c) How does the hypothalamus exert control over the endocrine system and when is this control particularly important? Therefore, what has the hypothalamus been called? (42)

5. a) Indicate the effects of electrical stimulation in the region of the reticular system. (42-43)

   b) In what way may the reticular system act as an attentional filter? (43)

*   6. a) Discuss the different roles served by the limbic system in instinctive behaviors in lower animals and mammals. (43)

Biological Basis of Psychology   23

b) Indicate the part of the limbic system that has a role to play in memory. What happens at the time of injury or removal of this structure? What happens during recovery? Cite examples. (43-44)

c) Discuss some of the evidence that suggests the importance of the limbic system in emotional behavior. (43, 46)

* 7. Do the three "concentric" brain structures operate independently of one another? Discuss in detail the "interrelated computers" metaphor used by your authors to describe the functions of these structures. (46)

CEREBRAL HEMISPHERES

* 1. What happens to the size of the surface area of the cerebral cortex as one goes up the phylogenetic scale? How is this accomplished? (47)

* 2. If you have not already, be sure to label the cerebral cortex in the figure in item 5, directly above. In addition, be sure that you can identify the parts of the cerebrum shown in the figures below. (See also Figure 2-8 in your text.) (47-48)

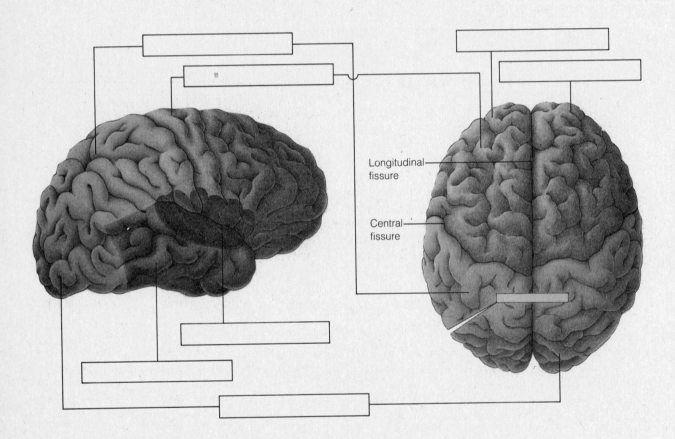

Longitudinal fissure

Central fissure

24   Chapter 2

* 3. In the table below, for each of the cortical areas, be able to indicate its location and functions. (47-50)

Cortical area	Location (in your words)	Functions
motor area		
somatosensory area		
visual area		
auditory area		
frontal and *posterior association areas*		

4. a) What happens to motor responses when a point on the motor area is electrically stimulated? When it is injured? (47)

* b) How is the body represented in the motor cortex? How is it represented in the two hemispheres? (47)

* 5. a) How are sensory impulses represented in the two hemispheres of the cortex? (49)

* b) In general, what is the relationship between the sensitivity and use of a body part and its amount of representation in the cortex? Give some examples. (49)

* 6. a) Discuss the relationship between the eyes and where the optic nerves go in the two hemispheres. Use the term *optic chiasma* in your response. (49)

b) What does this mean with respect to the effects of damage to the hemispheres and how might this relationship be helpful? (49)

7. Discuss the effects of cerebral lesions in each of the following cases. (50)

—frontal association area in monkeys:

Biological Basis of Psychology   25

—frontal association area in humans:

—posterior association area in humans:

ASYMMETRIES IN THE BRAIN

1. Are the two hemispheres of the brain perfectly symmetrical? What are some of the structural differences? (50)

* 2. a) What was Paul Broca's important discovery regarding the frontal lobe? What happens if the corresponding area in the other hemisphere is damaged? (50)

* b) Besides speaking, what other language functions are usually located in the left hemisphere? How does this relate to the effects of strokes? (51)

c) What is the relationship between handedness and the location of the speech center? (51)

* 3. a) Why does the brain normally function as an integrated whole despite its two hemispheres? When may this become a problem? (51-52)

* b) Therefore, what procedure may alleviate generalized seizures in some epileptics and what other aftereffects may be expected? (52)

4. a) Describe three of Sperry's procedures for investigating sensory and speech effects in split-brain subjects outlined in your text and in Figure 2-12. (52-53)

b) Discuss the results obtained in each of these types of studies. (52-53)

c) Why is it important when presenting visual material that it be flashed for only one-tenth of a second? What does this imply with respect to the usual effects of the split-brain operation? (In these terms, what do you think would happen if auditory material is presented?) (51)

* 5. a) For each of the following functions, indicate whether the left or right hemisphere appears to be dominant. Be able to illustrate with examples where possible. (53-55)

—expression in language:

—logical and analytical activities:

—mathematical computations:

—comprehension of abstract linguistic forms:

—spatial and pattern comprehension:

* b) From the above distinctions, which hemisphere should be able to identify verbal information more quickly and accurately? Which hemisphere should be able to recognize faces, expressions of emotions, and characteristics of lines or dots more readily? Cite the related experimental evidence. (55-56)

26   Chapter 2

* 6. Should one infer from the evidence regarding the functions of the two hemispheres that they work independently of one another? Explain. (56)

AUTONOMIC NERVOUS SYSTEM

1. How does the physiologist distinguish in appearance and function between the muscles controlled by the autonomic system from those controlled by the somatic system? (56)

* 2. a) From Figure 2-13, be able to identify some of the antagonistic actions of the two portions of the autonomic nervous system. (Can you see the role the neural *ganglia* may play in the unitary action of the sympathetic division?) (57)

   b) What is the "normal" state of the body and how is this maintained? (56)

* 3. Are the sympathetic and parasympathetic systems always antagonistic to one another? Cite two examples to support your answer. (58)

ENDOCRINE SYSTEM

1. a) How does the speed of the endocrine system compare with that of the nervous system? (58)

   b) Describe the mechanism by which target cells react to their respective hormones. (58)

   c) Indicate two mechanisms for the activation of the endocrine glands. (58)

* 2. List several functions of the pituitary gland. (58)

* 3. a) Describe the sequence of events that take place between the hypothalamus and the pituitary gland in response to stress. Use the term *coritcotropin-release factor (CRF)* in your answer. (58)

   b) What indicates that the endocrine system is under the control of the hypothalamus and other brain centers? (58)

* 4. List some of the specific effects of each of the following hormones. (59)

   —epinephrine:

   —norepinephrine:

* 5. a) In what way are hormones and neurotransmitters similar? Cite an example. (58-59)

*   b) In what way do hormones and neurotransmitter differ? (59)

GENETIC INFLUENCES ON BEHAVIOR

* 1. a) What does the DNA molecule look like, and what holds its two strands apartt? (60)

*   b) How is the "genetic code" determined and, in terms of the chemical composition of the molecule, what gives DNA the ability to express many different genetic messages? (60)

2. a) If all cells carry the same genes, how is it that different cells perform different functions? Give an example. (60-61)

*   b) Where do the two genes in each pair come from? Then, why is it so unlikely that two human beings have the same heredity, even if they have the same parents?

      c) Indicate one exception to your answer to c). (61)

3. a) Explain the mechanism of gene *dominance* and *recessiveness* as it applies to eye color. (61)

*   b) Do all gene pairs follow the dominant-recessive pattern? What is the usual basis for human characteristics? (61)

4. a) What is the actual cause of damage in the disease PKU? (61)

      b) How is this disorder now alleviated by making use of genetic information? (61)

5. How is the likelihood of Huntington's disease now diagnosed and what will eventually provide the mechanism for treating this genetic disorder? (62)

* 6. Whose chromosome, the mother's or the father's, determines their child's sex? Explain. (62)

* 7. Why is it that the male X chromosome is often responsible for expression of recessive characteristics? Give an example of one such sex-linked disorder. (62)

8. For each of the following syndromes, indicate the nature of the condition and related chromosomal abnormalities. (62-63)

—*Turner's syndrome* :

—*Klinefelter's syndrome* :

* 9. a) What was discovered about the incidence of an extra Y chromosome in imprisoned males, and what did this appear to imply as to the genetic basis for their difficulties? (63)

*   b) Outline the results of more recent research and indicate an alternative possibility for the higher rates of the XYY characteristic among convicts. (63)

10. Illustrate the polygenic aspect of most human traits with an example. (63)

* 11. a) Describe the method of selective breeding as it has been used to study the inheritance of learning ability in rats. (64)

*   b) From Figure 2-18, describe the results of this procedure. (64)

28   Chapter 2

c) List some other examples of selective breeding. (64)

d) When should a trait be modifiable through selective breeding, and what can we conclude if it is not? (64)

* 12. a) Since selective breeding cannot ethically be carried out with humans, what alternative method is used to study the heritability of traits? (64)

b) What difficulty is encountered in this method? Give some examples. (64)

c) In order to overcome this problem, to what do psychologists turn? (64)

* d) To demonstrate the importance of heredity, cite some characteristics on which identical twins are more similar than fraternal twins. (65)

13. Discuss the role of the environment in influencing gene action in each of the following cases. (65-66)

—diabetes:

—schizophrenia

Sample Quiz 2.1

1. Which of the following statements concerning axonal conduction is *true*? a) During depolarization, sodium ions leave the cell. b) Neural transmission takes place at the speed of electricity. c) When at rest, the inside of a nerve cell is more negative than the outside. d) Nerve impulses get weaker and weaker as they travel down the axon.

2. The neurotransmitter, GABA, is important in: a) memory storage in the hippocampus; b) inhibiting muscle movements; c) mood changes; d) homeostasis.

3. The normal level of functioning characteristic of a healthy organism is called: a) depolarized; b) dizygotic; c) polygenic; d) homeostasis.

4. In mammals, the limbic system appears to: a) inhibit instinctive behaviors and allow for greater adaptiveness; b) control stereotyped behaviors, such as, attack and mating; c) serve as the "stress center"; d) coordinate movement.

5. The reason the corpus callosum has been severed in some individuals is to: a) control generalized epileptic seizures; b) improve memory in victims of Alzheimer's disease; c) provide research subjects in brain asymmetry; d) none of the above; this surgical procedure has only been performed on lower animals for ethical reasons.

6. The right cerebral hemisphere is superior to the left with respect to: a) mathematical computation; b) language expression; c) spatial and pattern recognition; d) both a and b.

7. The autonomic nervous system: a) is in two parts that are often oppositional in function; b) controls the muscles and glands; c) is relatively self-regulating; d) all of the above.

8. Hormones and neurotransmitters are similar in that: a) they both carry messages between cells of the body; b) under certain circumstances the same substance can serve both functions; c) the effects of both can operate across long distances in the body; d) both a and b.

9. XY is to XX as: a) male is to female; b) zygotic is to dizygotic; c) female is to male; d) dizygotic is to zygotic.

10. In recent studies of the presence of the XYY chromosomal abnormality, it has been found that: a) men with this abnormality are shorter and less aggressive; b) women with this abnormality are more likely to develop Klinefelter's syndrome; c) males with this gene structure are more likely than normal males to be convicts; d) males with this genetic makeup have male reproductive organs but feminine characteristics.

Sample Quiz 2.2

1. Reception is to transmission as: a) dendrites are to axon; b) axon is to dendrites; c) synapse is to cell body; d) cell body is to neuron.

2. In depolarization: a) negatively charged sodium ions enter the neuron; b) negatively charged sodium ions leave the neuron; c) positively charged sodium ions enter the neuron; d) positively charged sodium ions leave the neuron.

3. With respect to the three main concentric layers of the brain, inhibition of instinctive behavior patterns occurs at the: a) central core; b) limbic system; c) cerebrum; d) none of the above; instinctive behavior patterns cannot be modified.

4. Specific areas of the cortex are functional in all but which of the following: a) control of motor responses; b) reception from sensory system; c) secretions of ACTH; d) association.

5. The progressively more wrinkled and convoluted appearance of the cortex as one proceeds up the phylogenetic scale reflects: a) the relative increase of amount of cortex as compared to total brain tissue; b) the relative increase in amount of total brain tissue as compared to cortex; c) the older age of the species at the higher end of the scale; d) none of the above; there are no essential differences in the appearance of the cortex across species.

6. The "split-brain" operation designed to control generalized seizures in epileptics involves severing of the: a) brain stem; b) thalamus and the hypothalamus; c) frontal and posterior association areas; d) corpus callosum.

7. The right hemisphere appears to be dominant in: a) expression of language; b) mathematical computations; c) comprehension of abstract language; d) recognition of faces.

8. Sympathetic and parasympathetic are divisions of the: a) autonomic nervous system; b) endocrine system; c) somatic nervous system; d) limbic system.

9. The Y chromosome: a) when present, produces a male offspring; b) contains almost all dominant genes; c) is inherited from the mother; d) all of the above.

10. Most human characteristics are determined by many genes; in other words, they are: a) dizygotic; b) polygenic; c) monozygotic; d) psychogenic.

Names

1. Roger Sperry

Vocabulary and Details

1. neuron
2. cell body; dendrites
3. axon
4. synaptic terminals; do not
5. synapse; synaptic gap
6. neurotransmitter
7. receptor
8. sensory neurons
9. interneurons
10. motor neurons; effector organs
11. nerve
12. glial cells
13. axonal conduction; ions
14. Na+; depolarization; less
15. nerve impulse
16. myelin sheath; increasing
17. all-or-none principle; threshold level
18. synaptic vesicles
19. acetylcholine (ACh); memory
20. norepinephrine (NE); stimulating
21. gamma-aminobutyric acid (or GABA); inhibitory; tranquilizing
22. N-methyl D-aspartate (NMDA); memory

1. central nervous system
2. peripheral nervous system
3. somatic system
4. autonomic system
5. spinal cord; sensory neurons; motor neurons; interneurons

1. central core; limbic system; cerebral hemispheres
2. homeostasis

1. cerebral cortex; cortex; more
2. cerebral hemispheres; left hemisphere; right hemisphere
3. sensory; motor; association

1. Broca's area
2. corpus callosum
3. split-brain
4. right; left

1. glands; smooth muscles; autonomous
2. sympathetic; excitement; parasympathetic; quiescence

1. endocrine system; hormones
2. pituitary gland

3. adrenocorticotrophic hormone (ACTH)
4. adrenal glands
5. epinephrine (adrenaline); norepinephrine (noradrenaline)

1. behavior genetics (psychogenetics)
2. chromosomes; 23; 46
3. genes; deoxiribonucleic acid (or DNA)
4. dominant; recessive
5. phenylketonuria (or PKU); recessive
6. Huntington's disease (or HD); dominant
7. 23rd; XY; XX
8. sex-linked disorders
9. polygenic
10. (zygote); identical twins; monozygotic
11. fraternal twins; dizygotic

Sample Quiz 2.1

1. c, 35
2. b, 39
3. d, 42
4. a, 43
5. a, 52
6. c, 53-55
7. d, 56
8. d, 59-60
9. a, 62
10. c, 63

Sample Quiz 2.2

1. a, 34
2. c, 35
3. b, 43
4. c, 47
5. a, 47
6. d, 52
7. d, 56
8. a, 56, 58
9. a, 62
10. b, 63

Psychological Development

Learning Objectives

1. Understand how heredity and enviornment interact to determine human development. Be able to define the concept of maturation and show how it relates to this interaction, using motor development as an example.

2. Be familiar with what psychologists mean by developmental stages and by the realted concept of critical periods.

3. Be able to describe the capacities of the newborn and the procedures used to assess these capacities.

4. Be able to discuss the influences of enviornmental events on early development, including the consequences of restricted or enhanced sensory-motor stimulation.

5. Know the sequence of Piaget's stages of cognitive development and the major events that characterize each stage. Be familiar with some objections to Piaget's theory and with the alternative view that emphasizes the development of information-processing abilities.

6. Be familiar with the research on attachment, including experiments using the Strange Situation and those with artificial monkey mothers. Be able to describe how parental responsiveness influences attachment and the relationship between early patterns of attachment and later behavior.

7. Understand what is mean by sex typing (as opposed to gender identity) and be able to describe some of the influences that create and maintain sex-typed behavior.

8. Be able to describe Kohlberg's stages of moral reasoning. Be familiar with criticisms of his theory, including the relationshipo between moral thought and moral behavior.

9. Be able to describe the biological developments that characterize puberty and the psychological changes that accompany these developments, including the research on early and late maturers and on adolescent-family relationships. Be familiar with the data concerning the sexual behavior of adolescents.

10. Understand the problems and confusion involved in the adolescents search for personal identity.

11. Be familiar with Erickson's psychosocial stages and how they relate to the problems faced by people at different times in their lives.

Names

1. The question of whether nature or nurture determines human development was answered by the seventeenth century British philosopher _____, who maintained that the mind of an infant is a *tabula rasa* , or "blank slate," in the sense that its contents are determined entirely by the baby's sensory experiences. (70)

2. Another important figure in the historical background of developmental psychology was _____, whose nineteenth century theory of evolution, by contrast with John Locke's view, emphasized the biological bases of human development, or heredity. (70)

3. A third important historical period for developmental psychology began in the twentieth century, during which psychologists such as _____ and _____ maintained an *environmentalist* position, asserting that human nature is completely influenced by early training and continuing interactions with the environment. (70)

4. The Swiss psychologist _____ is noted in part for his studies and his theory of cognitive development in children. (80)

5. From original investigations by Piaget, work on the development of moral reasoning was extended to adolescents and adults by the American psychologist _____. (97)

6. The notion that development from the cradle to the grave could be characterized in a series of eight stages was proposed by _____. (108)

Vocabulary and Details

BASIC QUESTIONS ABOUT DEVELOPMENT

1. One of the most debated issues in developmental psychology is whether _____ (_____) or _____ (_____) is more important in determining the course of human development. (69-70)

2. The other basic question that underlies theories of human development is whether development is a _____ process of change or a series of _____. (69-70)

3. Genetic determinants of development are expressed through _____, innately determined sequences of growth or bodily change that are relatively independent of the environment. (71)

4. As used by psychologists, the concept of developmental stages implies that a) behaviors at a given stage are organized around a _____, b) behaviors at one stage are _____ from behaviors in earlier or later stages, and c) all children go through the same stages _____. (73)

5. Crucial time periods in a person's life during which specific events must occur for physical development to proceed normally are called _____. (73)

6. With respect to psychological development, it is probably more accurate to speak of _____ periods that are optimal for a behavior to develop if it is to reach its full potential. (73)

EARLY YEARS

1. Literally, the term _____ means "without language." (74)

2. In _____, there is a reduction in the strength of a response to a repeated stimulus. (74)

3. Conversely, following habituation, if some aspect of the stimulus is changed, there may be a renewed increase in the strength of the response in the process called _____. (74)

4. A person's characteristic mood, sensitivity to stimulation, and energy level come together in the concept of _____. (77)

COGNITIVE DEVELOPMENT

1. Piaget designated the first _____ years of life as the _____. (80)

2. During the sensorimotor stage, Piaget maintained that children develop the concept of _____, an awareness that an object continues to exist even when it is not present, a phenomenon that suggests that the child possesses a _____ of the missing object. (81)

3. The next period of development, between the ages of _____ and _____, Piaget calls the _____ because the child does not yet comprehend certain rules. (82)

4. These rules or _____ are mental routines for transposing information, and are _____ in the sense that every operation has a logical opposite. (82)

5. As children leave the preoperational stage, they may begin to develop an understanding of the principle of _____, that the total amount or weight of a substance does not change when the shape or number of parts of the substance are altered. (82)

6. In Piaget's stage termed the _____, between the ages of _____ and _____, children use abstract terms and operations, but only in relation to objects to which they have direct sensory access. (83)

7. In Piaget's fourth stage, the _____, beginning around age _____, youngsters are able to reason in purely _____ terms, that is, without direct reference to concrete objects. (83)

8. _____ refers to a variety of approaches to the study of memory and thinking that emphasize processes of attention, representation, storage, and retrieval of information. (85)

9. The knowledge and control that people have over their own mental processes is called _____. (86)

PERSONALITY AND SOCIAL DEVELOPMENT

1. _____ is an infant's tendency to seek closeness to particular people and to feel more secure in their presence. (88)

2. The development of characteristics and behaviors considered appropriate for each sex is called _____; the degree to which individuals regard themselves as being male or female is known as _____. (93).

3. When referring to the belief that a person should behave in a certain way or display certain characteristics because of his or her sex, we speak of _____. (93)

ADOLESCENCE

1. The period of transition from childhood to adulthood is called _____. (100)

2. The period of sexual maturation that transforms a child into a biological adult, capable of sexual reproduction, is termed _____ and lasts 3 or 4 years. (101)

3. This period begins with a time of very rapid physical growth, called the _____, which is accompanied by the gradual development of the reproductive organs and the appearance of _____, such as breast development in girls, beard development in boys, and pubic hair in both sexes. (101)

4. A girl's first menstrual period is termed _____ and occurs relatively _____ (early/late) in puberty. (101)

5. When, in the face of conflict produced by different values between parents and peers, an adolescent tries one role after another and has difficulty synthesizing the diferent roles into a single identity, we speak of _____. (106)

DEVELOPMENT AS A LIFELONG PROCESS

1. Erikson called his eight stages of development _____ because he believed that psychological development depends upon the social relations a person forms at different points in life. (108)

2. The term _____ was used by Erikson to describe the concern that people in middle age have for providing for the next generation. (110)

Ideas and Concepts

1. a) Discuss the relationship between an organism's level on the phylogenetic scale and the time required for the development of maturity. (70)

   b) Is development complete when a person reaches physical maturity? Explain. (69)

* 2. Be able to distinguish by way of example between *physical, perceptual, cognitive,* and *social development*. (69)

*Basic ideas and concepts

BASIC QUESTIONS ABOUT DEVELOPMENT

* 1. a) Today, what is the view of most psychologists on the nature-nurture issue in human development? (70)

  b) Cite an example of the interaction of these classes of variables in one facet of development. (70-71)

  2. a) Why do we say that maturation is "relatively" independent of environmental conditions? (71)

* b) Is maturation strictly a childhood process? Cite an example. (71)

* c) Discuss the role of maturation in fetal development, citing examples. What kinds of factors may disrupt the regularity of development before birth? (71)

  d) Describe the role of maturation in one developmental process after birth. Do all children go through the stages in the same order? At the same rate? (71)

  3. How do sequences in development normally proceed? Cite an example. (71-72)

* 4. Outline two general positions on the nature of developmental sequences. (72-73)

  5. Cite an example of a critical period in human development. (73)

EARLY YEARS

* 1. a) Indicate the basic method used to study infant sensory capacities. Cite an example and a variation on this method. (74)

  b) Similarly, describe and give examples of the use of the methods of habituation and dishabituation. What has been found using this technique for the study of sensory capabilities of newborn infants? (74)

* 2. For each of the following sensory processes, indicate typical responses of newborn infants: (74-76)

  —Hearing:

  —Vision:

  —Taste:

  —Smell:

  3. a) Can infants distinguish the sound of the human voice from other sounds? Whose voice do they prefer and why? (75)

  b) Can infants distinguish important characteristics of human speech? How do we know? (75)

* c) What may be concluded with regard to the perceptual mechanisms of hearing in human infants? (75)

4. a) Indicate what characteristics of objects newborns look at and how this has affected the manufacture of crib toys. (76)

   b) What kinds of patterns do newborns prefer in the sense that they look longer at them? (76)

* c) Do newborns have a preference for looking at human faces because they are human? Explain and indicate what part of the face is generally attended to. (76)

5. a) Why was it once thought that infants could neither learn nor remember and what phenomenon shows this not to be the case? Explain. (77)

   b) Describe an experiment to show that infants can learn to discriminate between stimuli. (77)

   c) Cite a demonstration that infants as young as 3 months have very good memories. (77)

* d) From this kind of research, what is your authors' conclusion with regard to John Locke's notion that the infant's mind is a "blank slate"? (77)

6. a) Give some instances of temperament differences among infants. (77)

   b) What has been the traditional view of the origin of temperament differences and how has research altered this view to some extent? (77-78)

   c) Do researchers therefore assume that a child's temperament is unchangeable? Discuss. (78).

* 7. a) Can environmental conditions affect the rate of maturational processes? Cite the Iran orphanage examples that demonstrate such effects in the arena of motor development. (78-79)

   b) Can special training actually accelerate the development of basic motor skills? What procedures were used in classic studies on this issue and what general conclusion was reached? (79)

   c) Describe the recent studies of the stepping "reflex" that illustrate the acceleration of motor development through practice. (79)

* 8. a) Illustrate with two examples that the effects of early experiences may not be permanent, at least with respect to motor skills. (79)

* b) In what other areas of development may early deprivation produce lasting effects? Cite one example. (80)

   c) Outline a classic study concerning the effects of environmental stimulation on the intellectual development of orphaned children and indicate in detail the results of this research. (80)

COGNITIVE DEVELOPMENT

* 1. Be able to recognize the characteristics of Piaget's sensorimotor, preoperational, concrete operational, and formal operational stages, as outlined in Table 3-1. (81)

38   Chapter 3

2. a) What are infants discovering during the sensorimotor stage? What is the outcome of their "experiments" with the environment? Give an example. (81)

    b) To illustrate the concept of object permanence, indicate how a child early in this stage reacts differently to a cloth covering a toy than a child late in this stage. (81)

3. a) Can you cite an example other than that in your text to be sure that you understand the way in which conservation principles operate? (81)

    b) Why do children younger than about seven have difficulty with concepts of conservation? (82)

4. Describe some of the specific things that children between about 7 and 12 years of age (concrete operational stage) can do. (83)

5. a) Give an example of what a youngster in the formal operational stage can do when presented with a problem by contrast with a child in the concrete operational stage. (83)

    b) How would Piaget account for the adolescent tendency to be concerned with philosophical and ideological issues? (84)

*   6. a) Cite several positive contributions of Piaget's theory. (84)

    b) What do related studies tend to show with regard to the ages cited by Piaget as defining different stages of cognitive development? (84)

*   c) Indicate another problem with Piaget's theory with respect to the quality of children's thinking suggested by more recent methods of intellectual assessment. Give an example. (84)

*   d) With regard to the role of sensorimotor abilities in cognitive development, what sorts of issues are raised by recent research? (84-85)

7. a) By contrast with a focus on stages, what is the approach of some psychologists and what term applies to this view? (85)

    b) In the area of developmental psychology, how is the information processing approach applied? How are many performance differences between older and younger children viewed? (85)

    c) From this analysis, on what dimension do preschoolers perform poorly and what mainly changes with age? (85)

    d) By way of examples, illustrate how memory can be changed in children through instruction in rehearsal and organization of information. (85)

*   8. From the information processing perspective, discuss three aspects of cognitive development that affect performance as children mature. (86)

PERSONALITY AND SOCIAL DEVELOPMENT

*   1. a) Describe the early mutually reinforcing social interactions between "mothers" and their children. (86)

b) Cite evidence to indicate that infant smiling is maturational and innate. (86)

c) How do 3- and 4-month old infants demonstrate recognition and preference for familiar people, and what begins to happen around 7 or 8 months? (86-87)

*   2. a) Describe the time course and pattern of reactions in infant "stranger anxiety" and distress over separation from parents, noting also when these behaviors decline. (87)

b) What evidence suggests that conditions of child rearing have little effect on these behaviors. (87)

c) Explain in detail the two factors important in the onset and decline of stranger anxiety and separation distress. Use the term *object permanence* in your answer. (87-88)

3. a) What adaptive value does attachment have? (88)

b) Indicate the first view that psychologists held regarding the source of attachment and a conflicting piece of evidence. (88)

*   4. a) Describe the procedure of the classic Harlow experiment on attachment in monkeys. What was the question being asked in this study? (88)

*   b) Indicate the results of comparisons between artificial "mothers" along each of the following dimensions? (88-89)

—cloth vs. wire:

—rocking vs. immobile:

—warm vs. cool:

*   c) What conclusion regarding attachment in infant monkeys do these results support? (89)

5. Is attachment to an artificial mother sufficient for early social development in infant monkeys? Explain, citing typical responses. (89)

*   6. What was Bowlby's hypothesis regarding the failure to form secure attachments in human infants and, in general, what is the related evidence? (89)

7. a) Be familiar with the episodes in Ainsworth et al.'s *Strange Situation* and the measures recorded. (89)

*   b) Characterize each of the following types of babies and their mothers that were distinguishable in this procedure by completing the following table: (90)

Types of Babies	Observations at Home	Behaviors of Mothers
Securely attached		
Insecurely attached: Avoidant		
Insecurely attached: Resistant		

* 8. a) What conclusion did Ainsworth and his colleagues reach based on these and related data? (90)

b) How stable are results obtained in the Strange Situation procedure and what may influence them? (90-91)

9. a) Cite a study that showed a relationship between the pattern of early attachment and later coping with new experiences. (91)

b) Similarly, indicate the results of a study on social behavior in children as a function of early attachment styles. (91)

c) What conclusion may be drawn from these studies? However, what may be an additional *ongoing* variable to consider? (91)

d) Similarly, how may child-rearing practices affect behavior of the child in the Strange Situation? Cite an example. (91)

* 10. Cite your authors' general conclusion from these data. (91-92)

* 11. a) Overall, what do studies of the Strange Situation indicate regarding an infant's attachment to the father (when the latter is not the primary caregiver)? (92)

b) What happens if the father spends more time in child care? (92)

c) How do fathers typically interact with their children and how does this affect a baby's choices? (92)

12. a) Compare the course of social development with peers in young monkeys and young human children. (92)

b) Indicate two specific kinds of influences of peers on children's behavior. (92-93)

13. Cite two general variables determining what behavior is defined as appropriate for each sex. (93)

* 14. a) Cite an example illustrating the operation of sex-role stereotypes. Describe an experiment with college students that demonstrates this phenomenon. (93)

b) Describe the changes in sex-typed behavior that have been observed in boys and girls as they grow older. (93-94)

* c) Which sex shows more sex-typing--male or female? Give two possible reasons for this difference, citing experimental support for your answer where possible. (94-95)

* 15. a) Identify three basic sources of influence in the development of sex-typed behavior, illustrating each with examples. (96)

b) Which parent seems more concerned with sex-typed behavior? Is this concern restricted to children of only one sex? (96)

c) Can television modify sex-role stereotypes that tend to parallel reality? What may help? Cite some evidence. (96)

* 16. a) Would you expect a difference between a five-year-old and an older child in terms of whether each would say that it was wrong to lie, steal, or injure another? In what way *would* the two children differ with respect to their concepts of right and wrong? (97)

b) Cite some factors that affect a child's ability to make judgments about moral issues. (97)

17. Describe Piaget's method for studying the development of moral reasoning. What finding did he typically obtain? (97)

18. a) Describe Kohlberg's technique for studying the development of moral reasoning. What was Kohlberg attempting to determine with these methods? (97)

* b) In the table below, indicate the basis for resolving moral dilemmas for each level of moral development and suggest a possible explanation that might be offered for why it is wrong to cheat on a classroom examination that would be characteristic of each level. (98-99)

Level	Basis for Judgment	Sample Explanation
Preconventional Morality (Level I)		
Conventional Morality (Level II)		
Postconventional Morality (Level III)		

c)   Describe the results of two longitudinal studies of moral reasoning with respect to Kohlberg's analysis. What do these results suggest about postconventional morality in normal development? (99)

* 19.   a)   According to Kohlberg's analysis, where do moral standards come from? How does movement from one stage to the next come about? (99)

*   b) Present an alternative view concerning the development of conscience, citing some empirical findings to support your answer. (99)

* 20.   What conclusion do your authors reach concerning developmental trends in moral reasoning and what suggestion do they make concerning teaching children moral concepts? (99)

21.   a)   Discuss some data to show that there is a relationship between *moral reasoning* and *moral behavior*. Describe an experiment that shows that the relationship is not a perfect one when self-interest is involved, at least in children. (100)

*   b)   List three factors in addition to the ability to reason about moral dilemmas that can affect moral conduct. (100)

ADOLESCENCE

* 1.   a)   List three major tasks accomplished during adolescence. (100)

b)   Describe some of the changes that have taken place with respect to the transition between childhood and adulthood across the past few generations. What factors may be responsible for the lengthening of this transition period? (100)

c)   Cite an advantage and a disadvantage to having a gradual transition to adulthood. (100)

2.   a)   Are boys and girls immediately able to reproduce with the onset of puberty? Illustrate your answer by describing the menstrual cycles and ejaculations of young adolescents. (101)

b) Cite some statistics to illustrate the variation in duration and age of onset of puberty. In general, which sex enters puberty first and by how many years? (101)

3. a) Describe the methodology employed in a recent study by Petersen on the psychological effects of puberty. (101)

* b) Indicate the general findings of the Petersen study, noting in particular the nature of the experience for each sex and the conclusions of the authors. Do these results support the notion of adolescence as a period of "storm and stress"? (102)

* 4. a) Describe some of the dramatic changes that have occurred with respect to sexual behavior across the past 30 years. (102)

b) How have these changes produced more conflict for adolescents today? (102)

* c) Have these changes in attitudes had an effect on actual behavior? Summarize some statistics to defend your answer. (102-103)

d) What factors may be resulting in a reversal of these trends? (103)

* 6. a) Does research support the notion of a generation gap between parents and adolescents? Cite some research findings to support your answer. (103-104)

b) Characterize the family conflict that does *seem* to be more common during adolescence than other periods of development in terms of the following variables. (104)

—behaviors exhibited:

—bases for disagreement:

—intensity as a function of period of adolescence:

—parent most likely to be involved:

c) Despite the seemingly unimportant bases for conflict between adolescents and parents, what more important attempt on the part of the adolescent frequently underlies these arguments? (105)

* d) What differences have been found in the interpretation of issues between adolescents and their parents? Describe how parents and their teenagers are both torn between two positions in their interactions with one another. (105-106)

7. a) What type of working relationship is generally developed between the adolescent and his or her parents? (106)

b) According to Maccoby and Martin, what kind of parents are likely to ease the transition from childhood to adulthood? (106)

8. a) Describe some of the elements involved in the search for self-identity facing adolescents. (106)

b) Discuss the various sources of the adolescent's sense of identity. What can make the development of a consistent identity easier? (106)

c) Is the task of forming an identity easier in simple or in complex cultures? Why? (106-107)

d) How is role experimentation suppressed in today's world? In this view, what positive function might be served by political and religious youth movements? (107)

9. a) Distinguish among three ways in which the search for identity can be resolved. Use the terms *identity crisis, deviant identity*, and *identity confusion* in your answer. (107)

b) Does one's personal identity remain unchanged throughout life? Explain, citing an example. (107-108)

DEVELOPMENT AS A LIFELONG PROCESS

1. In what ways is development to be viewed as a continuous process? (108)

* 2. Look at Table 3-5. Be able to recognize the psychosocial crises associated with Erikson's eight stages of psychosocial development and the favorable outcome associated with each stage. (108)

3. a) During which psychosocial stage do most people marry? What type of people do individuals usually seek out as marriage partners? (109)

b) Which sex tends to take a more romantic approach to the selection of a mate and why is this not particularly surprising? (109)

* c) Compare how happy a married woman feels with her life as compared to unmarried women and married men. (109)

4. a) How common is divorce in this country? (109-110)

* b) Describe some of the characteristics of a successful marriage, as found in a survey of couples married 15 years or more. Be sure to note the degree of importance placed on sexual fulfillment in this survey. (110)

5. a) Describe how middle adulthood is the most productive period for many people. How imporant are people in this age group to society in general? (110)

b) What are the sources of the feelings of satisfaction and of despair that occur during middle adulthood? (110)

* 6. a) Characterize the "midlife crisis" found in several longitudinal studies. To what earlier psychosocial stage has the transition to middle adulthood been compared according to this view? (110)

* b) Is the notion of midlife crisis as a developmental stage accepted by everyone? Cite some evidence to support your answer. (110-111)

c) Nevertheless, in what ways is middle age a period of transition? (111)

7. a) Cite some reasons why it is no longer proper to call anyone over 65 "old." (111)

b) Does aging result in inevitable physical and mental deterioration? To what factors can extreme debility in the later years be attributed? (111)

c) Summarize what is known about changes in cognitive ability associated with aging. (111)

8. a) What are some of the variables that can make the later years a period of unhappiness? (111)

b) Describe some societal changes that have been brought about by the increasing proportion of older people in our society. (112)

c) According to Erikson, with what is the final psychosocial crisis concerned? (112)

Sample Quiz 3.1

1. Today, most psychologists take the view that: a) nature predominates in determining human development; b) nurture provides all of the significant bases for human development; c) both nature and nurture play important roles in human development; d) none of the above; modern psychologists no longer take a position on the contribution of nature and nurture to development.

2. A person's characteristic mood, sensitivity to stimuli, and energy are termed his or her: a) critical period; b) sex-role stereotype; c) temperament; d) maturational level.

3. In which of the following areas of development would we *not* expect lasting effects of early deprivation: a) motor skills; b) language ability; c) intellectual skills; d) emotional development.

4. According to Piaget, an important discovery made by the infant during the sensorimotor stage is the concept of: a) object permanence; b) conservation of mass; c) conservation of number; d) concrete operations.

5. In Piaget's theory, the ability to reason in purely symbolic terms is associated with the _____ stage of development: a) concrete operational; b) formal operational; c) sensorimotor; d) preoperational.

6. According to the information processing approach to cognitive development, as children mature they develop: a) knowlege of how to use good strategies for learning and remembering; b) knowing when something is not comprehended; c) monitoring of their own comprehension; d) all of the above.

7. The experiment described in your text, in which the reaction of an infant to a jack-in-the-box was labeled differently depending upon whether subjects thought the infant was a boy or a girl, was used to illustrate: a) the operation of sex-role stereotypes; b) how child-rearing practices can affect behavior in the Strange Situation laboratory setup; c) the importance of peer interaction in emotional

development; d) the fact that fathers are more concerned with sex-typed behaviors than mothers.

8. Kohlberg's classification of the level of a child's moral reasoning is based on the child's: a) agreement with parental values; b) reasoning in solving moral dilemmas; c) agreement with society's values; d) ability to reason in abstract terms.

9. Puberty: a) is defined as the period of sexual maturation that transforms a child into a biological adult; b) begins with the adolescent growth spurt; c) is accompanied by the appearance of secondary sex characteristics; d) all of the above.

10. The concern that people in middle age have for providing for the next generation is called: a) mid-life responsibility; b) menarche; c) generativity; d) the mid-life caretaking syndrome.

Sample Quiz 3.2

1. Nature is to nurture as: a) Darwin is to Skinner; b) Watson is to Piaget; c) environment is to heredity; d) both a and c.

2. Psychologists *agree* that: a) there are orderly sequences in development that depend on maturation and environment in interaction; b) developmental sequences are a continuous process operating to produce smooth effects; c) development occurs in a series of consecutive stages; d) development does not occur in an orderly fashion.

3. If an infant shows a reduction in the strength of a response such as heart rate to, say, a tone presented repetitively, we speak of: a) maturation; b) cognitive development; c) dishabituation; d) habituation.

4. Piaget's stage in which children can begin to think logically and to classify objects was termed the: a) sensorimotor stage; b) preoperational stage; c) concrete operational stage; d) formal operational stage.

5. Metacognition is: a) a child's first use of language to make a request; b) the most obvious evidence of a child's entry into the preoperational stage; c) knowledge and control over one's own mental processes; d) the type of cognitive processing found in nonhuman animals.

6. In the Harlow experiments, it was shown that baby monkeys prefer an artificial mother that is: a) cloth rather than wire; b) rocking rather than immobile; c) warm rather than cool; d) all of the above.

7. The belief that people should behave in certain ways characteristic of their sex is termed: a) sex typing; b) sex-role stereotype; c) role resolution; d) sex characteristic attribution.

8. In Kohlberg's view, the basis for resolving moral dilemmas at the conventional level of morality (Level II) includes: a) guidance by principles essential to the public welfare; b) upholding laws and social rules laid down by authorities; c) self-chosen ethical principles; d) conformance to obtain rewards.

9. Compared to his classmates, a boy who matures early will tend to be: a) happier; b) more shy and withdrawn; c) embarrassed by his physical appearance; d) more demanding of attention than others.

10. The crisis of intimacy in relationships versus isolation was said by Erikson to occur during: a) the aging years; b) the first year of life; c) early adulthood; d) age 3 through 5.

Key, Chapter 3

Names

1. John Locke
2. Charles Darwin
3. John Watson; B. F. Skinner
4. Jean Piaget; cognitive development
5. Laurence Kohlberg
6. Erik Erikson

Vocabulary and Details

1. heredity (nature); environment (nurture)
2. continuous; stages
3. maturation
4. dominant theme; qualitatively different; in the same order
5. critical periods
6. sensitive periods

1. infancy
2. habituation
3. dishabituation
4. temperament

1. 2; sensorimotor stage
2. object permanence; mental representation
3. 2; 7; preoperational stage
4. operations; reversible
5. conservation
6. concrete operational stage; 7; 12
7. formal operational stage; 12; symbolic
8. information processing
9. metacognition

1. attachment
2. sex typing; gender identity
3. sex-role stereotypes

1. adolescence
2. puberty
3. adolescent growth spurt; secondary sex characteristics
4. menarche; late
5. role confusion

1. psychosocial stages
2. generativity

Sample Quiz 3.1

1. c, 70
2. c, 77
3. a, 79-80
4. a, 81
5. b, 83
6. d, 86
7. a, 93
8. b, 98
9. d, 101
10. c, 110

Sample Quiz 3.2

1. a, 70
2. a, 72
3. d, 74
4. c, 81
5. c, 86
6. d, 88-89
7. b, 93
8. b, 98
9. a, 101-102
10. c, 108

Sensory Processes

Learning Objectives

1. Be familiar with the procedures for measuring absolute thresholds and difference thresholds. Know what is meant by the terms psychometric function, just noticeable difference (jnd), Weber's law, and Fechner's law.

2. Be able to discuss the process of sensory coding, including what single-cell recording experiments tell us about how sensory systems code the intensity and the quality of a stimulus.

3. Be able to describe the stimulus for vision. Know the main parts of the visual system, the sequence by which light passes through them, and the functions of the two types of receptor cells in the retina.

4. Understand the phenomena of color appearance, color mixing, color deficiency, and object color. Be able to discuss these phenomena from the perspective of trichromatic theory, opponent-color theory, and two-stage color theory.

5. Be able to describe the physical aspects of a sound wave. Know the main parts of the auditory system and the sequence by which sound passes through them and is transduced into an electrical impulse.

6. Be prepared to describe temporal and place theories of pitch perception. Be familiar with the problems encountered by each that led to the idea of duplicity theory.

7. Understand the evolutionary significance of smell and its function as a primitive means of communication. Know the stimulus for smell, the parts of the olfactory system, and how the system codes the quality of an odor.

8. Be familiar with the stimulus for taste, the nature of taste receptors, and how the gustatory system codes taste.

9. Be able to describe the three distinct skin senses in terms of the class of stimuli to which each responds and the receptors involved. Be familiar with the gate control theory of pain.

10. Be familiar with the body senses that inform us about our movements and our orientation in space.

Names

1. In what has become the cornerstone of the biological approach to sensation, ~~Weber~~ *Müller* (in the early 1800s) proposed that the stimuli reaching our sense organs produce different types of sensations in different nerves. (117)

2. The founder of the science of psychology in the late 1800s was ~~Wundt~~, who sought to break down conscious experience into its basic elements and analyze how they related, in a kind of "mental chemistry." (117)

3. The German physiologist *Fechner* first determined the psychophysical law that the greater the intensity of a stimulus the larger the change in the stimulus that is necessary for a change to be noticed. (120)

4. Assuming this law to be true, later the German physicist _____ proposed also that, for a given stimulus, every *just noticeable difference* is perceptually equal to every other one. (120)

5. The trichromatic or Young-Helmholtz theory of color vision was developed and quantified by _____ in the 1850s based upon an earlier theory. (133)

6. Limitations of the trichromatic theory led _____ to develop the opponent-color theory a little later in the nineteenth century. (134)

Vocabulary and Details

1. Wilhelm Wundt's method of _____ involved trained observers describing their own experiences of some object or event. (117)

2. In the current view, the experiences elicited by simple stimuli (such as a red patch) are termed _____, while those occasioned by complex and often meaningful stimuli (such as a fire engine) are called _____. (117)

3. Thus, perception involves the integration of _____. (117)

4. If we think of a system of processes for directly knowing the world, then _____ processes are associated with the sense organs and peripheral levels of the nervous system, while _____ processes are associated with the higher levels of the nervous system.

COMMON PROPERTIES OF SENSORY MODALITIES

1. Individual senses are also called *sensory* *modalities* (118)

2. Any one of the forms of physical energy to which we are sensitive is called a _____. (118)

3. The weakest magnitude of a stimulus that can be reliably discriminated is called the *threshold* defined as the value of the stimulus at which it is detected _50_ percent of the time. (118)

4. The procedures used to determine thresholds of stimuli are called _____. (118)

5. In the method called the _____, a set of stimuli of varying magnitudes is presented one at a time and a subject reports whether or not a given stimulus is detected. (118)

6. A graph of the data obtained in a psychophysical experiment that relates stimulus magnitude to subject reports is called a psychometric function. (118)

7. The smallest difference in stimulus magnitude necessary to tell two stimuli apart _50_ percent of the time is called the JND or differential threshold. (119)

8. The translation of physical energy into electrochemical energy in the nervous system is called transduction. (121)

9. Cells specialized for transduction are located in the sense organs and are called sensory transducers. (121)

10. In essence, a receptor is a specialized nerve cell or neuron. (121)

11. Experiments designed to determine which specific neurons are activated by a given stimulus use a procedure called _____. (121)

12. In the absence of a stimulus, the usual single-cell recording will depict a slow rate of excitation in the form of vertical spikes on an oscilloscope; by contrast, when a stimulus is presented, the rate of spike activity will be fast (fast/slow). (121)

13. Müller's notion (see Names, item 1) that different sensory modalities are represented by different sensory nerves to the brain is called the doctrine of _____. (124)

VISUAL SENSE

1. Light is energy produced by the oscillation of electrically charged matter; this energy (like X rays, infrared rays, or television waves), is called solar radiation and measured in quantum. (125)

2. Actually, only the small portion of such radiation visible to humans is ordinarily called visual spectrum that in the wavelength range of _400_ to _700_ nanometers. (125)

3. Light (or other electromagnetic radiation) may be specified in terms of a) the wavelengths it contains and b) its physical intensity at each wavelength, called the _____ of the light. (125)

4. The image-forming system of the eye consists of the retina lens, and conjunctiva (125)

5. When the lens of the eye does not flatten enough to bring far objects into focus, but does focus on near objects, a person is said to be short or _____. (125) sighted.

6. Conversely, when the lens of the eye does not become spherical enough to focus on near objects, but does focus on far objects, a person is said to be far (or _____). (125) sighted

Sensory Processes   53

7. Transduction in the eye occurs in the _retina_ (126)

8. In the retina, there are two types of cells: a) _rods_, elongated cells that are specialized for responding to light at low intensities (at night, for example); and b) _cones_, specialized for light at high intensity and in color (especially in daylight). (126-127)

9. Rods and cones contain chemicals that absorb light called _photopigments_ which start the process of nerve impulses. (127)

10. Seeing *what* happened is essentially what we mean by visual _____; seeing that *something* happened is essentially visual _____. (127)

11. The phenomenon of _adaptation_ refers to the fact that the sensitivity of the visual system changes as a person's visual system adjusts to the prevailing level of illumination. (128)

12. Experientially, a colored light may be characterized along three dimension, the first of which is _brightness_, its perceived intensity. (129)

13. The second dimension of color is _hue_, which refers to its quality (e.g., red or greenish-yellow). (129)

14. The third dimension of color is _hue_, its purity or "colorfulness," where a color that contains a large amount of white is said to be _pale_ and a color that contains little or no white is said to be _solid_. (129)

15. When we mix lights of different colors we obtain an _____ mixture; whereas when we mix colored paints or pigments we obtain a _____ mixture. (130)

16. People who have the ability to match a wide range of colors with three colored lights in a way that resembles the matching of most other people are called _____; those who match the colors differently or who are poor at discriminating wavelengths are called _____. (131)

17. People who are somewhat or completely unable to discriminate wavelengths are _colourblind_, including those who match colors using two wavelengths, called _____, and those who match colors using only the intensity of a single wavelength, called _____. (131)

18. According to the Young-Helmholtz, or _____ theory of color vision there are _3_ (how many?) types of cone receptors for color vision that act jointly. (133)

19. Alternatively, according to the _____ theory of color vision devised by Herring, there are _2_ (how many) types of color-sensitive units, one responding to either red or green and the other to either blue or yellow. (134)

Auditory Sense

1. A _sound_ is a wave of pressure changes that is transmitted through the air when an object moves or vibrates. (135-136).

2. The waveform of any sound may be decomposed into some number of simpler wave forms described mathematically as _____ and perceived as _pitch_. (136)

54   Chapter 4

3. Pure tones vary in terms a) _____, perceived as pitch; b) _____, perceived as loudness; and c) the time at which they start, called _____. (136-137)

4. Frequency of sound waves is measured in _____ (_____); intensity is measured in terms of the pressure difference between peak and trough of the sound wave, specified in _____. (137)

5. The ear consists of three parts: the _____ and _____, which function to amplify and transmit sound, and the _____ or _____, a coiled tube of bone which contains the sound receptors. (139)

6. The sound receptors are called _____ because they resemble tiny hairs that extend into fluids in the inner ear. (140)

7. The prime *quality* of sound is _____, which _____ (increases/decreases) as frequency increases. (141)

8. When two pure tones that are close in frequency are presented simultaneously and the threshold for one of the tones is increased, we speak of the phenomenon of auditory _____. (141)

9. The _____ theory of pitch perception holds that the basilar membrane vibrates at the same frequency as a sound wave, thus allowing us to hear different sound frequencies. (141)

10. The later _____ theory of pitch perception proposed by Helmholtz maintains that it is the place on the basilar membrane that vibrates the most that determines what neural fibers are activated, thus enabling us to distinguish pitches. (142)

11. Because a sound provides slightly different inputs at each of our two ears, we can determine the direction of its source; that is, we can _____ sound. (143)

Other Senses

1. The most primitive sense, and the one with the most direct neural route to the brain, is _____ (_____). (144-145)

2. Chemicals secreted by insects and some animals that may be smelled and that communicate various forms of information are called _____. (146)

3. Taste or _____ begins in taste receptors located in bumps on the tongue and around the mouth called _____. (147-148)

4. Sensitivity to pressure may be measured by the _____ method, the minimum distance between two points on the skin that pressure applied by thin rods can be discriminated. (150)

5. Temperature is sensed by _____ and _____ that respond to temperature decreases and increases, respectively, during transduction. (151)

6. According to the _____ theory of pain, a neural "gate" in the spinal cord may block transmission from pain receptors to the brain. (152)

7. In the phenomenon called _____, stimulation of a region of the midbrain acts like an anesthetic (pain reducer). (152-153)

8. A Chinese healing procedure that involves inserting needles into the skin to reduce pain is _____. (153)

9. A sense of the position and movement of the head and limbs is called _____. (153)

10. Orientation and body movement are made possible by receptors located in the inner ear's _____. (153)

Ideas and Concepts

1. a) What knowledge is needed in order to survive and how is it obtained? (117)

   b) Outline Democritus's ancient view of how the brain differentiates between different modalities of sensory stimuli. (117)

   c) Was Democritus's model completely erroneous? Explain. (117)

* 2. a) What was the main problem with Wundt's method of introspection, and to what did the goal of research on sensation shift? (117)

* b) Accordingly, how did the methods of sensory research change? (117)

   c) Currently, what are the dominant approaches to the study of sensory processes? (117)

3. How did Wundt distinguish between sensation and perception, and what kind of a distinction is made today? Cite examples. (117)

COMMON PROPERTIES OF SENSORY MODALITIES

* 1. a) What is a common way to determine the sensitivity of a sensory modality? (118)

   b) Cite an example of the use of the method of constant stimuli. (118)

   c) Be able to interpret a psychometric function, such as that in Figure 4-1. (118)

* 2. a) What is the most notable thing about the different thresholds shown in Table 4-1? (119)

   b) Cite some data to show the sensitivity of human vision. (119)

* 3. a) Besides the detection of a stimulus *per se*, in what other aspect of sensation have psychologists been interested? (119)

   b) Outline an experiment to find a jnd and the results that enable determination of its actual size. (119)

*Basic ideas and concepts

56   Chapter 4

*   c)   What is the relationship between intensity of the standard stimulus and the size of the jnd? (119)

*   4.   State *Weber's law* in your own words and indicate in the following equation what each term stands for. (120)

$$\frac{\Delta I}{I} = k$$

*   5.   a)   Similarly, state *Fechner's law* in your own words and indicate in the following equation what each term stands for. (120)

$$P = c \log I$$

        b)   What additional assumption did Fechner make as he generalized Weber's law? (120)

        c)   To show Fechner's law in operation, use specific values to demonstrate that the intensity of, say, a light bulb might not appreciably affect its perceived magnitude (P). What happens to perceived changes in magnitude as the physical intensity of a stimulus increases from low levels to high levels? (120)

*   6.   a)   What formidable problem is faced by the brain in sensing the world and how does it solve this difficulty? (120-121)

        b)   Cite some examples to illustrate the process of transduction. (121)

  7.   a)   Trace the progress of an electrical signal once a receptor is activated. (121)

*   b)   Where is the experience of sensation actually located? Then how do our sensory systems accurately relate external events to sensory experience? (121)

*   8.   a)   What two sensory experiences are coded for every modality of stimulus? Cite examples. (121)

        b)   Describe a single-cell recording experiment, noting especially how the signals are displayed and how they appear. (121)

*   9.   a)   What is the primary means for coding the intensity of a stimulus, as revealed by the single-cell recording method? (121, 124)

*   b)   Describe another means by which the intensity of a stimulus can be coded. Note especially the relationship between intensity and regularity of neural firing. (124)

*   c)   Discuss the coding of distinctive qualities *between* sense modalities, as formulated by Müller. (124)

*   d)   In what two ways are distinctive qualities of a stimulus coded *within* a sense modality. Use examples and the terms *specificity* and *pattern* in your answer. (124)

VISUAL SENSE

1. Which of the body's "six" senses obtain information that is at a distance? (124)

* 2. a) Be able to list the three main components of the human visual system and the two systems within the eye itself. (125)

*   b) Using the information in Figure 4-6 and the letters in the diagram below, enter the letter that corresponds to the location of each part of the eye in the corresponding cell of the table provided for item 2c). (125)

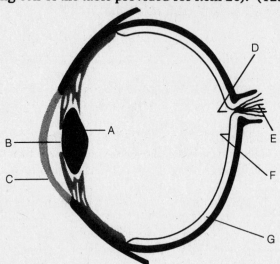

*   c) In the table below, where possible describe and indicate the functions of the various parts of the eye. (125-127)

Part of the eye	Location	Description (if possible)	Function (if possible)
cornea			
lens			
pupil			
retina			
fovea			
optic nerve			
blind spot			

58   Chapter 4

*   3. Are the receptor cells distributed evenly across the retina? What are some of the implications of their distribution? (127)

    4. Trace the course of a nerve impulse in the retina using the terms *bipolar cells* and *ganglion cells*. (127)

*   5. a) In detail, what two features of the eye determine our sensitivity to a light's intensity, or brightness ? (127)

*   b) What is one consequence of the difference in location of rods and cones? How may this be measured? (127)

*   c) Indicate yet another factor that plays a role in brightness sensitivity. Be able to interpret the related information presented in Figure 4-10. (127-128)

        d) Why do the differences discussed in 5c arise, and how does this fact explain changes in vision that take place as night falls? (128)

    6. a) Discuss the rates of light adaptation that take place when the change is to light of higher intensity versus to light of a lower intensity. Cite a familiar example of each. (128)

*   b) Why does the course of light adaptation illustrated in Figure 4-11 show essentially two different patterns? How do we know that this is largely a retinal process rather than a cortical one? (128)

*   c) What happens to the perceived brightness of light as we adapt to it? Describe a dramatic demonstration of this process possible with sophisticated equipment. (128)

*   d) What is the "hallmark of sensory systems" that is demonstrated by the process of adaptation to an unchanging visual stimulus? (128)

    7. Indicate what color corresponds to each of the spectrums of light below. (See also Figure 4-12.) (128)

        —short wavelengths:

        —medium wavelengths:

        —long wavelengths:

*   8. a) In your own words, what is meant by the term *color solid*, devised by Munsell? (129)

        b) How many different colors can people discriminate and how many can actually be named? (129)

    9. a) Why are the rules for additive mixtures of color different from those of subtractive mixtures? (130)

*   b) Be sure to note how many different wavelengths of light are necessary to match any color. Also, what must characterize the relative differences in

wavelengths of colors that are used to match other colors? (That is, should they be very different or very similar?) (130-131)

c) Discuss a practical application of the rule expressed in b). (131)

10. Indicate the origin of most color deficiencies. Why do they occur more in males than females? (131)

* 11. a) What physical dimension determines the color of an object? Cite some examples. (133)

* b) Name two other factors that may determine object color perception. Nevertheless, what is the critical factor? (133)

* 12. a) Outline the Young-Helmholtz theory of color vision. Use the terms *short, medium,* and *long receptor.* (133)

* b) How is quality of color (hue) coded in this theory? (133)

* c) How does this theory relate to the normal way we can match a color with a mixture, and how does it explain the two types of color blindness? (133-134)

* 13. a) Summarize the observations that led Herring to postulate the opponent color theory of color vision. Use the term *opponent pair.* (134)

* b) Discuss Herring's opponent-color theory in detail, indicating some of the limitations on color vision explained by the theory and how it accounts for the experience of hue. (134-135)

* c) Outline how the discovery of *color opponent cells* in the brain relates to Herring's theory. (135)

* 14. a) Indicate a theoretical solution to the problem faced by proponents of the trichromatic theory and opponent-color theory, namely that neither approach could explain all of the facts of color vision. (135)

b) Does this theory provide the last word in this area of sensation? Indicate two unsolved difficulties. (135)

Auditory Sense

1. a) Characterize the power of some sounds in terms of decibels and note the mathematical relationship between sound power and decibels. (137-138)

b) Are most sounds pure tones? Explain, using the terms *harmonies* and *fundamental.* (139)

60   Chapter 4

* 2. a) Using the information in Figure 4-25 and the letters in the diagram below, enter the letter that corresponds to the location of each part of the ear in the corresponding cell of the table provided for item 2b. (140)

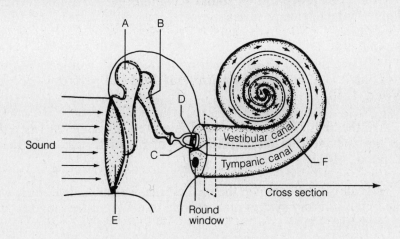

* b) In the table below, where possible describe and indicate the functions of the various parts of the ear. (139-140)

Part of the ear	Location	Description (if possible)	Function (if possible)
eardrum			
malleus			
incus			
stapes			
oval window			
basilar membrane			

* c) Trace the course of sound transduction in the inner ear from the basilar membrane to the auditory neurons. To what side(s) of the brain is sound information transmitted? (139-141)

d) Can you indicate what the relative number of neurons in the ear and the eye says about the relative sensitivity of each of these receptor organs? (140)

* 3. a) How does reception of sound resemble that of light? Therefore, in what relative frequency range is hearing best, low, middle, or high? (See also Figure 4-26.) (140)

* b) Describe the two kinds of hearing loss. Which would be more typical of rock musicians? Use the terms *conduction loss* and *sensory-neural loss* in your answer. (140)

* 4. a) Are the sensations when sound is mixed the same as when color is mixed? Explain and indicate the implications of the differences for theories of sound reception. (141)

* b) Indicate the rationale for the method that is used to determine whether there are cells in the auditory system that respond to different frequencies and one result of this method. (141)

* 5. a) Outline two important features of Rutherford's temporal theory of pitch perception. (141)

* b) What major problem did this theory encounter and how did Weaver propose to resolve it? (141)

c) Indicate the research support that this theoretical resolution received. (141-142)

* d) What problem is faced by even the modified temporal theory, and what answer was proposed by the anatomist, Duverney? In what respect is this notion essentially correct? (142)

* 6. a) Does Helmholtz's later place theory of pitch perception hold that we hear with our basilar membrane? Explain. (142)

b) What observations did von Békésy make that validate the place theory? (142)

7. a) What major problem is encountered by the place theory? (142-143)

b) How does *duplicity theory* provide a tentative solution to this difficulty as well as to the difficulty encountered by temporal theory? (143)

* 8. Discuss how we use *interaural time differences* and *interaural intensity differences* to localize sound and at what relative frequencies each is important. (143)

Other Senses

1. Why have vision and hearing been called the "higher senses"? (143)

* 2. a) What anatomical information tells us that olfaction is more important in many species than it is in humans? Cite an example to show the utility of this fact. (145-146)

b)   Describe examples of the power of pheromones in the love life and death of certain species. (146)

c)   Discuss two kinds of data indicating that humans have retained at least some remnants of an effective of olfactory communication system. (146)

*   3.   Trace the transduction pathway of olfaction from molecule to *cilia*, to *olfactory bulb*, and *olfactory cortex*. (146)

*   4.   a)   About how much *less* sensitive is a human's ability to smell than a dog's? Is this because our receptors are less sensitive? Explain. (147)

b)   What six basic odors have been postulated? Is there good agreement on these? (147)

*   c)   Is there agreement on how odors are coded? Describe this mechanism in detail. (147)

5.   a)   List some of the factors that determine taste. Cite examples. (147-148)

*   b)   Describe the gustatory system, including the nature of the stimulus for taste and the transduction process. (148)

*   c)   Be able to identify the locations of the four different kinds of taste buds on the tongue. (See also Figure 4-30.) (148)

6.   a)   Cite some examples of "masking" with taste. (148-149)

*   b)   Given the choice, how many basic tastes do people use to describe substances and what are they? (149)

*   c)   Describe the neural coding system that underlies the classification of tastes indicated in b) and provide some related empirical evidence. (149-150)

*   7.   What are the three senses of the skin? List four reasons why we conclude that there are three senses rather than just one, as is traditionally thought. (150)

8.   a)   What is the stimulus for sensed pressure? Does this mean that any steady pressure will be sensed? Explain. (150)

b)   Where are we the most sensitive to variations in pressure? (150)

*   c)   Describe two factors upon which pressure sensing depends, citing the anatomical evidence regarding the distribution of receptors and also the nature of underlying neural cells. (150)

*   d)   What do your authors mean when they say that pressure sensing "shows profound adaptation"? (Can you see how this characteristic of pressure sensing relates to your answer to a?) (150)

9.   a)   Does evidence obtained with the two-point threshold method correspond with that for the pressure threshold described in 8b)? In terms of the two-point threshold measure, where are we the most sensitive? (150)

b) Distinguish between active and passive touching. (150)

* 10. a) How are the qualities of temperatures coded and what are the limits of this system? Explain how we sense very "hot" objects. (151)

* b) Why is it important that we are so sensitive to temperature changes at the skin? (151)

c) Describe the process of adaptation of skin temperature and illustrate with an everyday example. (151)

* 11. a) In general, what is the stimulus for pain? Describe the process of pain sensing in the skin. (151)

* b) List some of the factors that may modify pain sensations. Cite one astonishing demonstration of the psychological aspects of pain control. (151-152)

* 12. a) In the gate control analysis of pain sensation, how can the "mind" alter the experiencing of pain? (152)

* b) Cite three forms of evidence that are consistent with gate control theory. (152-153)

* 13. a) What does kinesthesis enable us to do? (153)

b) Where are the receptors for kinesthesis located? Are these solely responsible for this sense? Explain. (153)

* 14. a) Discuss the mechanism for the sense of orientation and body movement using the terms *vestibular sacs* and *semicircular canals* in conjunction with the specific forms of movement detected. (153)

b) What form of stimulation may cause dizziness and nausea? (153)

c) In what respect are the body senses different from the other senses discussed in this chapter? (153)

Sample Quiz 4.1

1. Psychophysical methods are used to determine: a) the electrical activity in the receptors and neural pathways to the brain when subjects are presented various stimuli; b) stimulus thresholds; c) the physical properties of the stimuli to which a sensory modality is sensitive; d) the relationship between sensation and perception.

2. The two-point threshold method is used to measure sensitivity to: a) light; b) pressure; c) sound; d) smell.

3. The critical factor determining the color of an object is: a) the color of the other objects surrounding it; b) the wavelengths reflected by the object; c) the color normally associated with the object; d) the brightness of the setting in which the object is being viewed.

4. Which of the following phenomena was not listed as a piece of evidence consistent with the gate-control theory of pain: a) stimulation of a region in the midbrain can act as an anesthetic; b) acupuncture has made it possible to perform major surgery on a conscious patient; c) pressure stimulation near a wound may help alleviate pain; d) temperatures that are very hot will activate both warm and cold receptors in the skin.

5. The experiences elicited by simple stimuli are termed: a) perceptions; b) transductions; c) sensations; d) mental elements.

6. _____ are to low intensity as _____ are to high intensity: a) cones, rods; b) rods, cones; c) photoreceptors, retina; d) retina, photoreceptors.

7. People who match colored lights using three wavelengths are probably in the category of those we would call: a) color normal; b) color anomalous; c) dichromats; d) color blind.

8. The temporal theory of pitch perception holds that: a) it is the place on the basilar membrane that vibrates the most that determines which receptor cells are activated; b) there are three types of sound receptors that act together to determine the nature of sound; c) sound is perceived when opponent cells for sound reception are activated; d) the basilar membrane vibrates at the same frequency as a sound wave, enabling us to discriminate pitch.

9. The auditory hair cells are supported by the _____ which vibrates due to pressure changes when a sound is transmitted. a) cochlea; b) basilar membrane; c) malleus; d) stapes.

10. The more intense the stimulus, the _____ the change in intensity required for a person to notice a change: a) smaller; b) greater; c) more variable; d) none of the above; Weber's law states that the relationship between intensity and a jnd is a constant.

Sample Quiz 4.2

1. The absolute threshold of a stimulus is that value of the stimulus at which it is: a) always detected; b) never detected; c) detected 50 percent of the time; d) detected only sometimes, regardless of the percentage.

2. Perhaps the most notable thing about absolute thresholds for stimuli in different sense modalities is: a) how similar they are; b) how low they are; c) how variable they are; d) how high they are.

3. A single-cell recording of a receptor when a stimulus is absent: a) shows a slow rate of activity; b) shows a high rate of activity; c) shows spontaneous activity; d) both a and c.

4. "What happened" is to "something happened" as: a) hyperopia is to myopia; b) light adaptation is to dark adaptation; c) place theories are to temporal theories; d) visual acuity is to visual sensitivity.

5. Munsell's color solid: a) depicts hue; b) depicts brightness; c) includes a scale for saturation; d) all of the above.

6. Frequency, intensity, and phase are the three basic dimensions of: a) color; b) touch; c) sound; d) odor.

7. The gateway to the inner ear (the membrane separating the middle ear from the inner ear) is the: a) oval window; b) eardrum; c) basilar membrane; d) pinna.

8. With respect to transduction, the difference in smell between rotten eggs and milady's finest perfume is due primarily to: a) the pattern of activation in the receptors; b) the number of receptors activated; c) the type of receptor stimulated; d) the direction the cilia move when stimulated.

9. Taste: a) is a function of genetic makeup and past experiences; b) may be a function of four distinct qualities; c) is coded in the form of both the specific nerve fibers that are activated and the pattern of activation across nerve fibers; d) all of the above.

10. A sense of the position and movement of the head and limbs is called: a) gustation; b) olfaction; c) kinesthesis; d) vestibular localization.

66   Chapter 4

Key, Chapter 4

Names

1. Johannes Müller
2. Wilhelm Wundt
3. Ernst Weber
4. Gustav Fechner
5. Hermann von Helmholtz
6. Ewald Herring

Vocabulary and Details

1. introspection
2. sensations; perceptions
3. sensations
4. sensory; perceptual

1. sensory modalities
2. stimulus
3. absolute threshold; 50
4. psychophysical methods
5. method of constant stimuli
6. psychometric function
7. 50; difference threshold; just noticeable difference (jnd)
8. transduction
9. receptors
10. neuron
11. single-cell recording
12. spontaneous activity; fast
13. specific nerve energies

1. electromagnetic; wavelengths
2. light; 400; 700
3. energy spectrum
4. cornea; pupil; lens
5. myopic (nearsighted)
6. hyperoptic (farsighted)
7. retina
8. rods; cones
9. photoreceptors
10. acuity; sensitivity
11. light adaptation
12. brightness
13. hue
14. saturation; unsaturated; saturated
15. additive; subtractive
16. color normal; color anomalous
17. color blind; dichromats; monochromats
18. trichromatic; three
19. opponent-color; two

1. sound wave
2. sine waves; pure tones
3. frequency; intensity; phase
4. cycles per second (hertz); decibels
5. outer ear; middle ear; inner ear; cochlea
6. hair cells

7. pitch; increases
8. masking
9. temporal
10. place
11. localize

1. smell (olfaction)
2. pheromones
3. gustation; taste buds
4. two-point threshold
5. cold receptors; warm receptors
6. gate control
7. stimulation-produced analgesia
8. acupuncture
9. kinesthesis
10. vestibular apparatus

Sample Quiz 4.1

1. b, 118
2. b, 150
3. b, 133
4. d, 152-153
5. c, 117
6. b, 126-127
7. a, 131
8. d, 141
9. b, 139-140
10. b, 120

Sample Quiz 4.2

1. c, 118
2. b, 119
3. d, 121
4. d, 127
5. d, 129
6. c, 136-137
7. a, 139
8. a, 147
9. d, 147-149
10. c, 153

Perception

Learning Objectives

1. Be prepared to discuss the processes by which we segregate objects, including figure-ground organization and the Gestalt principles of grouping.

2. Be able to list and describe the various monocular and binocular cues that determine perceived distance (depth). Understand the difference between Helmholtz's notion of unconscious inference and Gibson's direct perception as explanations of distance perception.

3. Understand the phenomena of stroboscopic motion and induced motion. Be able to present evidence that the perception of real motion depends on the activation of specific cells in the the visual cortex as well as on information from the motor system about eye movements.

4. Be able to discuss the role of feature detectors in the early stages of object recognition and to cite the behavioral evidence for primitive features.

5. Know how connectionist models explain the process of matching an object's description with shape descriptions stored in memory to find the best match.

6. Be able to describe, with examples, how context influences our perception of objects.

7. Be able to describe the process of selective attention (both visual and auditory) and the role of attention in conjoining the features of an object.

8. Be able to show, with examples, how each of the five perceptual constancies contributes to our perception of stable wholes.

9. Understand how perceived distance contributes to size constancy and how the size-distance principle explains some perceptual illusions.

10. Be prepared to discuss the nativist and empiricist views of perception, presenting relevant evidence from research on the perceptual capacities of infants and the rearing of animals under conditions of controlled stimulation.

Names

1. The famous Gestalt psychologist who first noted the determinants of grouping (as well as many other perceptual phenomena) was _____. (159)

Vocabulary and Details

Functions of Perception

1. A _____ is the outcome of a perceptual process. (157)

2. The study of perception is the study of how we integrate _____ into _____ of the objects of our world, and the use of the latter in getting around the world. (157)

3. In vision, determining *what* objects are is referred to as _____(or _____). (157)

4. Also in vision, determining *where* objects are is called _____ (or _____). (157)

Localization

1. Localization in a three-dimensional world is made possible by three perceptual abilities: a) _____, separating objects from one another and from their background; b) determining the _____ of objects from us; and c) determining the _____ patterns of objects. (158)

2. An early twentieth century German approach to psychology that studied how we organize objects and stressed the importance of perceiving *whole* objects or forms was called _____. (158)

3. If a stimulus contains two or more distinct regions, we usually see part of the stimulus as a _____ containing objects of interest and the rest as _____. (158)

4. When objects cluster into pairs or sets of some kind, we speak of the perceptual phenomenon called _____. (159)

5. Among the determinants of grouping objects are: a) _____, the tendency to group elements that are near to one another; b) _____, the tendency to group elements to complete figures that are incomplete; c) _____, the tendency to group together objects that form an unbroken contour; and d) _____, the tendency to group similar objects. (159)

6. Cues our perceptual system uses to group features (shapes, for example) into a single object include: a) common _____, that is, two contours are likely to be features of the same object if they are the same distance from the observer; and b) common _____, that is two contours moving in the same direction are likely to be features of the same objects. (159-160)

7. _____ are two-dimensional cues that a perceiver uses to infer distance in a three-dimensional world; if these involve one eye they are said to be _____, and if they involve both eyes they are said to be _____. (160)

8. The monocular distance cues that artists use to create depth on a two-dimensional surface include _____, _____, and _____. (160)

9. A _____ is a device that displays a different image to each eye and creates the illusion of depth through binocular distance cues, including _____ and _____. (160-161)

10. One of the "invariant" cues in perception discussed by Gibson is the fact that, when a textured surface is viewed in perspective, its elements appear to be packed more closely together as the surface recedes; this phenomenon is termed the _____. (162)

11. In darkness, when a light is flashed followed by another light spatially close to it, it appears that the light has moved from the one position to the other in the perceptual event called _____. (163)

12. A second motion phenomenon, called _____, occurs when a large object surrounding a smaller one moves, causing the smaller one to appear that it is moving. (163)

13. Of course, we also perceive _____, caused by real movement across the retina. We appear to be more sensitive to _____ (an object is seen against a structured background) than we are to _____, (the background is dark or neutral and only the moving object can be seen). (163)

14. A loss of sensitivity to motion in a specific direction that occurs when we continuously view that motion is one form of _____. (164)

15. One effect of selective adaptation is apparent motion in the opposite direction of that which has just been viewed, termed _____. (164)

Recognition

1. The region of the retina that is associated with a specific neuron in the visual cortex is that neuron's _____; when a stimulus appears anywhere in the field, the associated neuron fires. (166)

2. Single-cell recordings in the visual cortex have identified three types of cells that can be distinguished by the features to which they respond; these are called _____, _____, and _____ cells. (166)

3. Collectively, the cells described in item 2 are referred to as _____, and may be called the "building blocks of perception" because the features they respond to approximate numerous shapes. (167)

4. A model of recognition--matching features with shape descriptions stored in memory--that incorporates a network of nodes with excitatory and inhibitory "connections" is called a _____. (168)

5. At the neural level, hypothetical connections may be either a) _____, if a feature is activated then activation spreads to a letter, or b) _____, if a feature is activated then activation of the letter decreases. (168-169)

6. Our ability to perceive an object is a function not only of the object itself but also everything in the surrounding situation, or _____, that we use to infer what the object is. (172)

7. The effect of context is extremely important to perception when a figure is _____, that is, when it can be perceived in more than one way. (172)

8. The process by which we select stimuli for awareness is termed _____. (173)

9. In "selective looking," the eyes are engaged in noncontinuous motion, or _____; the periods during which the eyes are still are called _____, and the brief movements are called _____. (173)

10. Besides selection, the process of attention brings together or "fuses" the features of an object in the phenomenon termed _____. (176)

Perceptual Constancies

1. The tendency to perceive an object as the same regardless of changes in, say, lighting, position, or distance is called _____. (177)

2. The _____ principle states that perceived size is a product of retinal size multiplied by perceived distance. (181)

3. An _____ is a percept that is false or distorted by when evaluated by means of physical measurement. (182)

Perceptual Development

1. In the age-old controversy regarding the nature of perception, the position of the _____ was that we are born with the ability to perceive the way we do, whereas the _____ held that we learn perception through experience with objects in the world. (183-184)

2. An infant's tendency to look at some objects more than others is studied through the _____ method. (185)

3. The method of _____ involves placing electrodes over the visual cortex in the back of the head to measure electrical activity generated by visual activity. (185)

4. To be able to discriminate one part of an object from another when perceiving forms is called _____. (186)

5. Closely related, the ability to discriminate between dark and light stripes is called _____. (186)

6. In the _____ method for the study of depth perception, an infant or animal is placed on a transparent surface and given a choice between standing over a "shallow" or "deep" checkerboard pattern. (187)

Ideas and Concepts

Functions of Perception

*   1.   According to the text, what two basic questions (problems) must our auditory and visual systems answer? (157)

      2.   Indicate the survival functions of pattern recognition and spatial location. (157)

      3.   Are the perceptual functions, recognition and localization, completely independent? Why can we assume that they are qualitatively different processes? (157)

Localization

*   1.   What kind of organization was of the greatest concern to Gestalt psychologists and is considered to be the most elementary form of perceptual organization? (158)

*   2.   a)   How do we know that figure-ground organization is not in the physical stimulus, but rather in the perceptual system? (158-159)

          b)   Must the stimulus in the figure-ground relationship contain identifiable objects? Can you cite an example? (159)

          c)   Give some instances of figure-ground relationships in other sense modalities. (159)

*   3.   Be sure you can recognize the determinants of grouping operating in Figures 5-3 and 5-5. (159-160)

*   4.   a)   Outline an example of the research strategy for the study of grouping used by Wertheimer. (159)

          b)   What has been the purpose of more recent variations on studies of grouping? Give an example of the kind of results that have been obtained and provide an explanation for these results. (159)

          c)   Using the information in Figure 5-5, explain the same phenomenon discussed in b) as it operates according to the principle of good continuation. (159-160)

      5.   Cite some examples of perceptual grouping in modalities other than vision. (160)

      6.   a)   Why has the idea of distance cues arisen in the context of perceiving depth? (160)

          b)   In what respect does seeing with both eyes have an advantage in depth perception? (160)

*Basic ideas and concepts

Perception   73

* c) In the table below, provide a definition in your own words and indicate the way in which each of the types of depth cues function in depth perception. (Also, be able to recognize the operation of these cues in the related figures in your text.) (160-161)

Monocular Cues	Definition, function
relative size	
superposition	
relative height	
Binocular Cues	Definition, function
binocular parallax	
binocular disparity	

7. a) In what respect is binocular disparity an especially powerful cue? (161)

* b) What physiological evidence indicates that binocular disparity is treated by the nervous system like, say, wave length of light? (161)

* 8. a) Explain in your own words what is meant by the term, *unconscious inference* in connection with Helmholtz's view of the nature of perception. (161)

* b) By contrast discuss Gibson's more recent notion that we use *invariant* cues in perception. Use an example to illustrate this important theoretical position in the context of perceiving depth. (162)

* 9. Distinguish between the three forms of motion perception by describing how each is produced. (163)

—stroboscopic motion:

—induced motion:

—real motion:

10. a) What are the limits of stroboscopic motion? What if the time between flashes is too short? Too long? (163)

b) Cite a real-life example of what happens when the time interval is too long and how this problem is addressed. (163)

11. a) Just how sensitive is the human eye to real motion? (163)

*   b)   In Gibson's view, why is it easier to distinguish relative than absolute motion? (163-164)

  12.   a)   In what sense is selective adaptation "selective"? Cite an example. (164)

*   b)   In physiological terms, why does selective adaptation apparently occur? (164)

*   c)   Discuss in detail additional evidence obtained with animals for the existence of movement cells. (164)

*   d)   On the other hand, cite the evidence that motion perception involves more than single cell activity. What sources of information does the visual system apparently combine in such cases? (164)

  13.   a)   Describe Michotte's demonstration of motion and causality. What are the limits of this phenomenon? (164)

       b)   Why does it appear that a Gibsonian analysis of this phenomenon in terms of direct perception is more accurate than an account in terms of inference? (164-165)

       c)   List three other sources of information besides that about location of an object provided us through motion perception. (165)

Recognition

*   1.   a)   Describe two kinds of recognition. What does recognition allow us to infer? (165)

*   b)   List some of the attributes we may use for recognition; which seems to play a critical role? Therefore, what is the critical question with regard to the perceptual function of recognition? (165)

  2.   Describe the two stages of recognition. (165-166)

*   3.   a)   What procedure was used by Hubel and Wiesel to study feature detectors in animals? (166)

*   b)   Indicate the features to which each of the kinds of cells identified by Hubel and Weisel respond. (Are these the only kind of cells there are?) (166)

—*simple cells*:

—*complex cells*:

—*hypercomplex cells*:

*   4.   a)   Describe and illustrate the behavioral procedure used by Treisman and colleagues to study feature detection. (167)

*   b)   What type of examination should an observer be able to use in a search for a target with primitive features and what should be the effect of changing the number of nontargets in the display? Use the terms *parallel* and *pop-out* effect in your answer. (167)

c) List three types of features identified by Treisman with this technique. (167)

d) What results suggest that not all primitive features relate to shape? (167)

* 5. a) Be able to discuss in your own words the application of a connectionist model to the recognition of letters in a *simple network*, such as that in Figure 5-14. Use the term "matching" in your response. (168)

* b) Why is this model considered to be too simple to account for all aspects of recognition? What is needed? (168)

* c) What does the term *augmented network* mean and how does this concept address the problem outlined in b) above? (See also Figure 5-15.) (168-169)

d) Indicate the two fundamental entities in the networks described in a) and c). What two types of processing are possible in this theoretical approach to recognition? (169)

e) What is the basic idea behind this theoretical model? (169)

* 6. a) Even with the added features of the augmented network, what problem arises in trying to account for the perception of letters? (169)

* b) Discuss the two solutions to this problem outlined in your text and in Figure 5-17. (169-170)

* 7. a) What two criteria have guided the search for object features that are used in the recognition of natural objects? (170)

* b) Outline two proposals for what constitutes the features of objects. (170)

c) What happens to the accuracy of recognition as the number of features of natural objects increases? Why? (171)

d) Discuss the matching process that takes place between a description of an external object and its representation in memory. (172)

* 8. a) Describe the effects of two types of context and be able to recognize them in the related figures, 5-22 and 5-23. (173)

b) Give an example to show that a stimulus object does not have to be ambiguous for there to be context effects. (172)

* c) Provide examples to illustrate when context provides conscious and unconscious expectations, respectively. Use the term *masking* in your second illustration. (172-173).

9. a) Describe the television technique for studying selective looking. (173-174)

b) In terms of the structure of the eye, what function does scanning a picture serve? (175)

c) What is the difficulty posed by *impossible figures*? (175)

* 10. a) In what respect is selective listening like selective looking? Under what conditions does this mechanism show limited utility? Use the term *cocktail party phenomenon* in your answer. (175-176)

b) Indicate several cues that enable us to select a verbal message from a background of conversation. Which can we use even in the absence of the others? (176)

* 11. a) Discuss a common experimental procedure in which a subject is asked to *shadow* a message. (176)

* b) What outcomes are obtained with this technique? (176)

* c) Does current evidence support the idea that we completely select out information that is not shadowed? Explain, and cite an example. (176)

* 12. a) Besides selection, in your own words, what other function does attention serve? (176)

* b) Give an anecdotal and an experimental example of the process of conjoining. In the experiment, what evidence was provided to show that conjoining requires attention? (176-177)

c) What is meant by the term *illusory conjunctions,* and how does this phenomenon provide additional support for the view that conjoining requires an attentional process. (177)

Perceptual Constancies

* 1. In the table below, be sure you can define each of the terms and provide at least one example. (177-181)

Perceptual Phenomenon	Definition and example
lightness constancy	
color constancy	
shape constancy	
location constancy	
size constancy	

* 2. a) Outline a perceptual demonstration of the phenomenon of lightness constancy and a procedure that will alter the apparent lightness of the object. (177-178)

*　　　b)　What does this demonstration tell us about the process that underlies lightness constancy? (178-179)

3.　a)　In part, what determines the color of an object and how is this complicated? Does that fact necessarily alter the phenomenon of color constancy? (180)

*　　　b)　What procedure can eliminate color constancy, and again, as in the case of lightness constancy, what does this tell us about the basis for the phenomenon? (180)

4.　In the case of location constancy, what two sources of cues must the perceptual system take into account? Physiologically, where does the integration of this information take place? (180)

5.　Discuss the relationship between shape and location constancy and the phenomena you studied earlier in this chapter, localization and recognition. (180)

*　6.　a)　What are the two major variables in the determination of size constancy? Cite a demonstration of the way in which they interact. (181)

*　　　b)　How does the size-distance invariance principle explain size constancy? Be able to interpret an example. (181)

*　　　c)　Outline the Helmholtz concept of unconscious inference as it accounts for the combining of information in size-distance invariance, including the general rule that Helmholtz proposed. (182)

*　7.　Apply Helmholtz's rule in item 6c) to the problem of the *moon illusion*. (182)

*　8.　What is the *Ames room* illusion? Of what is this illusion a dramatic demonstration? (182-183).

9.　a)　What other kind of perceptual constancy is possible? (183)

　　　b)　On what do all constancies depend and what is the role of the perceptual system in this process? (183).

Perceptual Development

1.　a)　Cite an example of an empirical point of view regarding perception already covered in this chapter. (184)

*　　　b)　What is the view of contemporary psychologists with regard to the role of heredity and learning in perceptual phenomena? (184)

*　　　c)　List three major questions guiding modern research in perception on issues related to the role of heredity and learning that, in turn, provide an outline for this section of your text. (184)

2.　a)　Since research on perceptual capacities in infants is often aimed at the question of what processes are inborn, why has it not been restricted to newborns? (184)

*   b) Describe in detail the preferential looking method, including how the experimenter may conclude that the infant is showing a lack of discrimination. (185)

*   c) Similarly, outline one use for visual evoked potentials in the study of infant perception. (185)

* 3. a) Describe the method typically used in the study of perceiving forms and one main result of this procedure. (186)

*   b) What results have been obtained in the study of contrast sensitivity? Use the term *spatial frequency* in your answer. (186)

*   c) Answer the question in your text, "what do these studies tell us about the infant's perceptual world" by completing the following table. (Be sure to note when an infant can discriminate facial expressions.) (186-87)

Age of infant	Ability to discriminate
1 month	
3 months	

4. What is the evidence regarding other forms of object discrimination besides dark and light edges? In particular, what shapes do young infants find more interesting and why? (187)

* 5. a) At what age does depth perception begin to appear in infants and at what point is it fully developed? How do we know this for the use of binocular cues? (187)

*   b) At what age do infants begin to use monocular cues to infer depth, and what procedures reflect this? (187-188)

* 6. Describe the development of perceptual constancies. (188)

* 7. a) What was the purpose and method of the earliest experiments on controlled stimulation? (188)

*   b) Indicate the idea behind these studies and the principal results. (188)

*   c) Discuss the difficulty with the dark-rearing procedure that argues for caution in interpreting these data. (188)

8. Discuss in detail results obtained with single-cell recordings in the study of effects of absence of stimulation. (188)

* 9. a) Indicate the relationship between the duration of light deprivation and effects on visual perception. (188)

*   b)   What results suggest that there is a *critical period* in visual development during early life? (189)

* 10.   a)   Why have researchers altered their strategy in the study of the effects of controlled stimulation of perceptual development, and what has become the preferred method? (189)

*   b)   In this method, describe the effects of deprivation of horizontal or vertical stripes. (189)

    c)   What do studies of cortical cells show as a result of these procedures? (189)

* 11.   a)   What conditions provide information about visual deprivation in humans? Discuss the effects of three of these conditions upon visual development. (189)

*   b)   Indicate the conclusion to be drawn from these observations, noting a probable critical period in humans for visual development. (189)

* 12.   a)   Do the effects of controlling stimulation on perceptual development favor a learning interpretation of the origins of perception? Explain. (189)

*   b)   Describe two cases that illustrate the role of learning in perception in humans more clearly. (189)

* 13.   a)   Discuss evidence obtained with kittens indicating the role of learning in the development of perceptual-motor coordination. (190)

*   b)   What additional evidence with kittens shows the importance of self-produced movements in response to stimulation in perceptual motor coordination. (190)

*   c)   Cite the results obtained with humans that show similar effects for self-produced movement. (190-191)

* 14.   Overall, based on the evidence presented in this section, what is your authors' conclusion with respect to whether perception is innate or learned? (191)

Sample Quiz 5.1

1. Pattern recognition refers to determining: a) *where* objects are located; b) *how many* objects there are; c) *what* objects are; d) *what color* objects are.

2. When the features of an object are brought together or fused through the process of attention, we speak of: a) size-distance invariance; b) visual acuity; c) receptive fields; d) conjoining.

3. Binocular disparity: a) is actually a form of monocular cue; b) while useful, is not an especially powerful cue to depth; c) appears to be coded directly by the nervous system, like wave length of light; d) refers to the fact that any visible point will differ slightly in its direction to the two eyes.

4. Induced motion refers to: a) apparent movement in a smaller object when actual movement occurs in a larger, surrounding object; b) assignment of two contours to the same object when they are moving in the same direction; c) apparent movement

80   Chapter 5

of two lights flashed in succession in a dark room; d) a loss of sensitivity to a given motion when it is viewed for a while.

5. The connectionist model: a) maintains that hypothetical "connections" enable the matching of features of letters with letters of the alphabet; b) was developed by Gibson to account for certain "invariants" in visual perception; c) was a major tenet of the Gestalt approach to the problems of depth perception; d) argues that there is an underlying "connection" between binocular and monocular depth perception.

6. Which of the following kinds of feature detectors responds only when a stimulus is in a particular orientation and is of a particular length: a) simple cells; b) complex cells; c) hypercomplex cells; d) grating-sensitive cells.

7. If a word, such as, "bread," is flashed on a screen, a subject will be more likely to recognize the word "butter" faster than if it is not preceded by "bread." This demonstrates the phenomenon of: a) context; b) masking; c) conscious expectations; d) ambiguous figures.

8. When a door swings open, it appears to be the same door irrespective of changes in its projection on the retina of the eye. This is the perceptual phenomenon of: a) lightness constancy; b) impossible figures; c) shape constancy; d) illusory conjunction.

9. With respect to the nature-nurture problem as it applies to perceptual development, modern psychologists believe: a) an integration between the empiricist and the nativist viewpoints is impossible; b) heredity is the most important factor; c) learning is all-important; d) both genetics and experience influence perception.

10. Results obtained using the preferential looking method with human babies have shown that: a) visual acuity increases rapidly over the first six months of life then improves more slowly after that; b) contrast sensitivity increases rapidly over the first six months of life; c) by age 3 months, an infant can perceive facial expressions; d) all of the above.

Sample Quiz 5.2

1. The most elementary form of perceptual organization deals with: a) the detection of motion; b) the arrangement of elements into figure and ground; c) the perception of distance; d) the grouping of objects.

2. In the history of psychology Max Wertheimer is famous for: a) his identification of the determinants of grouping; b) his theoretical position that we do not infer depth and motion, but rather perceive them directly; c) the development of the connectionist model for perceptual recognition; d) his pioneering research concerning perceptual development in infants.

3. The twentieth century theoretical approach to psychology that developed in Germany and that emphasized the importance of perceiving whole objects or forms is called: a) nativism; b) the connectionist model; c) empiricism; d) Gestalt psychology.

4. When an object has multiple features, such as shape and color, we may group these together perceptually on the basis of common: a) distance; b) motion; c) both a and b; d) none of the above.

5. After watching a spoked wheel turn counter-clockwise for a time, it will appear to begin turning in a clockwise direction even though there is no actual change in motion. This phenomenon is called: a) induced motion; b) a motion aftereffect; c) relative motion; d) stroboscopic motion.

6. Which of the following attributes seems to be most important when we recognize an object: a) its color; b) its shape; c) its orientation; d) its size.

7. Based on the experimental evidence, we can infer that conjoining requires attention because: a) subjects report that it does; b) the greater the number of nontargets, the longer it takes to identify a target requiring conjoining; c) impossible figures become possible if made small enough to project completely on the fovea; d) in shadowing experiments, only the physical characteristics of the sound are reported for unshadowed messages.

8. The size-distance invariance principle states that: a) perceived size is directly proportional to distance; b) perceived size is the quotient of perceived distance divided by retinal size; c) perceived size is the product of retinal size times perceived distance; d) size and distance are never related.

9. "A phenomenon of perception that is false or distorted when evaluated by means of physical measurement" was the definition provided in this chapter for a(n): a) hallucination; b) illusion; c) percept; d) ambiguous figure.

10. The fact that there is a relationship between length of visual deprivation and sight deficit in young animals but not in adults suggests that: a) there is a critical period for visual development early in life; b) absence of stimulation is probably a better technique for studying visual development than is limited stimulation; c) learning is the primary factor operating in the development of perceptual capacities; d) our perceptual capacity is severely limited at birth.

Key, Chapter 5

Names

1. Max Wertheimer

Vocabulary and Details

1. percept
2. sensations; percepts
3. pattern recognition; recognition
4. spatial localization; localization

1. segregation; distance; movement
2. Gestalt psychology
3. figure; ground
4. grouping
5. proximity; closure; good continuation; similarity
6. distance; motion
7. distance (or depth) cues; monocular; binocular
8. relative size; superposition; relative height
9. stereoscope; binocular parallax; binocular disparity
10. texture gradient
11. stroboscopic motion
12. induced motion
13. real motion; relative motion; absolute motion
14. selective adaptation
15. motion aftereffect

1. receptive field
2. simple; complex; hypercomplex
3. feature detectors
4. connectionist model
5. excitatory; inhibitory
6. context
7. ambiguous
8. selective attention
9. scanning; fixations; saccades
10. conjoining

1. perceptual constancy
2. size-distance invariance
3. illusion

1. nativists; empiricists
2. preferential looking method
3. visual evoked potentials
4. acuity
5. contrast sensitivity
6. visual cliff

Sample Quiz 5.1

1. c, 157
2. b, 158

3. c, 161
4. a, 163
5. a, 168
6. c, 166
7. a, 172-173
8. c, 180
9. d, 184
10. d, 186

Sample Quiz 5.2

1. b, 158
2. a, 159
3. d, 158
4. c, 159-160
5. b, 164
6. b, 165
7. b, 176-177
8. c, 181
9. b, 182
10. a, 188-189

Consciousness and its Altered States

Learning Objectives

1. Be familiar with the history of the study of consciousness. Be able to define consciousness in terms of its function in monitoring information and controlling our actions.

2. Know what is meant by the terms subconscious processes, preconscious memories, and the unconscious. Be familiar with the phenomenon of dissociation as illustrated by multiple personalities.

3. Be able to discuss in some detail sleep schedules, stages of sleep depth, and sleep disorders.

4. Be familiar with Freud's theory of dreams and with the theories proposed by Evans and by Crick and Mitchison. Know the answers to the questions about dreams discussed in the text.

5. Know what is meant by the term psychoactive drug and be able to give examples of each of the subcategories of psychoactive drugs discussed in the text. Be familiar with typical patterns of use of these drugs.

6. Be able to define physical dependence and psychological dependence. Know the stepping-stone theory of drug usage and some of the reasons people take drugs.

7. Be able to define meditation and describe the various techniques used to induce a meditative state. Be familiar with the research findings on meditation.

8. Be able to describe the procedure and typical effects of a hypnosis session. Be familiar with the phenomena of post hypnotic amnesia and other posthypnotic suggestions; understand the questions of conscious control that these phenomena raise.

9. Be familiar with the various theories of hypnosis. Understand what is meant by the "hidden observer" and how it is studied.

10. Be able to define the phenomena included under the term psi. Be familiar with the ganzfeld procedure, the results obtained, and the issues involved in evaluating these results.

Names

1. In the view of _____, the father of behaviorism, the data of psychology must be objective and measurable, thus limiting study to public events and substituting verbal reports for "consciousness." (195)

2. At the other end of the spectrum, according to the psychoanalytic theory of _____, some memories, impulses, and desires that are of great importance are in the unconscious and cannot enter consciousness. (195)

3. The French psychiatrist _____ is credited with the concept of dissociation. (199)

Vocabulary and Details

1. Whenever there is a change from an ordinary pattern of mental functioning to a state that *seems* different to the person experiencing the change, psychologists speak of an _____. Such states are personal and _____. (195)

ASPECTS OF CONSCIOUSNESS

1. Early psychologists defined psychology as the study of _____ and used the method of _____. (195)

2. Later, behaviorists reserved the term _____ events for those observable only to the experiencing person (such as those in consciousness), and restricted the term _____ events to actual behavior (such as verbal reports of consciousness). (195)

3. In the current definition, the term *consciousness* involves two processes: a) _____ ourselves and our environment so that our awareness of events is accurate; and b) _____ ourselves and our enviornment so that we can initiate and terminate behavior and cognitions. (196)

4. Stimuli may be registered and evaluated without conscious perception; in this case, the stimuli are said to operate at a _____ level of awareness. (197)

5. Memories that are not part of consciousness at a given moment but are accessible if you wish to retrieve them are termed _____; the collection of such memories is termed the _____. (197)

6. In the psychoanalytic view of Freud, some emotionally painful memories, wishes, and impulses are _____, that is, assigned to the _____, where they may continue to influence behavior even though we are not aware of them. (197)

7. One example of the influence of the unconscious upon behavior is an unintentional remark that is assumed to reveal hidden impulses; this is termed a _____. (197)

8. In Fodor's theory, termed the _____, the mind is seen to consist of a number of innate and independent mental structures or _____ that unconsciously control classes of activities, including language and visual perception. (198)

86   Chapter 6

DIVIDED CONSCIOUSNESS

1. When certain skills become so well-learned that they no longer require attention, they are termed _____. (198)

2. One interpretation of automatic processing is that the control is still there (we can focus on the automatic process if we wish to), but that it has been severed or _____ from consciousness. (199)

3. In Janet's concept of _____, under certain conditions some thoughts and actions become split off (dissociated) from consciousness and function outside of awareness (in the preconscious). (199)

4. _____ is the existence of two or more integrated and well-developed personalities within the same individual. (200)

SLEEP AND DREAMS

1. The _____ is the natural cycle or "internal clock," about _____ hours in length, that characterizes the course of many bodily functions. (202)

2. The fatigue and lack of alertness that may accompany travel, termed _____, is due to disruption of the normal circadian rhythm. (202)

3. The graphic recording of electrical changes on the scalp associated with brain activity, or brain waves, is termed an _____ or _____. (203)

4. During periods of relaxation with eyes closed, such as prior to sleep, the brain may show a regular pattern of slow waves, termed _____. (203)

5. _____ sleep, are periods of sleep detected with electrodes showing rapid eye movements, characteristically active EEG patterns, and dreaming; these periods occur repeatedly in alternation with the other four stages of sleep, termed _____ sleep. (203-204)

6. REM sleep is characterized by a brain that is _____ in a virtually _____ body; NREM sleep by an _____ brain in a very _____ body. (204)

7. A _____ exists whenever the inability to sleep well produces impaired daytime functioning or excessive sleepiness. (206)

8. When a person complains about dissatisfaction with amount or quality of their sleep, we speak of the sleep disorder _____. (206)

9. A very rare sleep disorder, _____, is characterized by recurring, irresistible attacks of drowsiness and the tendency to fall asleep at inappropriate times, for periods ranging from _____ to _____. (206)

10. A third sleep disorder is the condition called _____, in which the individual stops breathing from _____ to _____ (how many?) times while asleep. (207)

11. Deprivation of REM sleep has been found to produce a tendency to spend an abnormal amount of time in REM sleep during a recovery night, a so-called _____. (208).

12. _____ is an altered state of consciousness in which remembered images and fantasies are temporarily confused with external reality. (208)

13. In a _____, events seem so normal, without the illogical character of most dreams, that dreamers feel they are awake and conscious. (209)

14. In Freud's view, the _____ content of a dream consists of the symbolic representation of the repressed (unconscious) wishes and that underlie it; the _____ content of a dream consists of the characters and events that make up the actual dream narrative. (211)

PSYCHOACTIVE DRUGS

1. Drugs that affect behavior, consciousness, and mood are called _____. (212)

2. Through repeated use, _____ dependence on drugs, also called _____, may develop; this is characterized by a) _____, that is, a need for more of the drug to achieve the same effect, and b) _____, unpleasant physical symptoms if the drug is discontinued. (212).

3. By contrast, _____dependence refers to a need for a drug that develops through learning. (212)

4. A drug that depresses the central nervous system is called a _____; this class includes _____, _____, and the most commonly used member of the group, _____. (213)

5. Maternal drinking may cause _____, a condition of the child characterized by mental retardation and multiple deformities of the face and mouth. (215)

6. Alcoholism is defined in terms of the _____ from drinking and a _____ over drinking. (215)

7. Chronic alcoholics who stop drinking after a sustained period of heavy consumption may experience _____, severe withdrawal symptoms including confusion, hallucinations, and convulsions. (216)

8. Another group of drugs that diminish physical sensation and the capacity to respond to stimuli by depressing the central nervous system are collectively known as _____; these drugs include the substance from the poppy plant _____ and its derivatives _____ and _____, as well as the powerful derivative of morphine, _____. (217)

9. A group of neurotransmitters called _____ are the body's "natural opiates," in terms of molecular similarity. One of these neurotransmitters, _____, occupies a number of opiate receptors. (218)

10. A drug that has a greater affinity for an opiate receptor site than an opiate itself is called an _____, one example of which is _____. (218)

11. A synthetic opiate called _____ prevents symptoms of withdrawal from heroin by occupying unfilled opiate receptor sites. (218)

12. By contrast with depressants and opiates, drugs that *increase* arousal are called _____, for example, _____ and _____. (219)

13. Stimulants may induce experiences in the absence of stimulus input, that is, _____, in visual, auditory, and (in the case of cocaine) sensory forms. They may also cause _____, false beliefs that people are persecuting the user. (220)

14. Psychoactive drugs whose main effect is to change perceptual experience are called _____, including the natural substances from cactus and mushrooms, _____ and _____, respectively, and the laboratory produced drugs, _____ and _____. (221)

15. The plant _____ yields the substance _____ from its leaves and flowers and _____ from a solidified resin; the active ingredient is _____ . (222-223)

MEDITATION

1. In _____, a person achieves an altered state of consciousness by performing certain rituals and exercises, including controlling and regulating _____, restricting _____, assuming _____, and forming _____. (224)

2. Traditional forms of meditation follow either the religious practices of _____, from Hinduism, or _____, from Buddhism--including so-called _____ in which the subject clears the mind for receiving new experiences, and so-called _____ in which there is active attention to some object, word, or idea. (224-225)

3. The recent, secularized form of meditation, called _____ or _____, involves the repeated saying of a sound termed a _____ while sitting quietly and in relaxing conditions. (226)

HYPNOSIS

1. In _____, a cooperative subject relinquishes some control over his or her behavior to the hypnotist (becomes more suggestible) and accepts some reality distortion. (229)

2. Subjects who have been brought out of hypnosis may respond with movement to a prearranged signal in the phenomenon called _____. (231)

3. At the suggestion of the hypnotist, events occurring during hypnosis may be forgotten until a signal enables the subject to recall them, a phenomenon called _____. (231)

4. In _____ during hypnosis, some individuals are able to relive episodes from earlier periods of life. (231)

5. During hypnosis, a subject may see an object or hear a voice that is not actually present in the phenomenon of _____; conversely, the subject may also *not* perceive something that is present in the phenomenon called _____. (231-232)

PSI PHENOMENA

1. The term _____ refers to information and/or energy exchanges not currently explicable in terms of known physical mechanisms. These phenomena are the subject matter of _____. (234)

Consciousness and its Altered States   89

2. One class of such psi phenomena is _____, a response to external stimuli without known sensory contact. (234)

3. Three examples of ESP are a) _____, thought transference between two people without known sensory communication; b) _____, perception of objects or events that do not provide a physical stimulus; and c) _____, perception of a future event without the use of known inferential processes. (234-235)

4. Another class of psi phenomena is _____, mental influence over physical events without the intervention of known physical force. (235)

5. The term _____ as applied to research in parapsychology and other fields, is a statistical technique that treats accumulated studies as a single grand experiment and each individual study as a single observation. (236)

Ideas and Concepts

ASPECTS OF CONSCIOUSNESS

* 1. a) Discuss the changing views of "consciousness" from early definitions through the views of behaviorism. (195)

   b) Did behaviorism require a radical change in its views of private events? Explain, using the term *verbal responses* in your answer. (195)

   c) What difficulty with the behaviorist position espoused by John Watson did many psychologists see and what was said to be neglected in this view? (195-196)

* d) Indicate the view of consciousness that became prominent in psychology beginning in the 1950s. How, then, has the focus of psychology come "full circle" and what gain has been contributed by behaviorism in this journey? (196)

2. a) Why can we not attend to all of the stimuli that impinge on us? (196)

* b) In what sense is attention "selective" and what determines priority of selectiveness? (196)

* 3. a) List the three aspects of the controlling function of consciousness. What special function of consciousness can occur in planning? (197)

4. From the text and your own experience, give some examples of the following. (197)

   —subconscious phenomena (include the term "cocktail party phenomenon" in your answer).

   —preconscious memories.

* 5. a) List several ways in which unconscious thoughts and impulses can appear. (198)

*Basic ideas and concepts

90   Chapter 6

b) In Freud's view, what is the cause of most mental illness and what is the goal of psychoanalysis with respect to material in the unconscious and in consciousness? (198)

*   c) In what respect would many psychologists challenge Freud's view of the unconscious? Provide an example. (198)

DIVIDED CONSCIOUSNESS

1. a) Cite some examples of automatic processes from the text and your own experience. (198-199)

*   b) What is the apparent function of automatic processes? Cite an instance in which they may have negative consequences. (199)

2. a) In what respect does Janet's concept of dissociation differ from Freud's notion of repression? (199)

    b) Give some examples of mild forms of dissociation. (199)

*   3. a) Discuss some of the characteristics of multiple personalities. What provides a clue to the presence or this disorder? (200)

    b) On what dimensions may different personalities within the same individual differ? (200)

*   4. a) In terms of some of the common features of multiple personalities, indicate the nature of the initial dissociation and outline the mechanism by which this process may work. (201)

    b) Discuss another factor in the development of multiple personality. (201)

    c) What may happen when an individual discovers that an alternate personality developed through self-hypnosis works? (201)

SLEEP AND DREAMS

*   1. List four ways in which sleep and wakefulness are alike. (201)

*   2. Do people show the same patterns of sleep across their lifespan? Are the patterns the same from person to person? Discuss. (202)

3. Explain why jet lag does not occur when traveling in a north-south direction. (202)

*   4. Characterize the stages of sleep listed below in terms of their respective EEG patterns and, where possible, other features. Use the terms *spindles, delta waves,* and *non-REM sleep* in your answer. (203-204)

—Stage 1:

—Stage 2:

—Stages 3 and 4:

5. a) Describe the typical alternation of the various stages of sleep throughout the night, noting the common pattern of REM sleep. (204)

    b) Is the pattern of sleep cycles consistent across age? Explain. (204)

*   6. Discuss the evidence concerning the state of the brain and body in REM sleep. (205)

*   7. a) What are the data with regard to the incidence of dreaming in REM and NREM sleep? (205)

    b) Therefore, in what two respects is mental activity different in REM and NREM periods? (205)

*   8. What two separate functions may be fulfilled by sleep? Cite the evidence relative to these possibilities. (205)

9. Cite the statistics on normal sleep patterns. What happens if the usual requirement is not met? (206)

*   10. Why do your authors say that having insomnia is always a "subjective decision"? That is, is insomnia always accompanied by abnormal sleep patterns? Cite the evidence. (206)

11. a) Describe the intrusion of REM states in narcolepsy. (206)

    b) What evidence suggests that narcolepsy is genetic? (206)

*   12. a) Discuss two explanations for apnea attacks. (206-207)

    b) Why does the sleeper awaken during an apnea? (207)

    c) Who is especially afflicted by sleep apnea? Are sleeping pills a good remedy? Why or why not? (208)

*   13. a) Discuss the general effects of *sleep* deprivation. (208)

    b) Describe the procedures and outcomes of Dement's study of *dream* deprivation. (208)

*   14. a) Does everyone dream? Indicate the most widely accepted hypothesis concerning dream recall. (208-209)

    b) How long do dreams last? Cite the evidence relating the length of incidents in dreams versus real life. (209)

*   c) Do people know when they are dreaming? Be familiar with some of the "experiments" that have been conducted by individuals experiencing lucid dreams. (209)

92   Chapter 6

*   d)   Can people control the content of their dreams? Describe how is this made made possible by citing examples of *implicit predream suggestion, overt predream suggestion,* and *posthypnotic dream suggestion.* (209-210)

    15.   a)   When does sleepwalking always occur? (210)

*   b)   Cite some of the data on sleepwalking. (215)

*   16.   a)   Outline Freud's theory of dreams, using the terms *wish fulfillment* and *censor* in your answer. (211)

          b)   What is the function of "dream work," and what happens when it fails? (211)

*   17.   How do current cognitive interpretations treat Freud's theory of dreams? (211-212)

PSYCHOACTIVE DRUGS

     1.   a)   Discuss some of the factors that have contributed to the shift of this society from one that was relatively drug-free to one that is drug-using. (212)

          b)   Discuss two reasons that may underlie the current apparent decline in drug use. (212)

     2.   Give an example of a drug that may produce psychological dependence and one whose use may result in a transition from psychological to physical dependence. (212-213)

*   3.   a)   In neurological terms, why does alcohol seem to produce an initial stimulating effect? What accounts for its depressive effects? (213)

          b)   List some of the effects of the following *blood alcohol concentrations:* (213-214)

         —.03 to .05 percent:

         —.10 percent:

         —.20 percent:

         —.40 percent:

          c)   Can we state how much a person can drink without becoming legally intoxicated? Explain. (214)

*   4.   a)   Indicate some of the positive and negative effects of alcohol consumption among high school seniors including effects on physical health. What is the most serious problem? (214)

          b)   Cite some of the statistics on alcohol consumption and current trends. (215)

*   5.   a)   Is the stereotype of the "skid-row drunk" characteristic of most alcoholics? Explain. (215)

b) Discuss the relationship between age and drinking patterns in the average drinker and the average alcoholic. (215-216)

c) What are some other patterns of development of alcoholism and what is the vicious circle in which the alcoholic may become trapped? (216)

d) Do most alcoholics stay drunk until they die? Explain and indicate what is therefore the most useful criterion for diagnosing alcoholism. (216)

6. What is the common name for the "opiates" and why is it not a very accurate term? (217)

7. a) In what ways can heroin be taken into the body? Describe some of the cognitive and behavioral influences of the drug. (217)

* b) What effects of heroin apparently induce people to *start* its use? Outline the course of events that may lead to other methods of heroin ingestion, including "mainlining." (217)

* c) Then what seems to underlie the tendency to *continue* use of heroin? Use the terms **withdrawal** and **addiction** in your answer. (217)

* d) Indicate three other hazards of heroin use. (217-218)

* 8. a) What major breakthrough was made in the 1970s in understanding opiate addiction? (218)

* b) Discuss the mechanism by which morphine and heroin relieve pain. In this analysis, why does discontinuation of heroin use lead to withdrawal? (218)

* c) Describe two treatment advances that have resulted from increasing knowledge of the mechanism of opiate action at the receptors. (218-219)

9. a) Cite some of the trade names and colloquial terms for amphetamines. (219)

* b) What are two immediate effects of amphetamine consumption? List some other psychological and behavioral effects of their use. (219)

c) Describe the likely sequence that leads to overuse and the development of tolerance for amphetamines. What happens when oral ingestion is no longer effective and what is a common result? (Use the term "crash" in your answer.) (219)

* d) Discuss the effects of long-term amphetamine use. In what three respects do the behaviors of "speed freaks" resemble those of acute schizophrenics? (219)

* 10. a) List some of the psychological effects of cocaine. (220)

b) In what forms can cocaine be taken into the body (use the term "crack"). (220)

* c) What characteristic of cocaine did Freud discover under unfortunate circumstances and what current form of coke listed in b) above renders this effect even more serious? (220)

11. a) Identify the abnormal symptoms of heavy concaine use, including the terms "snow lights" and "cocaine bugs" in your answer. (220)

* b) Outline the effects of maternal use of cocaine and the mechanism that renders this particularly dangerous for a fetus. (220)

c) Indicate the connection between the use of coke and AIDS. (220)

12. Cite some of the data on cocaine usage and current trends. (221)

* 13. a) Outline some of the effects of the hallucinogens in terms of perceptions and hallucinations. (221)

* b) Indicate four adverse reactions to LSD. (221-222)

c) Why has the use of LSD declined? (222)

* 14. a) What is the second most widely misused drug and why is it technically classified as a "dissociative anesthetic"? (222)

b) Why was PCP first made and what caused the discontinuation of its legal manufacture? (222)

c) What are some typical effects of PCP at low doses and at high doses? Include discussion of sensitivity to input and *apparent* aggressiveness in your answer. (222)

* 15. a) Describe typical effects of THC, including the stages of reactions that occur and sensory and perceptual changes that have been reported. (223)

b) Are all marijuana experiences pleasant? Cite the data. (223)

* c) Discuss the effects of marijuana use upon performance on complex tasks and some of the implications of these findings for common activities, such as driving and flying aircraft. In what respect do such effects persist? (223)

* d) Outline a study of the long-term effects of marijuana use in large doses. Despite the results of this study, what is still not known insofar as potential adverse effects are concerned? (223)

MEDITATION

* 1. a) Indicate five results of meditative exercises. (224)

b) Cite some perceptual effects of concentrative meditation. (226)

2. Be familiar with Benson's five steps for a "relaxation response" through meditation. What effects can this procedure produce? (226-227)

* 3. a) List the physiological effects of meditation that indicate its effectiveness as a relaxation technique. (227)

b) Can the physiological effects of meditation be shown to be different from those of other methods, such as hypnosis, biofeedback, deep muscle relaxation, or even mere rest? (227-228)

4. Discuss some of the uses for meditation in the context of sports psychology, including for stress reduction and mental image formation. (228)

* 5. What is your authors' conclusion with regard to the evidence on meditation? (228)

HYPNOSIS

* 1. a) Describe three of the methods used in inducing a hypnotic condition, including one other than relaxation. (229)

   b) Does modern hypnosis use authoritarian commands? Explain, indicating when subjects enter the hyponotic state. (229)

* c) Summarize five changes to be expected in a subject when hypnotized. (229-230)

2. a) Describe differences between superficial and deep levels of hypnosis. What finding suggests that meditation may be a kind of self-hypnosis? (230)

* b) Is everyone equally susceptible to hypnosis? Cite the evidence. (230)

   c) Is a very hypnotizable subject also highly suggestible in social settings? Then what is a good predictor of responsiveness to hypnosis? (230)

* 3. Describe the effects of hypnotic suggestions on each of the following aspects of behaviors and experiences citing examples and the results of related studies, where possible. (230-233)

   —Control of movement (use the term *posthypnotic response*):

   —Posthypnotic amnesia:

   —Age regression:

   —Positive and negative hallucinations (be sure to note the uses of hallucinations in pain control):

* 4. a) Summarize the highlights of each of the historical periods and theories of hypnosis shown in the following table, being certain that you can define the related terms: (233)

Periods and Theories	Highlights
Historical views (including Bernheim's and Pavlov's)	
Psychoanalytic theory and *partial regression*	
Role enactment theory	
Dissociation theory	

b) What is the current status of theories of hypnosis? (233)

PSI PHENOMENA

1. Be able to recognize the terms *telepathy, clairvoyance,* and *precognition.* (234-235)

* 2. Discuss the current attitudes of some scientists on parapsychology. In your authors' view, what is the real question to be answered? (235)

3. a) Describe the method of parapsychology termed the *ganzfeld procedure.* (235)

b) What results have been obtained with this method and what is the likelihood of such results that lead your authors to state that this is the "most promising" of the methods of parapsychology. (235)

* 4. As an exercise in scientific methods, summarize the debate over evidence obtained from the ganzfeld studies in terms of:

a) *Problems of replication.* How replicable is the phenomenon when meta-analysis is employed? What happens when the potential motivational influence of the experimenter is taken into account. What role does the number of observations play in this issue? (236-237)

b) *Problems of inadequate controls.* By contrast with the typical history of parapsychology insofar as proper controls are concerned, how has meta-analysis been applied to the ganzfeld studies to deal with this issue and what have been the results? Use the term *sensory leakage* in your answer. (237-238)

c) *The file-drawer problem.* What is the file-drawer problem in the context of the ganzfeld studies? How has meta-analysis be used to address this issue? (238-239)

5. Discuss the three types of problems that emerge in the analysis of anecdotal evidence. Use the example of *precognitive dreams* to illustrate one of these problems. (239-240)

* 6. Discuss why there is such a level of continuing skepticism regarding psi phenomena in terms of:

a) *Extraordinary claims.* In the view of scientists, what do extraordinary claims demand and on what does extraordinariness depend? What model of reality do parapsychologists believe will accomodate psi phenomena? (240-241)

b) *The views of psychologists.* List four reasons why psychologists are so skeptical of the claims of parapsychology. In your authors' view, is all of this skepticism well-founded? Why or why not? (241)

Sample Quiz 6.1

1. The individual who argued that psychology must deal with objective and measureable events rather than states of consciousness themselves was: a) Freud; b) Benson; c) Watson; d) Janet.

2. The collection of memories that are not part of present consciousness but which can be readily retrieved is called the: a) preconscious; b) unconscious; c) subconscious; d) introconscious.

3. Psychological restoration is to physical restoration as: a) dreaming is to rapid eye movements; b) muscle relaxation is to diminished brain activity; c) REM sleep is to slow-wave sleep; d) logical dreams are to bizarre dreams.

4. The tendency to stop breathing while asleep is called: a) narcolepsy; b) the rebound effect; c) sleep apnea; d) insomnia.

5. Which of the following was *not* listed as a hazard of heroin use in your text? a) death from overdose; b) the development of bizarre visual hallucinations and feelings of being transported elsewhere; c) a deterioration of social and personal life; d) the acquisition of AIDS.

6. Freud changed his mind about the dangers of cocaine because he: a) found the drug impaired his ability to work; b) became concerned with the psychotic-like hallucinations that he began experiencing; c) discovered the drug was addictive; d) none of the above; Freud remained favorable to cocaine use throughout his life.

7. Which of the following statements concerning meditation is *false?* a) All forms of meditation involve a mystical element. b) Meditation is an effective means of inducing relaxation. c) The physiological state produced by meditation is no different from that generated by hypnosis or biofeedback. d) All of the above are false statements.

8. Which of the following would be classified as a negative hallucination when observed in a hypnotized subject: a) the hearing of voices of people not actually present; b) the experiencing of events appropriate to an earlier period in one's life; c) the inability to recall events occurring during the hypnotic session; d) the inability to see following the suggestion that one is blind.

9. The file drawer problem, a potential biasing factor in meta-analysis, occurs when: a) inadequate controls are employed in the individual experiments; b) too few observations are made; c) investigators finding no differences in their experiments fail to publish; d) the selection of test stimuli is poorly randomized.

10. Which of the following reasons for the skepticism of psychologists toward ESP phenomena was considered scientifically inappropriate by the authors of your text: a) the exaggeration of psychological findings in the popular press; b) the a priori view that psi is an impossibility; c) the fact that psychology would have to be radically revised if ESP existed; d) all of the above.

Sample Quiz 6.2

1. The view of consciousness that was prominent in psychology by the 1950s: a) emphasized introspection and the equating of consciousness with mind; b) maintained that a complete psychology must include the study of consciousness; c) argued that psychology should study only public events; d) defined psychology exclusively as the study of consciousness.

2. Which of the following statements concerning multiple personalities is false? a) One clue to the presence of multiple personalities is the occurrence of periods of unexplained amnesia; b) In most instances, some of the personalities are unaware of the experiences of the others; c) Different personalities can exhibit differences in blood pressure and electrical activity in the brain; d) Virtually all differences observed among the different personalities can be demonstrated by actors only pretending to have multiple personalities.

3. Which of the following is *true*? a) A person goes from wakefulness into deep sleep (Stage 4) very rapidly; b) Most REM sleep occurs in the early part of the night; c) There is typically one pronounced REM period each night; d) Sleep cycles contain either REM or NREM sleep, but not both.

4. Narcolepsy: a) is essentially the intrusion of NREM periods of sleep into daytime hours; b) tends to run in families; c) refers essentially to the cessation of breathing during sleep; d) especially afflicts older men.

5. A lucid dream refers specifically to: a) an altered stated of consciousness in which images and fantasies are confused with reality; b) the repressed wishes and ideas that underlie dreaming; c) a dream that includes spoken conversation; d) a dream that is so normal that the dreamer feels that he or she is awake.

6. Addiction to psychoactive drugs involves all of the following except: a) physical dependence; b) more rapid effects on increasingly lower doses; c) tolerance; d) withdrawal symptoms.

7. Alcohol seems to produce an initial stimulating effect because: a) excitatory synapses are suppressed earlier than inhibitory ones; b) it is in the stimulant class

Consciousness and its Altered States   99

of drugs; c) inhibitory synapses are suppressed earlier than excitatory ones; d) both b and c.

8. The evidence indicates that marijuana: a) significantly impairs motor coordination and signal detection in complex tasks; b) has effects that persist even after subjective experiences (such as euphoria) have passed; c) is dangerous when driving, when taken either by itself or with alcohol; d) all of the above.

9. When a person under hypnosis fails to perceive something that is actually present, we speak of a: a) posthypnotic amnesia effect; b) psi phenomenon; c) positive hallucination; d) negative hallucination.

10. Meta-analysis of the ganzfeld procedure: a) has shown the psi phenomenon not to be replicable; b) has demonstrated that the replicability of the ganzfeld effect is not dependent upon the experimenter (and therefore upon motivational influences); c) shows that the ganzfeld effect is so seriously dependent on the study of huge numbers of subjects that it has no apparent significance; d) all of the above.

100   Chapter 6

Key, Chapter 6

Names

1. John Watson
2. Sigmund Freud
3. Pierre Janet

Vocabulary and Details

1 altered state of consciousness; subjective

1. mind and consciousness; introspection
2. private events; public events
3. monitoring; controlling
4. subconscious
5. preconscious memories; preconscious
6. repressed; unconscious
7. Freudian slip
8. modularity thesis; modules

1. automatic processes
2. dissociated
3. dissociation
4. multiple personality

1. circadian rhythm; 24-25
2. jet lag
3. electroencephalogram; EEG
4. alpha waves
5. REM; NREM
6. wide awake (or active); paralyzed; idle; relaxed
7. sleep disorder
8. insomnia
9. narcolepsy; a few seconds; 15-30 minutes
10. sleep apnea; a few; several hundred
11. rebound effect
12. dreaming
13. lucid dream
14. latent; manifest

1. psychoactive
2. physical; addiction; tolerance; withdrawal
3. psychological
4. depressant; tranquilizers, barbiturates; ethyl alcohol
5. fetal alcohol syndrome
6. inability to abstain; lack of control
7. delirium tremens (or DT's)
8. opiates; opium; morphine; codeine; heroin
9. endorphins; enkephalin
10. opiate antagonist; naloxone
11. methadone
12. stimulants; amphetamines; cocaine
13. hallucinations; delusions
14. hallucinogens; mescaline; psilocybin; LSD (or lysergic acid diethylamide); PCP (or phencyclidine)

15. cannabis; marijuana; hashish; THC (or tetrahydrocannabinol)

1. meditation; breathing; attention; yogic positions; mental images
2. yoga; Zen; opening-up meditation; concentrative meditation
3. transcendental meditation; TM; mantra

1. hypnosis
2. posthypnotic response
3. posthypnotic amnesia
4. age regression
5. positive hallucination; negative hallucination

1. psi phenomena; parapsychology
2. extrasensory perception (or ESP)
3. telepathy; clairvoyance; precognition
4. psychokinesis (or PK)
5. meta-analysis

Sample Quiz 6.1

1. c, 195
2. a, 197
3. c, 205
4 c, 206
5. b, 217
6. c, 220
7. a, 227
8. d, 231
9. c, 238
10. b, 241

Sample Quiz 6.2

1. b, 195
2. d, 199-200
3. a, 204
4. b, 206
5. d, 209
6. b, 212
7. c, 213
8. d, 223
9. d, 232
10. b, 236-237

Learning and Conditioning

Learning Objectives

1. Be able to explain what is meant by the term associative learning. Know the distinction between the two forms of associative learning--namely, classical conditioning and operant conditioning.

2. Be familiar with Pavlov's experiments. Be able to define, and to differentiate between the CR, UCR, the CS, and the UCS. Know how these are related during both the acquisition and extinction of a classically conditioned response.

3. Know how generalization and discrimination function in classical conditioning. Be able to give examples of each in human learning. Be familiar with the role of temporal contiguity and predictability in establishing a conditioned response.

4. Be prepared to discuss the law of effect in relation to operant conditioning. Be familiar with the "Skinner box" and be able to define extinction and discrimination for operant conditioning in this apparatus. Know two measures of operant strength.

5. Be familiar with research on the operant conditioning of autonomic responses. Know how behavior can be shaped and why this is an important advantage of operant conditioning over classical conditioning.

6. Be able to define conditioned reinforcement and partial reinforcement; show, by examples, how each increases the generality of operant conditioning in everyday life.

7. Be prepared to discuss the nature of reinforcement, including a discussion of Premack's principle, brain stimulation, and punishment.

8. Be familiar with the ethologist's objections to a behavioristic approach to learning, and their notion of behavioral constraints. Know why experiments on taste aversion are critical to an ethological analysis of behavior.

9. Be familiar with the evidence the cognitivists cite in their challenge to the behavioristic approach to learning. Know what is meant by the term mental representation and the role it plays in a cognitive analysis of learning.

10. Understand what the study of learning in situations with less than perfect associations indicates about the role of cognitive processes. Know what the terms spurious associations, belief-driven learning, and data-driven learning mean in these experiments.

Names

1. The Nobel prize-winning Russian physiologist who pioneered research on classical conditioning in dogs was _____. (248)

2. The study of a form of operant conditioning began at the turn of the century with a series of experiments on problem solving in cats by _____, who became known for his related formulation of the law of effect. (255-256)

3. A more recent and influential psychologist who has reconceptualized the study of operant conditioning is _____. (256)

4. An early advocate of a cognitive view of learning was _____ who studied the behavior of rats in mazes and other tasks demanding complex solutions. (272)

5. The study of "insight" in chimpanzees and other primates in the 1920s was pioneered by the researcher _____. (273)

Vocabulary and Details

1. Learning that certain events go together is called _____. (247)

2. In one form of associative learning, termed _____, an organism learns that one event follows another; in the other form of associative learning, termed _____, an organism learns that a particular consequence will follow a response event. (247)

Perspectives on Conditioning

1. The study of behavior (including learned behavior) from an evolutionary-biological perspective is called _____. (247)

Classical Conditioning

1. Prior to classical conditioning, a stimulus, termed the _____ (_____), evokes a response, termed the _____ (_____). (249)

2. During classical conditioning, a second stimulus, termed the _____ (_____), is presented regularly with the UCS; as a result, a response to the second stimulus, termed the _____ (_____) comes to be evoked. (249)

3. After classical conditioning, we say that the organism has been taught or _____ to associate the CS (e.g., a light) with the UCS (e.g., food) such that it responds similarly (e.g., salivates) to both. (249)

4. Each time a CS is paired with a UCS, we speak of a _____. (249)

5. During the _____ stage of conditioning, pairings of the UCS with the CS are said to strengthen or _____ the association between them, as measured by the strength of the CR. (249)

6. Conversely, in the process called _____, the CS is presented alone repeatedly and there is no reinforcer (UCS); as a result, the strength of the association gradually diminishes, as measured by the CR. (249)

7. In _____, a stimulus (say, a tone) that has become a CS during previous conditioning may act like a "UCS" (say, an electric shock) in a new conditioning relationship; that is, the tone may now be used to condition a CR to a new stimulus (say, a light) by pairing the two stimuli. (249)

8. When a CR has been associated with a particular CS, other stimuli will tend to evoke the CR to the extent that they are similar to the CS, in the process called _____. (251)

9. Conversely, when a CR occurs to a CS but not to other stimuli that deliberately have not been reinforced with the UCS (or that are dissimilar to the CS), we speak of _____. (251)

10. To produce discrimination, we may selectively reinforce one conditioned stimulus, CS_1, and not reinforce another stimulus, CS_2, in the procedure called _____; as a result the strength of the CR to CS_2 will _____ (increase/decrease). (251)

11. Pavlov maintained that the critical factor in classical conditioning was _____ of the CS and UCS. (251)

12. More recent theorists, such as Rescorla, have maintained that the critical event in classical conditioning is that the CS be a _____ of the UCS. (251)

13. In the _____ phenomenon first demonstrated by Kamin, the learning of one association may "block" the learning of a second association to the extent that the second association fails to render the UCS any more predictable. (252)

Operant Conditioning

1. In _____ responses are learned because they _____ on (or affect) the environment. (254)

2. The likelihood that an operant response will be repeated depends on the nature of its environmental _____. (255)

3. The _____ states that when a reward immediately follows a behavior the learning of the action is strengthened. (256)

4. In a "Skinner box," an operant response, such as pressing a bar, may be followed by food (the "reinforcer") which is said to _____ bar pressing and _____ (increase/decrease) the rate of pressing. (256)

5. The conditioned response in an operant conditioning setting is simply termed the _____. (256)

6 If an operant is not reinforced, it will undergo _____, that is, its rate will _____ (increase/decrease). (256)

7. The strength of an operantly conditioned response is termed its _____, two measures of which are (a) _____, its frequency in a given time interval, and (b)

_____, the number of responses emitted after the reinforcer is withheld. (257)

8. In the procedure called _____ a subject is given information (feedback) about a physiological response (such as, blood pressure or heart rate) and is reinforced for altering the response. (258)

9. Some reinforcers, like food, are called _____ because they satisfy basic bodily needs. (258)

10. Most reinforcers, however, like money or praise, are called _____ or _____ reinforcers because they are stimuli that acquire their value through association with a primary reinforcer. (258-259)

11. In the technique called _____, only the responses that meet the experimenter's specifications are reinforced; other responses are extinguished. (259)

12. An easier way to shape a response in some species (such as key pecking in pigeons) may be achieved by merely pairing a stimulus with primary reinforcers and then reinforcing the operant response that begins to occur in the presence of the stimulus; this is called _____. (260)

13. Reinforcing a response only some of the time it occurs is termed _____. (261)

14. The _____ refers to the fact that extinction following partial reinforcement is slower than extinction following reinforcement of every response (that is, continuous reinforcement). (261)

Nature of Reinforcement

1. The _____ states that any activity may a) be reinforced when followed by a more probable activity and b) reinforce a less probable activity when it follows that activity. (263)

2. Another term for a positive event or reinforcer is _____, while another term for an aversive event is _____. (264)

3. Technically, when an operant response is followed by an aversive event in an effort to decrease the likelihood of the behavior, we speak of _____. (264)

Newer Approaches

1. In the phenomenon of _____, an animal learns to avoid a given taste because it has been associated with poison and sickness in a classical conditioning relationship. (269)

2. _____ refers to the type of learning that forms the basis for the attachment of young birds to their parents, other animals, or objects in their early environment, and that occurs only during a _____. (270)

3. In the _____ approach to intelligence and problems of learning, the organism is understood to "operate" on _____ of the world rather than on the world itself. (271)

4. In Tolman's approach to cognitive learning, he maintained that rats may develop a mental representation of the layout of mazes (and other spatial relationships), termed a _____. (272)

5. Nonexistent but plausible relations between events, called _____, are prior beliefs that may influence behavior. (276)

6. When a learner has no prior beliefs about relationships and associations are formed only with respect to objective data, learning is said to be _____; in such cases, the actual predictive strength of relationships is typically _____ (underestimated/over-estimated). (277)

7. By contrast, when prior beliefs about objective relationships influence learning, the learning is said to be _____; the actual predictive strength of relationships tends to be _____ (underestimated/overestimated). (277)

Ideas and Concepts

Perspectives on Conditioning

* 1. What perspective in psychology dominated the field of learning until about 20 years ago? To what two perspectives has the field shifted since then? (247)

* 2. a) Outline three assumptions of the behavioristic approach to learning. (247-248)

   b) To what outcomes for the field of learning did these assumptions lead? (248)

Classical Conditioning

* 1. Outline Pavlov's basic classical conditioning experiments by filling in the blanks in the diagram below. Use the technical terms and abbreviations for each of the stimuli and responses, and be sure you can cite a real example for each event from Pavlov's research. (See also Figure 7-1.) (249)

BEFORE CONDITIONING

DURING CONDITIONING

AFTER CONDITIONING

*Basic ideas and concepts

*   2. a) Using examples, outline the procedures and outcomes of acquisition and extinction. (Be sure to note the course of acquisition and extinction in Figure 7-2.) (249)

b) Describe the processes of classical conditioning in more intuitive terms, such as, "prediction" and "success." (249-250)

*   3. a) To illustrate classical conditioning in different species, for each of the following examples described in your text, be able to indicate the UCS, UCR, CS, and CR: (250)

—conditioning in flatworms:

—conditioning of human *vasoconstriction*:

—conditioning of fear:

*   b) Cite a practical use for the concepts of both conditioning and extinction in the case of human fears. (250)

*   4. a) Be able to describe the process of second-order conditioning in the following situation: During World War II, a musical passage from one of Wagner's operas is heard by a child playing in the background during the unfurling of a flag bearing a swastika emblem in a school program. The child is excited by the stirring music. Later, the flag is seen during speeches by a number of Hitler's followers, exciting the child's earlier emotions in the course of the speeches. (250)

b) By extension from the example in your text, what do you think would happen if the flag was never again paired with the music. (249-250)

*   c) What is the importance of second-order conditioning in understanding human behavior? (251)

5. a) Use the example of a classically conditioned *galvanic skin response* to demonstrate the process of generalization. (251)

*   b) What do your authors mean when they say that "Whereas generalization is a reaction to similarities, discrimination is a reaction to differences"? (251)

c) Cite some everyday examples of generalization and discrimination. Can you think of others? (251)

*   6. a) Cite some evidence favoring Pavlov's temporary contiguity view of classical conditioning. Note especially the most effective CS-UCS interval in many instances. (251)

b) In your own words, state Rescorla's view regarding the importance of predictability in classical conditioning. (251)

*   c) Outline the procedures of Rescorla's important experiment with dogs demonstrating the role of predictability in conditioning. (251-252)

*   d)   What were the results of this study and what conclusion may be drawn relative to the issue of contiguity vs. predictability? (252)

*   7.   a)   Outline the procedures and results of Kamin's blocking experiment. (252)

*   b)   In terms of the predictability concept, why did the earlier light-shock association apparently block the learning of the new association? (252)

*   8.   Discuss the main features of each of the cognitive models of classical conditioning in the following table and be able to apply them to Kamin's blocking phenomenon. (252-253)

Theorists	Main Features of Theory	Application to Blocking
Rescorla & Wagner		
Wagner	Use the term "short-term memory"	
Holyoak et al.	Use the terms "generation and testing of rules"	

*   7.   a)   Discuss some ways in which predictability and lack of predictability may play a part in emotional reactions. (253)

*   b)   Cite examples of the emotional effects of predictability at the human level. (253)

Operant Conditioning

*   1.   a)   Describe the nature of the response in classical conditioning. What kind of behavior cannot be learned through these types of procedures? (253-254)

*   b)   Cite examples of operant conditioning in humans and animals. What are the "goals" of the behavior in each example. (254-255)

*   2.   a)   Outline Edward Thorndike's problem solving procedures used in his classic studies with cats. Describe a typical pattern of behavior exhibited by an animal in the experimental cage. (255-56)

*   b)   Did Thorndike argue that the cats demonstrated "intelligence" or "insight" in this situation? Explain, using the term *trial-and-error* to describe the cats' behavior. (256)

*   c)   How does the law of effect apply to problem solving behavior such as this? (256)

Learning and Conditioning   109

d) What does it mean to say that the law of effect "promotes the survival of the fittest response"? (256)

* 3. a) Describe in detail the **Skinner box** procedure for the study of operant conditioning using the terms, *baseline level, reinforcement,* and *extinction*. (256)

* b) How would the experimenter set up a **discrimination** procedure in this setting? What would serve as the "discriminative stimulus"? (256)

* 4. In what respect are the temporal relations between events in operant conditioning important? Discuss the impact of delay of reinforcement on operant conditioning in general and in a specific example. (257)

5. Describe an application of operant conditioning principles in the case of a young boy with temper tantrums. (257)

* 6. a) What was the long-standing belief regarding the applicability of operant conditioning? How was this belief challenged? (257)

b) What is the difference between the type of bodily control over internal responses exercised by, say, yogis and the type of control that provides a demonstration of operant conditioning? (257)

c) List some of the difficulties in terms of the nature of the response, the reinforcer, and physical difficulties that may be encountered in demonstrating the kind of control discussed in b). What procedures did Miller and his colleagues use in an effort to overcome these problems? (Use the term *curare*.) (258)

d) What results were obtained in these initial studies by Miller and co-workers? (258)

* 7. Indicate the practical implications of biofeedback by outlining a range of disorders to which it might apply and how it might be effective. (258)

* 8. a) Why would operant conditioning be an uncommon event in our lives if only primary reinforcers were effective? Therefore, what extends the range of operant conditioning possibilities for us? (258)

b) Describe a demonstration of conditioned reinforcement in an animal experiment. (259)

* c) Why is money such an effective conditioned reinforcer? Why do you think that praise is so powerful? (259)

* 9. a) A psychologist friend of one of your authors has a dog that presses a button with its paw to sound a buzzer whenever it wants to go outside. Using the shaping example in your book, how would you have accomplished this training? (259)

b) Was "Priscilla, the Fastidious Pig" exceptionally bright? Why did she seem to be, and how do we know she was no Einstein? Cite some other examples of shaping as well. (259)

10. a) Describe in detail the autoshaping procedure. (260)

b) What two conditioning processes appear to be involved in this method? Cite the evidence that classical conditioning underlies the first appearances of the to-be-operantly-reinforced response. (260-261)

11. a) Cite an example of partial reinforcement in an animal experiment. (261)

*   b) Why does the partial reinforcement effect make intuitive sense? Illustrate with everyday examples of extinction following partial reinforcement and following continuous reinforcement. (261)

      c) How does the resistance of temper tantrums (or any other problem behavior) to extinction reflect a possible history of partial reinforcement? (261)

* 12. a) Contrast two possibilities for what serves as the critical factor in operant conditioning. (261)

      b) Outline the procedures of the Maier and Seligman study of learned helplessness in dogs. (261-262)

      c) What results were obtained in this study and which of the two alternative views of the operant conditioning process outlined in a) was favored by this research? Explain. (262)

Nature of Reinforcement

1. Cite three features of reinforcers that complicate their description. (262)

* 2. a) In what two ways may reinforcement be conceptualized? (262)

*   b) Outline the Premack experiment demonstrating the relativity of reinforcement when it is viewed as an activity. (262-263)

*   c) Discuss Premack's two-tiered conception of reinforcement. (263)

      d) Cite some practical applications of the Premack principle in classrooms. (263)

3. How did Premack go about demonstrating a reversal of the reinforcing qualities of activity through deprivation? Cite another example as well. (263-264)

4. a) Cite a human and an animal example of punishment. (264)

*   b) Discuss three disadvantages of the use of punishment to control operant behavior. (264)

      c) Do these disadvantages mean that punishment should never be used? Discuss the conditions under which punishment may be useful when dealing with "undesirable" behaviors. (264)

* 5. a) With what procedure were Olds and Milner experimenting, and what remarkable initial effects did they obtain? (Be sure to note the area of the brain important for these effects.) (265)

*   b) Outline the later discoveries regarding both the reinforcing and punishing effects of electrical stimulation of the brain. (265)

*   c)   Indicate one of the reasons why this research is considered so significant in the history of the field of learning. (265)

d)   What results with humans are suggestive that similar mechanisms operate at this phylogenetic level as well? (265)

6.   a)   What is a major difficulty with the view that electrical stimulation of the brain is merely one direct way to a "reward center." (265)

*   b)   Cite two lines of evidence to indicate that electrical stimulation of the brain has complex effects. (265-267)

*   c)   Discuss the theory that the neurotransmitter, *dopamine,* is involved in effects of brain stimulation. Also use the term *neuroleptics* in your answer. (267-268)

Newer Approaches

*   1.   Contrast the views of learning held by advocates of the newer approaches, ethology and cognitive psychology. (268)

*   2.   a)   Discuss two major areas of difference between the approaches of the ethologists and behaviorists. To what differing interests may these differences lead? (268)

*   b)   What is a "behavioral blueprint"? How does this concept relate to issues in the field of learning? (268)

c)   Indicate a line of reseach that lent early support to the ethological view of learning. (268-269)

*   3.   a)   Discuss the research that shows that an important event in the taste aversion studies is the particular CS that is chosen for study. (269)

*   b)   Similarly, how has it been shown that the particular CS-UCS combination, taste and sickness, are critical? (269)

*   b)   Why does this *selectivity of association* in the area of classical conditioning fit so well with the ethological approach but not with a more traditional view of the nature of learning? (Be sure to note in particular why taste should be a particularly good CS under some conditions whereas a visual CS may be effective under others.) (269-270)

c)   How does the species of the animal enter into the issue of selectivity of association in the taste aversion paradigm? (270)

*   d)   Indicate your authors' conclusion with regard to this line of classical conditioning research. (270)

4.   To show the importance of behavioral blueprints in operant conditioning as well, discuss the constraints on reward and escape learning that have been demonstrated in pigeons. (270)

*   5.   a)   Why is the phenomenon of imprinting considered to be another constraint on learning principles? (270)

*   b)   Indicate the respects in which bird songs also offer a challenge to traditional views of associative learning. Use the term *inborn template* in your response. (270-271)

*   6.   a)   What has been one counterargument of behaviorists to recent challenges to traditional views of learning? Give an example. (271)

*   b)   In your authors' view, what is the general point of these discussions? Is it clear that the behaviorists' arguments will be persuasive? (271)

*   c)   Therefore, what is likely to be the continuing impact of the ethological approach and what is the "synthesis" that your text says is called for? (271)

*   7.   a)   In what sense is the cognitive challenge to traditional views of learning the opposite of the ethologists' challenge? (271)

*   b)   What is the cognitive view of the "trial-and-error" process in learning and in what two respects does this contradict the behavioral approach? (271-272)

    c)   What is one reason why the cognitive view of learning has become so popular so quickly? How is behavior necessarily understood in this model? (272)

*   8.   a)   Describe a typical maze learning procedure used by Tolman. (272)

*   b)   What type of results did he obtain and how did he interpret these findings? (272)

    c)   Describe a more recent maze learning problem and results. Do rats favor the strategy that humans might in analogous situations? What does this imply the rats are learning? (272)

*   9.   a)   How have Köhler and others allowed for the occurrence of *insight* in higher species? (273)

    b)   Describe some of the typical results obtained using the *multiple-stick problem* in Köhler's studies. (273)

*   c)   Cite three critical aspects of the performance of Köhler's chimps that were unlike those typically obtained in animal learning studies with lower species. (274-275)

    d)   Therefore, as opposed to trial-and-error problem solving, what may the chimpanzee's solutions reflect? Explain. (274)

* 10.   Describe in detail Premack's demonstrations of even more sophisticated learning of "abstract" linguistic concepts in chimpanzees. List three such abstractions that chimps appear able to learn. (275)

* 11.   a)   In what sense does classical conditioning typically involve the learning of *perfectly predictable relations*? At what phylogenetic level has the study of *less than perfect relations* largely been carried out, and what processes have been implicated? (276)

b) Describe one line of research on less than perfect relations. In technical terms and your own words, what seemed to be the source of the subjects' reports of relationships in the stimuli? (276)

c) Cite the example of spurious associations in the clinical use of the Draw-a-Person test, indicating the nature of the actual correlation of the test with emotional difficulties. (276)

* 12. a) Describe a procedure for the study of data-driven learning and the typical results that are obtained with this method. (277)

* b) By contrast, what happens when subjects *do* have prior beliefs about objective relationships? (277)

13. How do such studies as those on pp. 276-277 of your text have a connection to the ethological approach? (277)

Unit Quiz 7.1

1. Which of the following is an assumption of the behavioristic approach to learning: a) Learning can be better understood in terms of internal or intentional causes than external or environmental ones. b) The laws of learning are different for different species. c) Simple associations learned through classical or operant conditioning are the building blocks of all learning, no matter how complex. d) All of the above.

2. The law of effect is to classical conditioning as: a) Skinner is to Kohler; b) Kohler is to Thorndike; c) Thorndike is to Pavlov; d) Pavlov is to Tolman.

3. When a conditioned stimulus is presented alone repeatedly, with no pairings with an unconditioned stimulus, the procedure is called: a) generalization; b) extinction; c) acquisition; d) second-order conditioning.

4. The fact that conditioning is typically most effective if the interval between the CS and the UCS is about half a second provides support for the notion that the critical factor in classical conditioning is: a) rule generation and testing; b) temporal contiguity; c) predictability; d) cognitive rehearsal.

5. Responses are learned because they affect the environment in the process called: a) classical conditioning; b) operant conditioning; c) second-order conditioning; d) spurious associations.

6. According to Premack, in operant conditioning you can reinforce an activity by: a) following it with a less probable response; b) following it with a more probable response; c) following it with an equally probable response; d) none of the above; the Premack Principle applies to classical conditioning, not operant conditioning.

7. As discussed in your text, taste aversion is an example of: a) imprinting; b) classical conditioning; c) autoshaping; d) operant conditioning.

8. The imprinting phenomenon creates a challenge for traditional behaviorism because: a) it demonstrates the importance of mental representation in even the most basic learning situations; b) it illustrates a selectivity of association with

114   Chapter 7

respect to CS-UCS pairings; c) it suggests that some forms of association learning can occur only very early in life; d) none of the above; the imprinting phenomenon supports the behavioral perspective rather than challenges it.

9. Tolman found that rats allowed to explore a complex maze prior to reinforcement, as compared to rats not allowed such exploration, subsequently: a) learned the maze less rapidly; b) learned the maze more rapidly; c) learned the maze equally rapidly; d) did not learn the maze at all.

10. Critical periods are an important element in which of the following learning phenomena: a) imprinting; b) the development of spurious associations; c) taste aversion; d) the partial reinforcement effect.

Unit Quiz 7.2

1. Learning that one event follows (or is predicted by) another is called: a) operant conditioning; b) associative learning; c) classical conditioning; d) both b and c.

2. _____ is to CS plus UCS as _____ is to CS alone: a) acquisition, extinction; b) extinction, acquisition; c) discrimination, generalization; d) generalization, acquisition.

3. Second-order conditioning is important at the human level because: a) it helps us to understand the mechanisms of operant conditioning; b) it is at the basis of virtually all punishment effects; c) it greatly expands the scope of classical conditioning; d) none of the above; second-order conditioning is not relevant to the understanding of human behavior.

4. By contrast with the response in classical conditioning, an operant: a) resembles the UCR; b) is reflexive; c) is novel and may occur spontaneously; d) does not have an effect upon the environment.

5. Conditioned reinforcers: a) commonly satisfy basic bodily needs; b) acquire their value through association with a primary reinforcer; c) include such everyday rewards as money or praise; d) both b and c.

6. A dog presses a buzzer to notify its owner to open the door and be let outside. The immediate conditioned reinforcer in this example is: a) the buzzer; b) being let outside; c) food in a tray outside the door; d) the dog's owner.

7. If you wanted to develop persistence with respect to a given behavior in your child, you should: a) use classical conditioning procedures instead of operant ones; b) use partial reinforcement; c) use continuous reinforcement; d) not use reinforcement at all.

8. Research on electrical stimulation of the brain: a) has shown that rats will press a lever at a very high rate to obtain such stimulation; b) has consistently shown reinforcing effects but has not demonstrated punishing effects; c) is important because it demonstrates the Premack principle; d) has been limited to demonstrations with rats.

9. Which of the following is *false?* a) Imprinting forms the basis for attachment only during a critical period. b) In the cognitive view, an organism is said to operate on

mental representations of the environment. c) In taste aversion, avoidance of a specific taste is developed by associating it with electric shocks. d) In punishment a response is followed by an aversive stimulus in an attempt to lower its probability.

10. Köhler's chimps behaved differently from the typical laboratory rat or pigeon in problem situations in that the former: a) came to a sudden solution; b) transferred their learning to a novel situation; c) showed few "irrelevant" moves once a problem was solved; d) all of the above.

Key, Chapter 7

Names

1. Ivan Pavlov
2. E. L. Thorndike
3. B. F. Skinner
4. Edward Tolman
5. Wolfgang Köhler

Vocabulary and Details

1. associative learning
2. classical conditioning; operant conditioning

1. ethology

1. unconditioned stimulus; UCS; unconditioned response; UCR
2. conditioned stimulus; CS; conditioned response; CR
3. conditioned
4. trial
5. acquisition; reinforce
6. extinction
7. second-order conditioning
8. generalization
9. discrimination
10. differential reinforcement; decrease
11. temporal contiguity
12. reliable predictor
13. blocking

1. operant conditioning; operate
2. consequences
3. law of effect
4. reinforce; increase
5. operant
6. extinction; decrease
7. response strength; rate of response; number of responses during extinction
8. biofeedback
9. primary reinforcers
10. secondary; conditioned
11. shaping
12. autoshaping
13. partial reinforcement
14. partial reinforcement effect

1. Premack principle
2. reward; punisher
3. punishment

1. taste aversion
2. imprinting; critical period
3. cognitive; mental representations
4. cognitive map
5. spurious associations

6. data driven; underestimated
7. belief driven; overestimated

Unit Quiz 7.1

1. c, 247
2. c, 248, 255-256
3. b, 249
4. b, 251
5. b, 254
6. b, 263
7. b, 269
8. c, 270
9. b, 272
10. a, 270

Unit Quiz 7.2

1. d, 247
2. a, 249
3. c, 251
4. c, 253-254
5. d, 258-59
6. a, 259
7. b, 261
8. a, 265
9. c, 269
10. d, 274

Memory

Learning Objectives

1. Understand the distinctions between the three stages and the two types of memory described in the text.

2. Know the difference between acoustic encoding and visual encoding in short-term memory.

3. Be able to discuss the limits of short-term storage represented by the number seven plus or minus two (7 ± 2). Explain how this is related to memory span, displacement, decay, and rehearsal. Be familiar with research on the time required to retrieve information from short-term memory.

4. Understand the role that short-term memory plays in problem solving, language comprehension, and higher mental processes such as reading. Be able to describe how chunking uses information stored in long-term memory to increase the capacity of short-term memory.

5. Be prepared to describe the Atkinson-Shiffrin theory of dual memory and show how free-recall evidence supports it. Be familiar with some of the problems encountered by the theory.

6. Understand the concept of encoding for meaning in long-term memory and how elaboration can improve memory.

7. Be able to discuss forgetting in terms of storage versus retrieval failure, citing evidence for both types of loss. Be familiar with research on interference, the importance of organization in encoding, and the effect of context on recall.

8. Be familiar with the various ways that emotion can affect memory.

9. Be able to differentiate between retrograde amnesia and anterograde amnesia. Be familiar with the evidence indicating that there may be different kinds of memories (fact versus skill memory, personal-fact versus general-fact memory).

10. Be able to describe the various methods for improving both short-term and long-term memory. Be able to explain the mnemonic systems called the "method of loci" and the "key word method." Be familiar with the PQRST method.

11. Know what is meant by constructive memory. Be able to show how inferences, stereotypes, and schemata each contribute to constructive memory processes.

Vocabulary and Details

Distinctions about Memory

1. In the three stages of memory, the first is _____, which refers to transforming information (such as, visual or verbal) into a code that memory accepts. (281)

2. In the second stage of memory, _____, the information is maintained or stored. (281)

3. In the third stage of memory, _____, information is recovered from storage. (281)

4. The concept _____ refers to the fact that information may be stored in memory for relatively short periods, say, a few seconds, whereas _____ refers to storage for longer intervals, from minutes to years. (282)

5. Another term for severe (partial or total) memory loss is _____. (282)

Short-Term Memory

1. _____ of material in short-term memory means to repeat material over and over to keep it active. (283)

2. A rare phenomenon, but one more likely in children, is the ability to recall photographically detailed information about previously viewed visual material, termed _____. (284)

3. It appears that short-term memory has a capacity limited to _____ items, a constancy referred to by George Miller as the _____. (284-285)

4. The maximum amount of material that a subject can recall in a short-term memory task is called the subject's _____. (285)

5. Forgetting of items in short-term memory may be due to their _____ by newer items or to _____ with time. (285)

6. Larger, meaningful units of material in short-term memory are called _____. Based on the information in item 3 directly above, we would expect a person to be able to remember about _____ (how many?) units when "chunking" information. (289)

7. According to Atkinson and Shiffrin's theory, termed the _____, information that is attended to enters short-term memory and then is either a) lost through displacement or decay, or b) rehearsed and transferred to long-term memory. (289)

8. In the _____ method for assessment of memory, a number of items are provided one at a time for a subject to remember and then the subject is asked to recall them in any order. (290)

Long-Term Memory

1. A _____ is anything that helps us to retrieve a memory; the better these cues are, the _____ (better/worse) our memory. (294)

2. In a _____ test of memory, we are asked if we have seen a particular item before; in a _____ test, on the other hand, we have to produce the memorized material with minimal retrieval cues. (294)

3. An important factor that can impair retrieval from long-term memory is _____; that is when we try to use a retrieval cue, other items associated with that cue may become active and interfere with the item we are trying to retrieve. (294)

4. An electric current applied to the brain that produces a brief seizure and momentary unconconsiousness is called _____. (296)

5. When memory is partly dependent upon the internal conditions that prevailed during learning, we speak of _____. (298)

6. A vivid and permanent record of the circumstances surrounding a significant, emotionally charged event is called a _____. (299)

7. In Freud's analysis of memory, traumatic experiences may be actively blocked from consciousness; this is a view called the _____. (301)

8. A partial or total loss of memory is called _____. (301)

9. In one form of amnesia, the primary symptom is a serious inability to acquire new factual information or to remember everyday events; this is termed _____. (302)

10. In another form of amnesia, there is an inability to remember events that occurred prior to the event causing the memory loss; this is termed _____. (302)

11. Amnesiacs appear to often suffer losses in their memory of specific events or people, termed _____ , but not in their ability to remember a variety of skilled activities, termed _____. (302)

12. Among memories for skills, _____ are those involved in motor responses, such as, riding a bicycle; _____ are those that demand attention and perception, such as, reading; _____ are those that require active cognitive processing, such as, defining a word. (302-303)

13. In further distinction between kinds of memories, it appears that perceptual or cognitive *skills* are often learned without conscious recollection of the experiences during learning, a process that is called _____. (305)

14. In contrast, memory of a personal *fact*, or _____, is often a conscious recollection of something in the past. (305)

Improving Memory

1. A system that aids memory is called a _____. (308)

2. One mnemonic, connecting items of information to an ordered sequence of imaginal locations, is termed the _____. (308)

3. Another mnemonic involves finding a part of a term to be remembered, such as part of a foreign word, that sounds like some object that can be imagined; this is the technique called the _____. (308)

4. Another technique for improving long-term memory is the PQRST method, in which the letters stand for _____, _____, _____, _____, and _____. (311)

Constructive Memory

1. We tend to use our general knowledge of the world to build a more complete memory of complex, meaningful events; that is, memory may be _____. (312)

2. In one form of construction, when we fill in material based on available facts, we are making use of _____. (313)

3. In another form of construction, the use of social _____, we may rely on inferences about the psychological or physical traits of a class of people. (314)

4. In general, mental representations of a class of people, objects, events, or situations, including the use of stereotypes, are called _____ (singular: _____). (315)

Ideas and Concepts

* 1. Give three reasons why we must give a central place to the concept of memory in the understanding of human psychology. (281)

Distinctions about Memory

* 1. Cite examples of encoding, storage, and retrieval of a memory. At what stage can memory fail? (281)

2. a) Give an example to illustrate the difference between short-term and long-term memory. (282)

* b) Distinguish between short-term and long-term memory in terms of conscious versus preconscious, or active versus passive, knowledge. (282)

* c) In what ways do different forms of amnesia also support the distinction between short- and long-term memory? (282)

* 3. a) What has been the assumption of psychologists about memory until recently? What different kinds of long-term memories may there be for different kinds of information? (282)

b) What kind of memory forms the basis for this chapter and why? (282-283)

*Basic ideas and concepts

Short-Term Memory

* 1. What is first necessary in order to encode information into short-term memory? Therefore, when we have "memory problems," does this necessarily mean that our memory is not functioning properly? Explain. (283)

* 2. a) In what three forms may material be encoded in short-term memory? What form do we seem to favor, at least unless verbal rehearsal is being employed? (283)

* b) Cite some evidence that demonstrates this tendency to code acoustically. (283)

   c) Describe another study, this one with readers of Chinese, that shows the effects of acoustic coding. (284)

   d) What other kind of coding is demonstrated in the study cited in c)? Give another example. (284)

* 3. Describe a procedure for demonstrating Miller's "magic number seven." (285)

* 4. a) In what respect does the notion of forgetting through displacement accord with what we know about short-term memory? (285)

   b) Provide an everyday example to demonstrate how displacement in short-term memory would work. (285-286)

* c) Describe an experiment that clearly demonstrates the fixed capacity of short-term memory. Use the term *probe* in your answer. (286)

   d) Discuss the "activation" view of short-term memory as it applies to these displacement demonstrations of its fixed capacity. (286)

* 5. a) Discuss two lines of evidence that favor the alternative "decay" view of forgetting of material in short-term memory. (286)

   b) As an aside, linguists have long noted that there is a tendency in human language to gradually adopt abbreviated versions of words across time, such as, "TV" for "television" and "car" for "automobile." Using the information in a), can you speculate as to why this might be the case? (286)

* 6. What is the one exception to the rule that items in short term memory may be displaced or undergo decay? How might this process affect each of these forgetting factors? (286)

* 7. a) Intuitively, why should retrieval of information in short-term memory *not* depend on the number of items being remembered at one time? Is this assumption correct? (287)

* b) Describe an experiment in detail that demonstrates clearly that retrieval times are directly proportional to the number of items in short-term memory. Use the terms *serial* search, *memory list* and *decision time* . (287)

   c) What is so remarkable about the relationship obtained in the experiment outlined in b) and how much time is required for a decision whether or not an item is present in short-term memory? Is this function dependent upon the type of material that is remembered or the type of subject that is employed? (287)

* 8. a) Illustrate with a demonstration that short-term memory plays an important role in conscious thought. Why is the term "working memory" applied to the functions of short-term memory? (287-288)

* b) How do we know that this same working memory function does not apply to understanding simple sentences? Discuss the evidence showing the existence of a special memory for language. (288)

* c) On the other hand, what happens as we progress to memory for relatively complex sentences? (288)

d) Discuss additional evidence to show the role of short-term memory in helping us to relate material in conversation or reading to previously known material. (288)

9. a) Cite a demonstration of chunking and indicate how this phenomenon demonstrates so well the interaction between short-term and long-term memory. (289)

* b) Use some additional examples to illustrate the principle that we can facilitate short-term memory through chunking, using units that already exist in long-term memory. (289)

10. To test your own memory of the basics of dual-memory theory, draw a little diagram like that in Figure 8-6 and see if you are able to fill in the appropriate terms without looking. What should you do to be sure that these terms are in your long-term memory? (289)

* 11. Describe in detail three variations on a basic free-recall procedure to demonstrate the predictive power of dual-memory theory. (290)

* 12. a) On the other hand, indicate one source of dispute concerning the validity of dual-memory theory. Cite a related anecdotal report. (290)

* b) Describe yet another challenge to dual-memory theory, using the term *recency effect* in your answer. To what have these arguments led in our progressive understanding of the nature of memory? (291)

Long-Term Memory

1. Indicate two complications in the study of long-term memory from the standpoint of encoding, storage, and retrieval processes. (291)

* 2. a) What is the major form of information storage in long-term memory? Give some examples to support this observation. (291)

b) List some other forms of information storage in long-term memory. (292)

* 3. a) How can we improve on long-term memory for material that has no inherent meaning? Try to think of an example other than the one in your text. (292-293)

124   Chapter 8

*   b) What is one of the best ways to add connections to material during memorization? Cite an example and a related experiment. (Can you see the relationship between the outcome of this experiment and the benefits of using this *Study Guide* for *Introduction to Psychology*?) (293)

*   4. a) Contrast the nature of forgetting in the case of long-term memory to that of short-term memory. (293-294)

*   b) Describe several types of everyday experiences, including some that may happen in psychotherapy, indicating that apparent forgetting may at times be a failure of retrieval. Use the term *tip-of-the-tongue* phenomenon. (294)

     c) Discuss an experiment to show the powerful role that retrieval cues play in helping us to remember. (294)

     d) From the information in your text, why would we expect the multiple-choice sample quizzes at the end of this section of the *Study Guide* to show better memory performance than questions that called for short answers or essays? (294)

*   5. a) Cite an everyday and an experimental example of interference. (294-295)

*   b) Why was recognition slower for one set of facts than the other set in this experiment, and what does this suggest regarding the nature of the process of retrieval from long-term memory? (295)

     c) Discuss yet another interpretation of the retrieval process that could be applied to this experiment. (296)

*   6. a) Are retrieval failures the only cause for forgetting? Indicate a procedure that appears to cause actual loss of storage in long-term memory. How do we know? (296)

*   b) In your own words, what do your authors mean when they say that electroconvulsive shock disrupts the process of *consolidation*? (296)

     c) Indicate the brain structures that play a role in consolidation; cite some observations about the relative importance of these structures. (296-297)

     d) Are these brain structures the actual site of memory storage? If not, what is? (297)

*   7. a) Indicate two encoding factors that increase the chances of successful retrieval (in addition to ones you learned earlier). (297)

     b) Cite an everyday and an experimental example of the role of organization in improving memory. (297-298)

*   c) In detail, give two reasons why hierarchical organization improves memory. (298)

*   8. a) In terms of retrieval cues, how important is the context in which you acquired a memory? Can you think of an example in your own life? (298)

*   b)   Must contextual cues always be external to the memorizer? Again, give an example. (298)

*   9.   Emotions can influence memory in five distinct ways. Using the items in the left-hand column of the following table as a cue, describe or explain each of these ways in your own words and cite an example. (299-301)

	Description or Explanation	Example
rehearsal and organization		
flashbulb memories		
anxiety		
context effects		
repression		

*   9.   Describe some of the specific causes and consequences of amnesia. Aside from anterograde and retrograde memory losses, how would the typical amnesia be characterized in terms of intellectual functioning? (301-302)

*   10.   a)   Give examples to illustrate that memory losses due to amnesia can occur at each of the particular stages of memory. (302)

          b)   Outline the controversial hypothesis that different kinds of amnesia are related to damage to different regions of the brain. (302)

*   11.   a)   What features of amnesia indicate that there are different types of memory skills? (302-303)

          b)   Describe an experiment demonstrating the aspects of cognitive skill learning that apparently are affected and those that are not influenced by amnesia. (303)

          c)   How do the distinctions developed in a) and b) correspond with the view that there are two forms of knowledge, "knowing how," and "knowing that"? (303)

*   12.   a)   Distinguish between *personal facts* and *general facts* and be able to cite examples. (303)

*   b)   How do amnesiacs differ with regard to their memory for personal and general facts, and what does this imply with regard to the existence of different memories? (303-304)

   13.   a)   Give some examples to illustrate the differences between implicit and explicit memories in skill and fact learning, respectively. (305)

*   b)   Discuss an experiment that shows how elaboration affects memory for facts but not for skills. (306)

*   c)   Conversely, describe two studies to show the effects of modality of stimulus presentation upon skill memory but not upon fact memory. (306)

*   d)   What conclusion may be drawn from experiments such as these? (306)

Improving Memory

*   1. a)   In terms of chunks, what can we do to enlarge the capacity of short-term memory? (307)

    b)   What do your authors mean by "general-purpose recoding system"? Give one example. (307)

    2. a)   How can we improve the recall of unrelated items and what is particularly useful for this purpose? (307-308)

*   b)   For each of the following mnemonics, provide an example from the text or from your own experience. (308)

    —*method of loci:*

    —*key-word method:* (Also, be sure to note what kind of learning this method is especially useful for.)

*   c)   Why does *elaboration* improve recall? Be able to provide an example. (308-309)

*   d)   Illustrate how we might recreate *context* both in physical terms and by mental methods. (309)

*   3. Demonstrate for yourself the power of *organization* for improving memory: Develop a scheme for organizing all of the methods discussed in this section on improving memory, including *retrieval* and the *PQRST* method (see items 4 and 5, below), using all of the italicized terms in items 2 and 3 or the section subheadings. (308-312)

    4. Describe the best way to be sure you can effectively retrieve information for a class assignment. (311)

*   5. a)   Be sure you understand what each step means in the PQRST method. (311-312)

    b)   Upon what three factors for improving long-term memory does the PQRST method mainly depend? (312)

Constructive Memory

    1. In your authors' speculation, why do we engage in construction when remembering? (313)

* 2. a) Provide examples of the use of simple inferences in memory for stories and for visual scenes. In the latter, what compelling evidence was obtained for constructive memory? (313)

   b) At what stage does the constructive process take place, in the forming of the memory or in the process of remembering? (313-314)

   c) For what area of human affairs might constructive memories have particularly important implications and why? (314)

3. a) Give an example for how a racial stereotype may impact on memory. (314)

* b) Describe an experimental demonstration of the retroactive influence of stereotypes on memory. In what two ways might the stereotypes have been used by the subjects in this study? (314-315)

* 4. a) Provide some illustrations of schemata. For what two purposes can schemata be used? (315)

   b) What does the use of schemata in perceiving and thinking permit and what price do we pay for their use? (315)

* c) What was the psychologist Bartlett's suggestion regarding the use of schematas in recalling stories, and how has this been confirmed? (315)

* d) In contrast, illustrate a way in which a schema may serve as an aid to memory. (315-316)

5. What two stages of memory are aided by schemata? Cite some examples. (316-317)

Sample Quiz 8.1

1. Encoding is the technical term used in discussions of memory to refer to: a) the recovery of information from storage; b) the transforming of information into a form that memory accepts; c) the maintenance or storage of memory; d) the transfer of information from short-term to long-term memory.

2. Short-term memory is to long-term memory as: a) active knowledge is to passive knowledge; b) preconscious memory is to conscious memory; c) passive knowledge is to active knowledge; d) both b and c.

3. Which of the following is *true?* a) Retrieval from short-term memory is independent of the number of items remembered. b) We use the process of a serial search when looking for information in short-term memory. c) Total decision time for all items in short-term memory is independent of the number of items remembered. d) None of the above.

4. If you are asked to recall your classmates in high school in any order without additional cues, the method for assessment of your memory is: a) free recall; b) the method of loci; c) recognition; d) none of the above.

128   Chapter 8

5. Dual-memory theory has been challenged by the fact that: a) rehearsal always facilitates long-term memory; b) the recency effect applies to long-term as well as short-term memories; c) our memory span for materials that have not been rehearsed is limited to about 7 items; d) the recency effect applies only to short-term memory.

6. If you have a very vivid recollection of events surrounding, say, the Challenger disaster, you have what is technically termed: a) a traumatic flashback; b) intrusive counter-repression; c) a flashbulb memory; d) displacement override.

7. The Freudian notion that traumatic experiences can be actively blocked from consciousness is termed: a) interference; b) repression; c) amnesia; d) displacement.

8. Memory for events that demand coordinated muscular responses, such as, typing at a word processer, is called _____ memory: a) perceptual skills; b) cognitive skills; c) motor skills; d) short-term.

9. The first step in the PQRST method is to: a) ponder; b) peruse; c) preview; d) procrastinate.

10. In construction through simple inference, we specifically make use of: a) filler material based on available facts; b) a mental representation of a class of events; c) a mental representation of a class of situations; d) the key word method.

Sample Quiz 8.2

1. Which of the following represents the proper sequence for the three main stages of memory: a) retrieval, storage, encoding; b) storage, encoding, retrieval; c) encoding, storage, retrieval; d) retrieval, encoding, storage.

2. George Miller's "magic number" was between: a) 3 and 6; b) 5 and 9; c) 4 and 6; d) 8 and 12.

3. Decay and displacement are to interference as: a) encoding is to storage; b) short-term memory is to long-term memory; c) amnesia is to emotional factors; d) organization is to elaboration.

4. According to dual-memory theory, the reason individuals engaging in a free recall task tend to remember items in the middle of a list better than those at the beginning is that the middle items: a) are more likely to be in short-term memory; b) are more readily related to prior memories; c) have more opportunity to be rehearsed; d) none of the above; in fact, items at the beginning of a list tend to be remembered better than those in the middle.

5. One reason why we may remember emotional events so well is that we think so much about them. This indicates the role of what emotional factor in forgetting: a) anxiety; b) flashbulb memories; c) rehearsal; d) context.

6. "Blocking" on a major examination illustrates the effects of emotion on memory in terms of: a) context effects; b) anxiety; c) flashbulb memories; d) repression.

7. Implicit memory refers to: a) unconscious recollection of experiences during learning; b) the type of memorization that often occurs during perceptual and cognitive learning; c) memory of a personal fact; d) both a and b.

8. Your text suggests that elaboration enhances long-term memory because the technique: a) increases the number of associations established among items during encoding; b) speeds up the transfer of information from short-term to long-term memory; c) re-establishes relevant context cues during retrieval; d) none of the above; elaboration hinders long-term memory, due to interference.

9. To refer to the fact that we tend to use our general knowledge of the world to build a more complete memory of complex, meaningful events, we use the term: a) fact memory; b) implicit memory; c) explicit memory; d) constructive memory.

10. Schemata can include: a) knowledge about how to act in certain situations; b) stereotypes; c) knowledge about particular objects and events; d) all of the above.

Key, Chapter 8

Vocabulary and Details

1. encoding
2. storage
3. retrieval
4. short-term memory; long-term memory
5. amnesia

1. rehearsal
2. eidetic imagery
3. 7 ± 2; magic number seven
4. memory span
5. displacement; decay
6. chunks; 7 ± 2
7. dual-memory theory
8. free recall

1. retrieval cue; better
2. recognition; recall
3. interference
4. electroconvulsive shock
5. state-dependent learning
6. flashbulb memory
7. repression hypothesis
8. amnesia
9. anterograde amnesia
10. retrograde amnesia
11. fact memory; skill memory
12. motor skills; perceptual skills; cognitive skills
13. implicit memory
14. explicit memory

1. mnemonic
2. method of loci
3. key word method
4. preview; read; question; self-recitation; test

1. constructive
2. simple inference
3. stereotypes
4. schemata (schema)

Sample Quiz 8.1

1. b, 281
2. a, 282
3. b, 287
4. a, 290
5. b, 290-291
6. c, 299
7. b, 301
8. c, 302-303
9. c, 311
10. a, 313

Sample Quiz 8.2

1. c, 281
2. b, 284-285
3. b, 285, 294
4. d, 290
5. c, 299
6. b, 300-301
7. d, 305
8. a, 308
9. d, 312
10. d, 315

Thought and Language

Learning Objectives

1. Be able to define three modes of thought. Understand the distinction between the prototype and the core of a concept, including the role these properties play in classical and fuzzy concepts and the way we use them to acquire concepts.

2. Know how concepts are organized into hierarchies based on levels of abstraction and be able to describe the use of exemplar and hypothesis-testing strategies in acquiring concepts.

3. Explain what a proposition is and how concepts can be combined into propositions. Illustrate how some concepts take the role of subject in the proposition, while others take the role of predicate.

4. Be able to distinguish between deductive and inductive reasoning; know the rule we use in evaluating both types of arguments and the biases that influence our judgments.

5. Be able to describe the three levels of language in both production and comprehension, including the units (phonemes, morphemes, and sentences) involved at each level. Explain the differences between comprehension and production and the effects of context on each.

6. Be familiar with children's development of language at all three levels.

7. Explain why imitation and conditioning are not likely to be the principle means by which children learn to produce and understand sentences. Describe the operating principles children use in forming hypotheses about language.

8. Be familiar with the evidence suggesting that humans have some innate knowledge of language and with the controversy over whether other species are similarly endowed.

9. Be able to explain what is meant by visual thinking, how it has been studied experimentally, and how it may be involved in creative thought.

10. Describe three problem-solving strategies that can be used to decompose a goal into subgoals.

11. Describe three basic ways in which expert problem solvers differ from novices.

Vocabulary and Details

1. One mode of thought, called _____, corresponds to the stream of sentences expressing propositions that we seem to "hear in our mind." (321)

2. Another mode of thought, termed _____, involves images (usually visual) that we "see in our mind." (321)

3. Yet a third mode of thought, called _____, corresponds to sequences of movements we make in our minds. (321)

Concepts

1. A _____ is a statement that expresses a factual claim. (321)

2. The components of a proposition are called _____; they are our means of dividing the world into manageable units, such as, classes of objects. (321)

3. Every concept has a _____ that contains the properties that describe the *best examples* of a concept. (322)

4. In addition, every concept contains a _____, the properties that are *most important* for being a member of the concept. Such properties are diagnostic of concept membership. (322-323)

5. With concepts that are _____, the core properties are as salient as are the prototype properties, so we can be sure of our classification of the concept. (323)

6. In contrast, with concepts that are _____, the core is less salient, so we mainly depend upon prototypical properties for classification and we may be less sure of our decision. (323)

7. When concepts are grouped on levels, in what is called a _____, two types of knowledge are represented: _____ of concepts and _____ between concepts. (324)

8. In the simple strategy for learning of concepts, termed the _____, children store a representation (that is, _____) of the concept and then note similarities to it. (325)

9. Later in life, we tend to use another strategy, termed _____, which involves conjecturing whether an item belongs to a concept, analyzing an instance, and determining the correctness of our decision. (326-327).

10. The simplest way to *combine* concepts is to join a _____ and a _____ (description) to form a _____. (327)

Reasoning

1. The term _____ refers to a sequence of thoughts, often in the form of an argument leading to a conclusion, and propositions that are reasons, or _____, for the conclusion. (328)

2. The strongest arguments are said to be _____, meaning that it is not possible for the conclusion to be false if the premises are true using rules that are _____. (328)

3. To solve deductive problems, besides logical rules people may use _____, that is, rules that are less abstract and more relevant to everyday problems. (329-330)

4. In reasoning, the use of shortcut procedures that are applied easily and that often work is called the use of _____. (330)

5. In contrast with a deductive argument, in an _____ argument it is *improbable* (rather than certain) that a conclusion is false if the premises are true. (330)

6. In violation of rules of probability theory, people may use one form of heuristic called the _____ in which they use estimates of similarity to come to inductive conclusions. (332)

7. Yet another heuristic that we employ to estimate probabilities when inducing conclusions is the _____, an estimate of the probability of causal connections between events. (332)

Language and Communication

1. In the _____ of language, we start with a propositional thought, translate it into a sentence, and express the sentence with speech sounds. (333)

2. In the _____ of language, we start by hearing sounds, attach meanings (words) to the sounds, combine the words to form a sentence, and extract a proposition. (333)

3. The smallest unit of speech sound is called a _____. (333)

4. The smallest linguistic unit that carries meaning is termed a _____. (334)

5. Words that are _____ name more than one concept. (334)

6. _____ units include sentences and phrases. (335)

7. Analyzing a sentence into noun and verb phrases and smaller units is called _____. (336)

8. The relations between words in phrases and sentences (or the *structure* of language) is termed _____. (336)

Development of Language

1. One way in which the specifics of language may be learned is through _____, simply copying what is heard; another way is through _____, being rewarded for specific structures and contents of speech. (340)

2. A third way in which language may be learned is through _____, that is, a child may form a notion about a rule of language, test it, and if it works, retain it. (341)

Imaginal Thought

1. Thinking using visual images is termed _____. (347)

Thought in Action: Problem Solving

1. In _____ we are striving for a goal but have no ready means of obtaining it. (349)

2. One strategy in problem solving is to reduce the difference between our _____ and our _____ in the process called _____. (350)

3. A second strategy in the solving of problems is to compare our current state to the goal state in order to find the most important difference between them; this process is termed _____. (350)

4. A third problem solving strategy is _____, that is, reasoning from the goal to a subgoal, and on backward to a subgoal that is obtainable. (350)

5. Using verbal reports obtained from people during problem solving, researchers may program a computer to solve the problem and then match the results of the program to those obtained by the people; this is the method called _____. (353)

Ideas and Concepts

Concepts

1. a)   Give some examples to show the use of concepts. (321)

*   b)   What do we achieve by treating objects as members of the same concept? (321)

*   c)   Cite an example of categorization and indicate what enormously important function concepts can serve once an item is categorized. (321-322)

*   d)   In addition to concepts regarding objects, what other types of concepts exist? With what are commonly used concepts usually associated and what function is thereby served? (322)

* 2. Using the concepts for "bachelor" and "bird," distinguish between prototype and core properties. Based upon this distinction, differentiate between classical and fuzzy concepts using specific examples. (323)

* 3. Discuss and exemplify the effects of the *typicality* of a concept upon each of the following mental processes. (323)

—categorization:

—memory:

*Basic ideas and concepts

—inferences:

—thinking:

4. a)   What does a hierarchy allow us to infer? Illustrate using the concepts "apple" and "pear." (324)

    b)   If it is not known whether a concept has a particular property, how does one proceed using a hierarchy? What is implied about how long that will take and what is the related evidence? (324)

*   c)   Again using the "apple" and "pear" examples, distinguish among the notions *basic-level, abstract,* and *concrete* concepts in hierarchies. (324)

5. a)   Indicate the two main origins of concepts. (325)

*   b)   In what two ways may concepts be learned? How do these ways relate to whether we are learning cores or prototypes? Use an example. (325)

*   c)   What must children learn about the relative importance of cores and prototypes, and at what age is this type of learning apparently easier? Illustrate. (325)

6. a)   What is one reason why young children may emphasize prototypes of concepts and what strategy do they use? (325)

*   b)   With what kinds of instances is the exemplar strategy best? Explain, using an example. (326)

*   c)   For what concepts is the hypothesis testing strategy appropriate and why? (326-327)

7. a)   Be sure you can distinguish subjects from predicates by example, noting three different types of predicates. (327)

*   b)   Discuss some of the ways, from the easiest to the most complex, that thoughts are formed by combining concepts. Use the term *embedded* in your answer. (328)

Reasoning

*   1.   Indicate two ways by which thoughts are organized. (328)

2. a)   Give an example of a deductively valid argument. How might people decide if this were a valid argument? (328-329)

    b)   Is the application of rules of logic to determine validity a conscious or an unconscious process? When does it become more conscious? (329)

*   c)   Cite some evidence to suggest that people do use logical rules in determining validity. (329)

*   3.   a)   Point out two bases on which we may evaluate a deductive argument. (329)

*   b)   Describe some evidence to show *content* effects in deductive reasoning. In what respect is this an example of the use of pragmatic rules? (329)

        c)   What is meant by the term ***permission rule*** ? (330)

*   4.   a)   Give an example of the use of heuristics as an alternative to rules in reasoning. How do we reason according to this idea? (330)

        b)   What do pragmatic rules and heuristics have in common and how does this affect our logically intuitive reasoning process? (330)

*   5.   a)   Give an example of an inductively strong argument. How is inductive strength expressed? (330)

*   b)   Distinguish by definition and by example between the rules of probability used by logicians. (331)

        —*base-rate rule:*

        —*conjunction rule:*

   6.   a)   Do people use such probability rules in everyday reasoning? Describe a study by Tversky and Kahneman to show a violation of the base-rate rule. (331)

        b)   Similarly, using an experiment, illustrate a violation of the conjuction rule. (331-332)

        c)   Describe the applications of the similarity heuristic in the studies discussed in a) and b). (332)

        d)   Similarly, illustrate a use of a causality heuristic in inductive reasoning. (332)

*   7.   Restate your authors' conclusion regarding the use of rational rules for inductive reasoning in everyday situations. On the other hand, when *do* we use these rules and what can increase the extent of their use? (332)

Language and Communication

*   1.   a)   Using the terms in Figure 9-3, what do your authors mean when they say that "language is a multilevel system"? (333)

*   b)   Indicate two of the basic properties of language. What is the function of linguistic ***rules*** ? (333)

   2.   a)   How many different phonemes are in the English language? Are we good at discriminating phonemes under all conditions? Explain. (333)

*   b)   What is one reason why learning a foreign language can be difficult? Give some examples. (334)

*   c)   Provide some illustrations of the assertion, "we conform to rules we cannot verbalize" with respect to combining phonemes. (334)

* 3. a) Distinguish between four types of morphemes; include the term *grammatical morpheme* in your answer. (334)

   b) Cite some examples of the use of rules in production and comprehension of prefixes and suffixes. (334)

   c) What is the evidence that we consider multiple meanings of a word when it is ambiguous in meaning? (334-335)

* 4. a) What is an important property of sentence units, and what does this property allow? (335)

* b) What do people do when reading or listening to a sentence? Give an example using the terms *noun phrase* and *verb phrase*. (335)

   c) Cite some evidence for the practice outlined in b). (335)

   d) Cite an example of what happens when normally unconscious syntactic analysis of language fails. Why might this happen? (336)

* 5. a) What does Figure 9-5 suggest about understanding and producing sentences? Be sure to use the terms *top-down processing* and *bottom-up processing* in your answer. (336)

* b) In what respect is this analysis of comprehension and production oversimplified? Use the term *context*, and cite an illustration. (336)

   c) Discuss the most salient part of context in terms of an example. (336-337)

Development of Language

1. What must all children master, and what is amazing about the process? (337)

* 2. a) At the level of development of phonemes, what remarkable ability do infants demonstrate at birth, and by what experimental procedure did this become known? (337-338)

* b) In the table below, for each level of language development, characterize the changes that take place at the ages indicated. (337-339)

Level of Language	Age	Description of Development and Examples
Phonemes	0-1 year 4 years	
Words and concepts	1 year 1-2 years 2 1/2 years	Use the term *overextend*
Sentence units (syntax)	1 1/2-2 1/2 years 6 years	Characterize changes in vocabulary

*   3.   What observations suggest that both learning and innate factors play a role in language development? (340)

     4.   a)   Give an example of imitation and indicate three reasons why it cannot be the primary way in which language is acquired. (340)

         b)   Similarly, what may be a limit on the possibility that conditioning experiences account for language development? (340)

*   c)   What do your authors consider to be a central problem with imitation and conditioning and how might more general aspects of language learning come about? (341)

*   5.   a)   Cite an example of the learning of linguistic rules through hypothesis testing. (341)

         b)   List six *operating principles* used by young children to form hypotheses about language. (341)

*   c)   What challenge has recently been made to the notion that language learning is a process of learning rules. Use an example. (341)

*   6.   a)   What is the first question posed by your text regarding the role of innate factors in language development? (342)

*   b)   Cite one line of evidence to suggest that there are innate constraints on syntax across human languages. (342)

         c)   How does the sequence of language acquisition pose another constraint for language development? Discuss a related study. (342-343)

* 7. What is the second question that is raised regarding innate factors in language? Cite some examples to show that there are critical periods in the development of phonemes. (342, 343)

* 8. a) State the third question raised in your text regarding innate factors in language. What answer is given by some experts? (342, 343)

* b) In what four respects is the communication system of chimpanzees more limited than that of humans? (344)

* 9. a) Describe each of the following stages of attempts to teach chimpanzees to communicate including what was taught and what results were obtained. (344-346)

—training in speech:

—training in American Sign Language:

—keyboard training:

* b) In general, from these studies what does it appear that chimpanzees *can* learn; by contrast, in what areas of language learning is the evidence considerably less definitive, especially in the case of the chimp, Washoe? (346)

Imaginal Thought

* 1. a) Give some illustrations of the use of images in thinking. What aspects of imaginal thought suggests that we rely upon perceptual processes in forming the images?

* b) Cite evidence from studies of *visual neglect* that imagery may be mediated by the same brain areas as perception. (347)

c) Discuss additional evidence from studies of brain activity indicating that specific parts of the brain may be involved in imaginal thought. (347-348)

* 2. Describe the results obtained in each line of experimentation below to support the view that imaginal operations are similar to perceptual operations. (348-349)

—rotation:

—scanning:

—"grain size":

3. Illustrate the use of imaginal thought in creativity with the two examples from your text. (349)

Thought in Action: Problem Solving

* 1. What is necessary in order to solve a problem? Illustrate. (349)

* 2. a) What is Newell and Simon's typical method for studying problem-solving strategies? (350)

* b) Give an example of the difference reduction strategy for problem solving. What is the critical element of this approach? (350)

* c) Similarly, provide an example of means-end analysis. Why is this strategy considered to be more "sophisticated" than difference reduction? (350)

d) Cite an illustration of the third problem-solving strategy, working backward. (350)

* 3. a) Besides strategy, upon what does solving a problem depend? (351)

b) Distinguish between a propositional mode and a visual mode of representation and show by example that visual images may be the most efficient method for some problems. Are some problems soluble by either method? (351)

c) Show that, besides the mode of representation, problem solving can also depend upon what is represented. (351-352)

* 4. Discuss and exemplify differences between experts and novices in a field along the following dimensions. (352-353)

—representations:

—strategies:

* 5. a) What is Simon's answer to why we should use computers to learn about human problem solving? How would we find support for the claim? (353)

b) What is the parallel between the rules we use in problem solving and a computer's program? Find at least one such parallel in the example of solving an equation. (354)

* 6. State three criticisms of computer simulation and your authors' replies. (355)

Sample Quiz 9.1

1. Propositional thought involves: a) images that we "see in our mind"; b) sequences of movements we "perform in our minds"; c) streams of sentences we "hear in our minds"; d) all of the above.

2. Which of the following statements concerning concepts is *false?* a) Treating different objects as members of the same concept increases the complexity of the world we have to represent mentally. b) Commonly-used concepts usually are associated with a one-word name. c) We possess concepts of activities, states, and abstractions as well as of objects. d) Concepts allow us to go beyond information immediately available.

3. When core properties are used to determine whether or not something is an instance of a concept, we speak of _____ concepts: a) typical; b) classical; c) categorical; d) fuzzy.

4. In reasoning, shortcut procedures that are applied easily and often work are called: a) premises; b) heuristics; c) pragmatic rules; d) logical rules.

5. When we conclude that someone who calls in sick for work has a cold rather than tuberculosis, we are employing the _____ in our inductive reasoning: a) similarity heuristic; b) base-rate rule; c) causality heuristic; d) conjunction rule.

6. The smallest linguistic unit that carries meaning is called a: a) morpheme; b) syntactic unit; c) sentence unit; d) phoneme.

7. Sentence comprehension is to sentence production as: a) noun phrase is to verb phrase; b) verb phrase is to noun phrase; c) top-down processing is to bottom-up processing; d) bottom-up processing is to top-down processing.

8. Based on the attempts to teach language to chimpanzees, there seems to be no doubt that apes can learn to: a) use signs that are equivalent to human words to refer to concepts that are equivalent to human concepts; b) combine signs into sentences; c) alter the order of signs to produce new sentences; d) all of the above.

9. Striving for a goal with no ready means of obtaining it is the definition offered in your text for: a) reasoning; b) concept formation; c) problem solving; d) hypothesis testing.

10. Which of the following is *not* characteristic of the differences between expert and novice problem solving: a) experts have many more specific representations stored; b) experts represent novel problems differently, for example in terms of general principles; c) experts tend to reason from the solution to a problem to its givens; d) novices tend to use the working-backward strategy.

Sample Quiz 9.2

1. Concepts: a) are statements that express a factual claim; b) are the components of a proposition; c) help us to divide our world into manageable units; d) both b and c.

2. Early in life, children are more likely to learn prototypes by the _____ strategy: a) exemplar; b) hypothesis testing; c) fuzzy; d) classical.

3. The exemplar strategy: a) works best with typical instances of concepts; b) works best with classical concepts; c) is more likely to be used as we grow older and begin to make abstractions; d) both b and c.

4. In inductive reasoning, we may use the strength of the causal connections between events to estimate the probability of a situation; this method: a) is called the causality heuristic; b) is called the similarity heuristic; c) violates the rules of probability theory; d) both a and c.

5. A sentence unit contains: a) sentences; b) phrases; c) hierarchies; d) both a and b.

6. Which of the following is *false?* a) A morpheme may be either a word or part of a word. b) Understanding a sentence is the inverse of producing a sentence. c) Infants appear to be able to discriminate primarily those phonemes that are appropriate for their own language. d) To understand comprehension and production of sentences, it is necessary to take into account the effects of context.

7. Critical periods in the development of human language have been observed for: a) phonemes in one's native language; b) phonemes in a foreign language; c) learning syntax; d) all of the above.

8. Experiments on rotation, scanning, and grain size support the view that: a) imaginal operations are similar to perceptual operations; b) language learning has critical periods; c) both learning and innate factors play a role in language development; d) computer simulation is an effective way to study human problem solving.

9. Thinking using visual images is called: a) problem solving; b) imaginal thought; c) motoric thought; d) fuzzy thinking.

10. The problem-solving strategy that involves comparing our current state to the goal state in order to find the most important difference between them is called: a) syntactic analysis; b) difference reduction; c) working backward; d) means-end analysis.

Key, Chapter 9

Vocabulary and Details

1. propositional thought
2. imaginal thought
3. motoric thought

1. proposition
2. concepts
3. prototype
4. core
5. classical
6. fuzzy
7. hierarchy; properties; relationships
8. exemplar strategy; exemplar
9. hypothesis testing
10. subject; predicate; preposition

1. reasoning; premises
2. deductively valid; logical rules
3. pragmatic rules
4. heuristics
5. inductively strong
6. similarity heuristic
7. causality heuristic

1. production
2. comprehension
3. phoneme
4. morpheme
5. ambiguous
6. sentence
7. syntactic analysis
8. syntax

1. imitation; conditioning
2. hypothesis testing

1. imaginal thought

1. problem solving
2. current state; goal state; difference reduction
3. means-end analysis
4. working backward
5. computer simulation

Sample Quiz 9.1

1. c, 321
2. a, 321-322
3. b, 323
4. b, 330
5. b, 331
6. a, 334
7. d, 336
8. a, 346
9. c, 349

10. c, 352-353

Sample Quiz 9.2

1. d, 321
2. a, 325
3. a, 326
4. d, 332
5. d, 335
6. c, 337
7. d, 343
8. a, 348-349
9. b, 349
10. d, 350

Basic Motives

Learning Objectives

1. Be able to define motivation and to distinguish among survival motives, social motives, and curiosity motives.

2. Be able to define homeostasis in terms of a sensor, ideal value, and comparator. Understand the distinction between need and drive.

3. Be prepared to discuss body temperature regulation and thirst from the perspective of a homeostatic system. Include the regulated variables, sensors, and behavioral and physiological adjustments in both cases.

4. Be familiar with variables that affect hunger and the location of satiety detectors. Be able to describe the LH syndrome and the VMH syndrome.

5. Be familiar with research on obesity, including restrained versus unrestrained eaters, emotional arousal, and responsiveness to external cues.

6. Understand the relationship between exercise and metabolic rate; be able to discuss various approaches to weight control and the role of genetic factors.

7. Be familiar with the major male and female sex hormones and their role in sexual behavior.

8. Be familiar with research on the role of early experience and cultural factors in shaping sexual behavior and the environmental and biological determinants of homosexuality.

9. Be prepared to discuss the influence of prenatal hormones and early environment on gender identity.

10. Be familiar with the biological and environmental determinants of maternal behavior.

11. Be familiar with curiosity motives and research on the need for sensory stimulation.

Vocabulary and Details

1. The study of wants and needs is the study of _____. (361)

2. Motivation deals with factors that give behavior _____ and _____. (361)

3. Unlearned motives in humans and other animals are called _____. (361)

Survival Motives and Homeostasis

1. The body's tendency to maintain a constant internal environment in the face of a changing external environment is termed _____. (361)

2. Any substantial physiological departure from the ideal value is a _____; its resulting psychological counterpart is an aroused state or urge, termed a _____. (362)

3. A small collection of cell nuclei at the base of the brain that functions in temperature regulation is the _____. (363)

4. Water inside the body's cells is called _____; water outside the cells (such as, in the blood) is called _____. (364)

5. When water leaves the cells through *osmosis*, cells that respond by becoming slightly deformed, called _____, act as sensors within the hypothalamus and preoptic area (slightly in front of the hypothalamus). (364)

6. The substance _____ produced by the kidneys responds to reduced blood pressure in part by _____ (constricting/dilating) the blood vessels (which, in turn, helps to raise blood pressure). (364)

7. A second function of renin is the production of the hormone _____, which induces thirst and an appetite for salt. (364-365)

Hunger

1. Extreme overeating leads to _____; extreme undereating may progress to an eating disorder called _____. (366)

2. We appear to have detectors, called _____, located in the digestive system which signal the brain during feeding that needed nutrients are on the way and feeding can stop. (367)

3. Originally it was believed that the hypothalamus served as a "dual hunger center," with the _____ (which part?) serving as a *feeding center* and the _____ (which part?) serving as a *satiety center*. (368)

4. Today, one alternative hypothesis holds that these two areas of the hypothalamus have reciprocal effects on the overall body weight at which an individual functions best, called the _____. (369)

5. Another alternative view proposes that the disturbances in weight control produced by destruction of LH and VMH tissue result from interference with some of the _____ that pass through these locations. (368-369)

Obesity

1. Three major causes of weight gain are a) _____ (eating too much), b) _____ (expending too little effort); and _____ (hereditary predispositions to be overweight). (370-371)

2. Energy that is devoted to basic bodily functions is termed _____ activity, expressed in terms of _____. (373)

3. Cells in which body fat is stored are called _____; genetics largely determines the _____ (number/size) of these cells, whereas eating patterns determine their _____ and _____. (375)

Adult Sexuality

1. Hormonal changes that serve to distinguish between males and females begin during _____, roughly ages _____. (378)

2. The hypothalamus is the first step in the hormonal control of sexual behaviors through its secretion of _____ which, in turn, acts to stimulate the pituitary to produce the hormones called the _____. (378)

3. Gonadotropins exert their influence on the _____, that is, the ovaries or testes. (378)

4. Hormones produced by the gonads are called the _____, and include the female hormones _____, _____, and the male hormones called _____. (378)

5. Removal of the testes, which affects androgen production, is called _____; the same effect may be obtained by _____, using synthetic hormones to block androgen production. (378)

6. Hormones fluctuate cyclically with accompanying changes in fertility in the _____ (or _____) cycle. (379)

7. The occurrence of sexual relations within the immediate family is called _____; this practice is prohibited in nearly all cultures. (382)

8. Whereas most people are *heterosexual*, that is, have sexual relations with the opposite sex, some are considered _____ if they are sexually attracted primarily to members of the same sex; females in this category are more often called _____. (385)

9. People who are _____ have sexual relations with members of both sexes. (386)

Early Sexual Development

1. The influence of androgens upon anatomy and brain cells is called _____. (388)

2. Individuals who are born with both male and female tissue are called _____. (389)

Basic Motives   149

3. Individuals who have the anatomical characteristics of one sex but whose gender identity is with the opposite sex are called _____. (390)

Maternal Behavior

1. It is possible that "cute" features of babies, such as certain facial features, as well as smiling, may serve as _____ of parental feelings and behaviors. (392)

Curiosity Motives

1. Motivation to seek stimulation and explore the environment is in a class of motives we may term _____. (394)

2. Limiting or restricting incoming stimuli is termed _____ (formerly, "sensory deprivation"). (395)

3. A scale developed by Zuckerman for the measurement of desire for adventure, new sensory experiences, and the avoidance of boredom is termed the _____. (397)

Common Principles for Different Motives

1. A view that maintains that motives are directed at the reduction of a psychological state of tension is termed the _____ principle. (397)

2. An alternative view of motivation maintains that organisms will seek an _____; thus, increases as well as decreases in sensory stimulation, novelty, and complexity may be preferred depending upon recent levels of stimulation. (397-398)

Ideas and Concepts

1. Use examples to illustrate the concepts of direction and energy in motivated behavior. (361)

* 1. Distinguish among survival needs, social needs, and curiosity motives. (361)

Survival Motives and Homeostasis

1. Cite some instances of homeostasis. (361)

* 2. Using the terms *sensor, ideal value,* and *comparator,* be able to outline a mechanical homeostatic system and describe a human analogue. (361-362)

3. Illustrate the use of the terms *need* and *drive* using hunger as an example. (362)

* 4. a) What is the range in which temperature must be regulated, and what specifically is the variable that is regulated? (362)

*Basic ideas and concepts

150   Chapter 10

*   b) Where are the sensors, comparator, and ideal temperature value (or zone) for temperature regulation located? Describe related experiments with animals supporting these conclusions. (362-363)

*   c) What specific kinds of adjustments can be made if body temperature is too high or too low? (363)

     d) Distinguish betweeen physiological and behavioral adjustments and identify the part of the brain involved in each case. (363)

—physiological:

—behavioral:

5. a) What makes our homeostatic system for the regulation of water intake more complex than that for temperature? (364)

*   b) Discuss the mechanism for the typical cause of intracellular fluid loss. (364)

*   c) What happens once the hypothalamus detects these changes? Use the term *antidiuretic hormone (ADH)*. Also, what happens if the water deficit is too great? Use examples. (364)

* 6. a) What is another major variable for thirst besides intracellular fluid levels? Indicate two circumstances under which this variable may become significant. (364)

     b) Where are the sensors for total volume of fluid in blood located, and what do they detect? (364)

* 7. a) Will dehydrated subjects drink until intracellular and extracellular water levels are reestablished? Explain, and indicate what this implies about additional receptors for water in the system, noting the name for these sensors. (365)

     b) Where are these receptors located? Cite a related experiment. (365)

Hunger

1. a) How do we know that each of the following factors is not sufficient to trigger eating: arrival of mealtime, "hunger pangs," or the taste of food? (365)

*   b) What *does* trigger eating, and what specific observation suggests that the system is homeostatic? (366)

*   c) Indicate three complications to a simplistic homeostatic analysis of hunger. (366)

2. a) List three nutrients needed for the body cells to function. (366)

*   b) Discuss in detail the homeostatic mechanism for the body's sensitivity to glucose, including the body structures involved and related experimental results. (366)

c) What does the hypothalamus detect in the regulation of fat? (366)

* 3. Indicate three locations for the satiety sensors and describe the research that demonstrates the existence of each. Use the term *cholecystokinin (CCK)*. (367)

* 4. a) Describe the patterns of eating in animals that have had tissue in the lateral and ventromedial portions of the hypothalamus destroyed. Use the terms *LH syndrome* and *VMH syndrome*. (368)

   b) What characteristics of the eating disorders discussed in a) have raised difficulties for the dual hunger center hypothesis? (368)

* 5. a) Indicate two aspects of the regulation of overall body weight of animals with damage to the either the lateral or ventromedial hypothalamus that suggests that overall body weight regulation has been affected. (368-369)

* b) What happens if both areas of the hypothalamus are damaged equally? (369)

* 6. a) Outline the argument that implicates extraneous nerve tracts rather than the hypothalamus itself in the regulation of hunger. (369)

* b) Indicate another finding that suggests that nerve fibers may affect hunger even outside of the hypothalamus. (370)

* c) Summarize your authors' conclusion from this research. (370)

Obesity

1. a) What is the most frequent deviation from homeostatic regulation of eating? Cite some statistics. (370)

   b) Why is dieting usually not successful in controlling weight? (370)

   c) Is obesity just one disorder? Explain. (370)

* 2. a) List some factors that *increase caloric intake* by noting the subheadings for this section. (371-372)

   —*i:*

   —*ii:*

   —*iii:*

* b) What two types of people are differentiated by questionnaires concerning diet and weight? Which type of individual eats more like an obese person? (371)

* c) Cite the results of one study on differing feeding behaviors of restrained and unrestrained eaters. Give an explanation for these results. (371-372)

* d) Give another reason for binge eating and an underlying explanation for this tendency in human behavior. (372)

152   Chapter 10

* 3. a) What differences appear in the eating behaviors of obese and normal-weight subjects under conditions of low and high anxiety? (372)

* b) Cite some additional findings to implicate emotional arousal in general in the tendency for obese people to overeat. (372)

* 4. a) How do obese people differ from underweight people in their sensitivity to external cues for food? Describe a related study. (372)

  b) Is *externality* a perfect indicator of degree of obesity? Explain. (372)

* 5. a) List two factors that *decrease energy expenditure* by noting two of the subheadings for this section. (373-374)

  —*i:*

  —*ii:*

* b) Indicate the relationship between rate of metabolism and body weight. Then why do obese people stay fat even when their caloric intake is normal? (373)

* c) Discuss the relationship between deprivation and metabolic rate, including implications for dieters. (373)

  d) How might evolution account for the relationship between deprivation and metabolic rate? (373)

  6. Discuss the "vicious cycle" between lack of exercise, obesity, and metabolic rate. (373)

* 7. a) What three things must overweight people do to lose weight and maintain the loss? (374)

* b) Describe in detail the results of the Craighead et al. study supporting the conclusion that to control weight an individual must establish new eating and exercise behaviors. (374)

  c) What do you think your authors mean when they say that perhaps "self-efficacy" may have been a factor in the behavior modification group? What was yet another possibility? (374)

* 8. a) What observations support the role of genetic factors in obesity? (375)

* b) Describe some data that implicate numbers of fat cells in obesity. (375)

  c) Is the number of fat cells entirely genetically determined? Explain and note the role that age may play. (375)

* d) Indicate the relationship between overeating and deprivation and the size of fat cells. (375)

* 9. a) State the *set-point hypothesis*. (375-376)

* b) In terms of the set-point hypothesis, outline Stunkard's view of the role that appetite-suppressant drugs may play in weight control (and subsequent gain). (376)

c) Does the set-point hypothesis serve as a general theory of obesity? Why or why not? (376)

Adult Sexuality

1. a) Compare sex and maternal motives on the one hand and the survival motives on the other hand. (377)

   —two similarities:

   —two differences:

   b) Outline two important distinctions with regard to sex. (377-378)

* 2. a) In the table below, indicate the origin and functions of the hormones involved in sexuality. (See also Figure 10-6.) (378-379)

Hormone	Origin	Function
follicle-stimulating hormone (FSH)		Use the terms *follicles, estrogen*
luteinizing hormone (LH)		Use the term *progesterone*
interstitial-cell stimulating hormone (ICSH)		Use the term *androgen*

* b) Summarize the three basic steps in the process outlined in the table above. (378)

* 3. Discuss the body changes at puberty produced by the following sex hormones. (378)

   —*estrogen:*

   —*testosterone:*

* 4. a) Describe two general methods used in studying the contribution of sex hormones to sexual arousal in males. (378)

* b) What is the effect of "castration" for animal subjects and for human subjects? (378)

* c) What is the relationship between hormonal fluctuation and sexual interest? Be sure to distinguish between sexual *arousal* and *desire*. (378-379)

5. a) Outline the course of the estrous cycle and its effects on sexual motivation in most mammals. (379)

* b) By contrast, what is the effect of the fertility cycle upon human female sexual desire and arousal? (379-380)

* 6. What is your authors' conclusion regarding the role of hormonal control in humans? (380)

7. a) Discuss the role of the spinal cord in sexual responses of men and women. (380)

* b) Where is "the most erogenous zone"? Describe some effects of control via this area in both humans and lower animals. (380)

* 8. a) Contrast in general terms the effects of early experience on sexual behaviors in lower and higher mammals. (380)

b) Discuss in detail the influence of early experiences of monkeys on their sexual responses. (380)

* c) Outline the influence of social deprivation on interpersonal sexual activities in monkeys. What do these findings suggest concerning the determinants of normal heterosexual behavior in primates? (381-382)

* d) What general clinical statements may be made regarding the role of early experience in human sexuality? (382)

9. a) Cite some examples of culturally specific sexual practices in primitive and very restrictive societies. (382-383)

* b) Describe the changes that took place in sexual activities in the United States from the 1940s to the 1970s. For which sex were the changes the greatest and during what period? (383)

10. a) What may be bringing an element of cautiousness to the "sexual revolution"? (383)

* b) Indicate the data suggesting that changes between the 1940s and 1970s pertained more to behaviors than to traditional values. (384)

c) In the same vein, illustrate two kinds of differences between men and women with respect to sexual attitudes. (384)

11. a) Is homosexuality an either-or matter? Explain, citing some observations. (385)

*   b)   Describe the changes in attitudes toward homosexuality from before the 1960s to today. (385)

*   c)   In what areas of life do homosexuals fare about as well as heterosexuals and in what area do they not? Under what circumstances do differences between homsexuals and heterosexuals tend to disappear? (385)

        d) Cite two reasons for the greater unhappiness of a homosexual today. (385)

* 12.   In the table below, summarize the essence of each hypothesis concerning the determinants of homosexuality and the related evidence. (385-387)

Hypothesis	Summary	Evidence
the "mothering" hypothesis		
"first encounter" theory		
fetal hormone exposure		

13.   Describe some of the parallels between sexual attitudes and behaviors among male and female homosexuals and heterosexuals. (388)

Early Sexual Development

* 1.   a)   Describe the genital development of the fetus from conception to about 3 months and the determining factor operating. (388)

*   b)   What happens when the testes or ovaries develop? What is the critical hormone at the prenatal stage of development? Explain. (388)

        c)   What structure is particularly involved in the effects of prenatal androgen upon the brains of rats, and why is this significant? (388-389)

*   d)   Discuss the effects of *testosterone* (a kind of androgen) when injected into female monkeys. Relate this finding to the hypothesis discussed earlier concerning the role of prenatal hormones in homosexuality (see item 12 above). (389)

2.   a)   Describe the observations made in each of the following cases and cite the conclusions to be drawn from each. (389-390)

—two hermaphroditic children who were raised as different sexes:

—male children raised as females in the Dominican Republic:

156   Chapter 10

—identical twin boys, one of whom was treated surgically and hormonally as a girl:

* b) What two things are striking about the case of the identical twin boys? (390)

* c) What conclusion can be drawn about the impact of environment and hormones upon gender identity? (390)

Maternal Behavior

1. a) Discuss some observations that support the role of hormones in the maternal behavior of lower species. What hormones are involved? (391)

* b) Cite one set of findings to indicate that hormones have less influence on maternal behavior at the human level than in lower mammals. (391)

2. By contrast, what have some *ethologists* argued about possible biological determinants of human parenting? (392)

* 3. What happens to parental behaviors if female monkeys are raised in isolation? What do your authors suggest is the parallel to human parenting? (393-394)

Curiosity Motives

1. Cite some observations concerning exploration and manipulation in humans and monkeys, including Piaget's reports on young infants. (394-395)

* 2. a) What may be the function of exploration and manipulation? Indicate some early results to suggest that humans need sensory stimulation. (395)

* b) Describe more recent methods of Suedfeld's that yield results that contradict the findings of the early "sensory deprivation" studies. (What performance decrements do result from such manipulations?) (395)

c) List some positive applications of reduced stimulation. (395-396)

3. Outline some of the relationships obtained between scores on the Sensation Seeking Scale and various activities. What result suggests that stimulation seeking may be a trait that accounts for individual differences on this dimension? (397)

Common Principles for Different Motives

1. a) Be able to apply the drive-reduction principle to a common activity. (397)

* b) With what motives is the drive-reduction principle consistent and with what motives does it have difficulties? Why? (397)

* 2. a) Apply the optimal-level-of-arousal principle to the effects of physiological deprivation and the effects of sensory reduction. (397-398)

* b) In your authors' view, which principle, drive-reduction or optimal level of arousal, is more likely to be the basis for a unifying principle of basic motives? (398)

Sample Quiz 10.1

1. Physiological is to _____ as psychological is to _____: a) need, drive; b) intracellular, extracellular; c) basic motives, social motives; d) anorexia, bulimia.

2. Which of the following is *false?* a) When the hypothalamus detects losses in intracellular fluids, the antidiuretic hormone is released. b) Dehydrated subjects will drink until intra- and extracellular fluid levels are reestablished. c) Eating is triggered when levels of specific nutrients fall below certain values. d) Not every person is able to maintain homeostasis with respect to hunger.

3. Receptors important in signaling the brain that feeding can stop even though not all nutrients are yet in the bloodstream are called: a) osmoreceptors; b) satiety sensors; c) proprioceptors; d) gonadotropin receptors.

4. Metabolic rate is higher: a) in active people than in sedentary people; b) during periods of deprivation; c) in fat tissue than in lean tissue; d) all of the above.

5. Eating patterns may determine the _____ of fat cells: a) number; b) size; c) complexity; d) both a and b.

6. The hormonal control of body changes occurring at puberty proceeds from: a) the pituitary to the gonads to the hypothalamus; b) the hypothalamus to the gonads to the pituitary; c) the hypothalamus to the pituitary to the gonads. d) the gonads to the pituitary to the hypothalamus.

7. Which of the following appears to be generally *true* of homosexuals? a) Job stability and satisfaction are equal to that of heterosexuals. b) Male homosexuals have more partners than female homosexuals. c) "Close-coupled" homosexuals manifest about the same number of problems of tension and depression as heterosexuals. d) All of the above.

8. People who have sexual relations with members of both sexes are technically called: a) homosexual; b) heterosexual; c) bisexual; d) transexual.

9. Ethologists have argued that certain "cute" facial features of babies may serve as _____ for parental feelings and behaviors: a) innate releasers; b) inhibitors; c) learned cues; d) drive reducers.

10. Exploration and seeking of stimulation are in a class of motives called: a) drive reduction motivation; b) social motivation; c) curiosity motivation; d) none of the above; there is not a distinct class of motives reserved for these behaviors.

Sample Quiz 10.2

1. Motivation deals with factors that give behavior: a) purpose and meaning; b) interest and appeal; c) direction and energy; d) substance and authority.

2. In maintaining body temperature, the specific variable that is regulated is: a) blood temperature; b) temperature of the outside skin; c) brain temperature; d) temperature of the digestive system.

3. The collection of cell nuclei at the base of the brain that functions in temperature regulation is: a) the hypothalamus; b) the pituitary; c) the thyroid; d) the thalamus.

4. Energy devoted to basic bodily functions is called: a) motivation; b) drive; c) metabolic activity; d) homeostasis.

5. The hormones released by the pituitary in the control of sexual behaviors are called: a) angiotensin; b) androgens; c) progesterone; d) gonadotropins.

6. Relative to underweight people, it has been found that obese people are: a) less sensitive to external hunger cues; b) more sensitive to internal hunger cues; c) equally as sensitive to both external and internal hunger cues; d) none of the above.

7. Testosterone is important in: a) increasing sexual arousal in men; b) causing the voice to deepen during puberty; c) influencing sexual desire in men; d) both b and c.

8. Which of the following was *not* listed as a factor important in the development of normal heterosexual behavior in primates: a) the ability to observe sexual activity among others; b) the establishment of an affectional bond between two members of the opposite sex; c) the development of specific sexual responses; d) hormones.

9. The data on child abuse is cited by your authors to show that: a) hormones may impact on early embryonic sexual development; b) hormones play a lesser role in human maternal behavior than in lower mammals; c) curiosity motives are strongly influenced by early parental attention to investigative behaviors; d) biological factors underlie human aggression even in parents.

10. Your text suggests that a unifying principle of basic motives can be found in: a) the optimal-level-of-arousal principle; b) the concept of homeostasis; c) the ethologists' notion of innate releasers; d) the drive-reduction principle.

Key, Chapter 10

Vocabulary and Details

1. motivation
2. direction; energy
3. basic motives

---

1. homeostasis
2. need; drive
3. hypothalamus
4. intracellular fluid; extracellular fluid
5. osmoreceptors
6. renin; constricting
7. angiotensin

---

1. obesity; anorexia
2. satiety sensors
3. lateral hypothalamus (or LH); ventromedial hypothalamus (or VMH)
4. set point
5. nerve tracts

---

1. calorie intake; calorie expenditure; genetics
2. metabolic; metabolic rate
3. fat cells; number; number; size

---

1. puberty; 11 to 14
2. gonadotropin-releasing factors; gonadotropins
3. gonads
4. sex hormones; estrogen; progesterone; androgens
5. castration; chemical castration
6. fertility (estrous)
7. incest
8. homosexual; lesbians
9. bisexual

---

1. androgenization
2. hermaphrodites
3. transexuals

---

1. innate releasers

---

1. curiosity
2. reduced sensory stimulation
3. Sensation Seeking Scale (or SSS)

---

1. drive reduction
2. optimal level of arousal

Sample Quiz 10.1

1. a, 362
2. b, 365
3. b, 367
4. a, 373-374
5. d, 375

6. c, 378
7. d, 385
8. c, 386
9. a, 392
10. c, 394

Sample Quiz 10.2

1. c, 361
2. a, 362
3. a, 363
4. c, 373
5. d, 378
6. d, 372
7. d, 378-379
8. a, 381
9. b, 391
10. a, 398

Emotion

Learning Objectives

1. Know the distinction between motives and emotions and the four components of an emotion.

2. Understand the role of the sympathetic and the parasympathetic divisions of the autonomic nervous system in emotional arousal.

3. Be able to discuss the research relating physiological arousal to the intensity of an emotion and to the ability to differentiate among emotions. Know the James-Lange theory, Cannon's objections to the theory, and Ekman's relevant findings.

4. Understand the concept of cognitive appraisal and its role in emotional experience. Be familiar with research on the experimental manipulation of cognitive appraisal and emotion without cognition.

5. Be familiar with attempts to classify emotions in terms of situations and consequences.

6. Be familiar with research on facial expressions of emotion, including the communication of emotions and the brain mechanisms involved in the recognition of emotions. Know what is meant by the facial feedback hypothesis.

7. Be able to discuss the general consequences of being in an emotional state, including the relationship between arousal level and performance, attention to events, and the effect of mood on our evaluation of people and events.

8. Be able to discuss the idea of aggresssion as a drive and the frustration-aggression hypothesis. Be familiar with research on brain-stimulated aggression in animals.

9. Be able to discuss the social-learning theory of aggression as a learned response. Be familiar with research on imitation and the reinforcement of aggression, and the relevance of the research to social-learning theory.

10. Understand the concept of aggression as cathartic and the implications of such a concept.

11. Be able to discuss research concerning the effects of viewing violence on television and to list several reasons why such viewing can lead to aggressive behavior.

Names

1. The famous American psychologist _____ is noted for his dictum, "We are afraid because we run," which derives from the James-Lange theory of emotion. (404-405)

2. The physiologist _____ countered the James-Lange theory with observations that the autonomic nervous system could not play the differentiating role in emotion that James and Lange had suggested. (405)

3. Another historically prominent figure in the field of emotion was _____, who emphasized the importance of innate expressions of emotion in communication and species survival. (413)

Vocabulary and Details

Components of an Emotion

1. Intense motions include four components; these are internal _____ (such as, rapid heart beat and trembling), _____ (such as, appraisal of emotional stimuli), _____ expressions, and other overt _____ to an emotional stimulus (such as, aggression). (401)

Arousal and Emotion

1. Most of the physiological changes that occur during emotional arousal stem from activition of the _____ division of the autonomic nervous system, which functions to increase energy output. (402)

2. As an emotion subsides, the _____ division of the autonomic nervous system takes over to conserve energy and return the organism to a state of lower arousal. (402)

3. The _____ theory of emotion holds that activity in the autonomic nervous system and other bodily changes differentiate the emotions. (405)

Cognition and Emotion

1. _____ refers to the process of analysis of a situation in which we interpret events or actions in terms of our personal goals and well-being; the immediate outcome is a positive or negative _____. (408)

Expression and Emotion

1. Facial expression has been shown to play an important role in the _____ of emotions. (413)

2. The interpretation of emotional expressions appears to be largely localized in the _____ of the brain. (415)

3. Besides communication, facial expression might contribute to our _____ of emotions, a notion termed the _____. (416)

General Consequences of Emotion

1. In the classic function relating performance to levels of emotional arousal, efficiency of performance is highest when arousal is _____ (moderate/high or low) and lowest when arousal is _____ (moderate/high or low). (420)

Aggression as an Emotional Reaction

1. An emotional reaction in anger is _____, that is behavior *intended* to injure or destroy. (422-423)

2. According to Freud's _____ theory, aggressive behaviors stem from an underlying instinctual _____. (423)

3. A related notion is that whenever goal-directed activities are blocked, an aggressive drive motivates attack behavior; this view is termed the _____. (423)

4. The approach that focuses on the role of environmental contingencies and cognitions in human social behavior is termed _____. (425)

5. Social-learning theory emphasizes the importance of learning by observation, or _____, and the role of _____ in transmitting specific behaviors and emotional responses in this form of learning. (425)

6. Discharge of an emotion by experiencing it intensely is called _____. (429)

Ideas and Concepts

*   1. a) Compare the concepts of emotions and motives. (401)

        —two similarities:

        —two differences:

        b) Are these distinctions absolute? Explain. (401)

Components of an Emotion

1. Cite examples of the components of emotions. (401)

    —internal bodily responses:

    —cognitive events (beliefs):

    —facial expression:

*Basic ideas and concepts

—overt reactions:

*   2.   Discuss two questions that have guided research in the field of emotion. (401-402)

Arousal and Emotion

*   1.   List some of the changes during emotional arousal that result from activation of the sympathetic nervous system. (402)

    2.   a)   Outline the role of the *hypothalamus* and the *limbic system* in emotional arousal. (403)

       b)   Of what emotions in particular is emotional arousal characteristic and why? (403)

*   3.   a)   Outline the well-known study by Hohmann relating the role of the sympathetic system in emotional intensity through observations of spinal cord injury victims. Note which emotions were assessed. (403-404)

*   b)   What is the significance of the response of Hohmann's subjects cited in your text, that "It's a mental kind of" emotion that they experienced? (404)

       c)   Cite a second more objective experiment that yielded similar results. (404)

*   4.   a)   Discuss Lange's contribution to the James-Lange theory of emotion through restatement of James' theory in terms of autonomic arousal. (404-405)

*   b)   Discuss three of Walter Cannon's criticisms of the James-Lange theory. (405)

*   c)   What evidence was recently obtained by Ekman and his colleagues that provides support for the James-Lange theory. (405)

*   d)   Give three reasons why your authors contend that results like Ekman's do not "provide unequivocal evidence" for the view that autonomic arousal differentiates the emotions. Therefore, what is the view of most psychologists on this issue? (405, 408)

Cognition and Emotion

    1.   a)   Cite some instances of the impact of "cognitive appraisal" on emotional experience, a concept developed by Lazarus and his colleagues. (408)

*   b)   Provide three arguments why cognitive appraisal might help in differentiating the emotions? (408)

*   2.   a)   Describe the procedures of the classic Schacter and Singer experiment, being sure to distinguish clearly between the *informed* and *misinformed* conditions. (408-409)

*   b)   What were the results of these manipulations? (409)

164   Chapter 11

*   c)   Describe some follow-up experiments, noting in particular how the results of these studies contrasted with those of Schacter and Singer. (409)

*   d)   Discuss in detail your authors' conclusions regarding the role of both cognitions and autonomic arousal in the experience of emotion. Be sure you can identify each of the terms in Figure 11-3. (409-410)

*   3.   In the table below, distinguish between three theoretical approaches to the dimensions of situations determining emotions. Note how many dimensions are identified in each approach and provide some examples of situational dimensions with their corresponding emotions. (410)

Theory	Dimensions and Emotions
Plutchik's primary emotions approach	
Roseman's situational aspects approach	
Smith & Ellsworth's multiple dimensions approach	

*   4.   Discuss some of the clinical implications of the cognitive appraisal analysis of emotion along each of the following lines. (411-412)

—Freud's concept of repression:

—Brenner's views on emotional development:

—the effects of past experience:

*   5.   a)   Your text points out that Zajonc (pronounced "Zeye-yonz") has challenged Lazarus's notions concerning the role of cognitive appraisal in emotional experience. Outline the idea that emotion may occur without cognition and cite some everyday examples. (412)

*   b)   Describe the key results of a related experiment. (412)

c)   What is your authors' reconciliation of these differing points of view? (Can you relate this approach to the diagram in Figure 11-3, discussed in item 2d, above?) (412)

Expression and Emotion

*   1.   a)   Cite some evidence obtained by Ekman to support that assertion that certain facial expressions appear to have meanings that are not culture specific? (413)

*   b) How does the universality of expression support Darwin's evolutionary analysis of emotion? (413)

*   c) Are all facial expressions and gestures clearly innate? Explain and cite some examples of the effects of both culture and of training on emotional expression. (413-414)

  2. a) What do the facts of universality and cultural specificity in emotional expression suggest about the underlying neurology? (415)

*   b) Discuss three lines of evidence to suggest that the right hemisphere is where emotional expression is localized. (415)

   c) Outline some evidence on even more specialized levels of localization obtained from the study of *prosopagnosics* and from electrical stimulation of the brain. (415)

  3. a) What is another way in which emotional expression is communicated? Cite three dimensions along which this information is conveyed. (416)

   b) Where is this function localized in the brain and how do we know? (416)

* 4. a) Discuss the key aspects of Tomkins' facial feedback hypothesis. (416)

   b) Cite two sources of support for this theory. (416-417)

*   c) Outline the idea that facial expressions may determine the quality of emotions. How does this possibility relate to the James-Lange theory presented earlier in this chapter? (417)

* 5. a) Discuss Zajonc's proposal for a bodily mechanism by which facial expressions may determine the positivity or negativity of emotion. (417)

   b) Describe an innovative study that provided some preliminary evidence on Zajonc's temperature hypothesis. (417)

General Consequences of Emotion

* 1. What three consequences result from being in an emotional state? (420)

  2. a) Can you cite a personal example to illustrate the relationship between level of arousal and performance efficiency? (Hint: Have you experienced a difference in studying for an examination days in advance versus hours before?) (420)

*   b) How does the degree to which a task is well-learned affect the performance-arousal relationship? (420)

*   c) Cite evidence to show that individual differences constitute another variable in the performance-arousal function. (420)

   d) What may happen when intense emotion problems are not quickly resolved? (420)

* 3. a) Illustrate each of the following assertions with experimental results. (421)

166 Chapter 11

—we tend to pay more *attention* to events that are congruent with our mood than those that are not:

—*learning* is also a function of congruence of moods with material to be learned:

b) Discuss the memory mechanisms by which congruence between mood and material may affect learning. (421)

* 4. a) Cite the evidence with respect to the effects of mood states upon judgments we may make in each of the following cases. (421-422)

—evaluations of people and objects:

—estimation of frequency of risks:

b) What do your authors mean when they say that "the general consequences of a mood serve to perpetuate that mood"? (422)

Aggression as an Emotional Reaction

1. Illustrate by example the meaning of the term "intent" in the definition of aggression. (423)

* 2. Discuss two critical aspects of the frustration-aggression hypothesis. Which is especially controversial? (423)

* 3. a) What is the relationship between the popular view that docile people may commit sudden acts of violence and the notion that there is an aggressive drive? (424)

* b) Discuss the related evidence. (424)

* 4. a) Outline the evidence on biologically-based aggression in each of the following species. (424)

—cats:

—laboratory rats:

* b) Contrast the above findings on the biological control of aggression in lower mammals with those of the higher mammals. In particular, note the role of the cortex. (424-425)

—monkeys:

—humans:

5. According to social-learning theory how do people come to select certain behavior patterns over others? (425)

* 6. After reading this subsection, indicate two respects in which social-learning theory differs from each of the following alternative approaches to aggression. (425-426)

—classical behaviorism:

—psychoanalytic theory:

* 6. Why do your authors say that "it is no surprise that social-learning theory rejects the concept of aggression as an instinct or . . . drive"? Apply the social-learning view to the case of aggression in a frustrating situation. (425)

* 7. a) Outline the methods, results, and conclusion of the classic Bandura study of aggressive behaviors in nursery-school children. (429)

* b) Discuss the observations made by Patterson and his co-workers on the role of consequences for aggression and counteraggression. (429)

8. How does research on catharsis relate to the issue whether aggression is an unlearned drive or a learned response? (429)

* 9. a) Summarize several research results that favor the view that acting aggressively fosters aggression rather than catharsis. (429-430)

b) Similarly, outline some observations made in a real-life situation that make the same point. (430)

c) Is there any instance in which behaving aggressively may reduce its subsequent occurrence? How do your authors account for this phenomenon? (430)

* 10. a) Outline the results of studies on the effects of viewing television violence on children's behavior in natural settings. (431)

* b) Does televised violence influence aggression, or is it simply the case that children who are more aggressive already prefer to watch violent television programs? Discuss the methods of a study designed to evaluate this important issue. (431)

* c) What results were obtained in this experiment that specifically addressed the issue raised in b)? (See also Figure 11-10.) (431)

* d) Discuss the differences in the effects of viewing violence on girls versus boys. How do these differences reflect on the catharsis hypothesis? (431)

11. What are some additional causes of anger and aggression? (431-432)

Sample Quiz 11.1

1. In general, emotions and motives are alike in that: a) they both are activated from within; b) they both can activate and direct behavior; c) they both can be elicited by a wide variety of stimuli; d) all of the above.

2. Parasympathetic is to sympathetic as: a) negative emotions are to positive emotions; b) subsiding of emotion is to arousing of emotion; c) William James is to Carl Lange; d) communicating emotion is to experiencing emotion.

3. The major critic of the James-Lange theory of emotion was: a) Charles Darwin; b) Walter Cannon; c) Sigmund Freud; d) Albert Bandura.

4. Plutchik's primary emotions approach: a) maintains that at least six dimensions of emotion are needed for adequate description, including effort and attention to and control over the situation; b) emphasizes cognitive processes and begins with a primary set of situational aspects to which a person attends; c) assumes that there is a small set of universal "primary" emotions; d) argues that the quality of emotions is largely determined by cognitive appraisal.

5. The interpretation of emotional expression appears to be largely localized in the: a) spinal cord; b) hypothalamus; c) right brain hemisphere; d) left brain hemisphere.

6. Zajonc has suggested that one's own facial expressions can determine the positivity or negativity of emotion being experienced by means of: a) cognitive appraisal mechanisms related to one's self concept; b) directly altering one's level of arousal; c) affecting the temperature of the brain; d) communicating an emotional state to other people, who then behave in accordance with that state.

7. According to Freud's _____, aggressive behaviors are caused by an underlying instinctual drive: a) social-learning theory; b) frustration-aggression hypothesis; c) cognitive appraisal theory; d) psychoanalytic theory.

8. Which of the following is *true* ? a) Stimulation of a cat's hypothalamus may produce rage or stalking and killing reactions dependent on the specific placement of electrodes; b) Most aggressive people have led relatively docile lives and then suddenly commit aggressive acts; c) Aggressive behavior in monkeys is automatically elicited by electrical stimulation of the hypothalamus; d) It is now clear that lower brain mechanisms primarily determine the occurrence of aggressive behavior in humans.

9. Social-learning theory differs from strict behaviorism in that social-learning theory emphasizes: a) learned behavior patterns; b) environmental contingencies; c) differential reinforcement; d) cognitive processes.

10. In a study by Patterson in which interpersonal aggression and its consequences were observed across a 10-week period, it was found that the most common reaction to the children with the highest level of overall aggression was: a) wincing and crying on the part of the victim; b) ignoring of the attacker by the victim; c) counterattack by the victim; d) verbal reprimand by the victim.

Sample Quiz 11.2

1. Which of the following is *not* a defining component of emotion: a) facial expressions; b) overt reactions; c) internal bodily responses; d) external emotional events.

2. A question that has guided research in emotion is: a) how do the components of emotion contibute to the intensity of emotion; b) how do the components of

emotion contribute to the differentiation of emotional feelings; c) both a and b; d) neither a nor b; research in emotion has been largely guided by a few well-articulated theories.

3. In Roseman's situational aspects approach to the determination of emotion, when an event is undesirable and it occurs, it gives rise to the emotion of: a) distress; b) joy; c) sorrow; d) relief.

4. Based on Ekman's research, which of the following is *false*? a) Certain facial expressions appear to have universal meanings; b) No facial expressions have meanings that are strictly culture specific; c) The same facial expression may have different meanings in different cultures; d) All of the above.

5. Facial expression has been implicated in the _____ of emotions: a) communication; b) experiencing; c) feedback; d) all of the above.

6. The idea that when you are down you should "Put on a happy face" is most consistent with: a) Lazarus's cognitive appraisal theory; b) Tomkin's facial feedback hypothesis; c) Plutchik's primary emotions theory; d) Darwin's universal emotional communications idea.

7. The aspect of the frustration-aggression hypothesis that is particularly controversial is the notion that: a) aggression has the property of a basic drive; b) frustration causes aggression; c) it is the intent of an act that defines whether it is aggressive; d) some aggression may be triggered without prior cognition.

8. Freud is to _____ as social-learning theory is to _____: a) sympathetic, parasympathetic; b) drive, vicarious learning; c) James-Lange, Cannon; d) left hemisphere, right hemisphere.

9. Discharging an emotion by experiencing it intensely is called: a) frustration; b) catharsis; c) vicarious learning; d) drive reduction.

10. Which of the following is a result obtained in efforts to extend research on aggression to natural settings: a) There is no consistent relation between television watching in girls and their aggressive behaviors; b) Children who watch violent cartoons show more aggression in interpersonal relations than those who watch nonviolent cartoons; c) Boys who prefer violence on television are more likely to exhibit aggressive behavior irrespective of initial aggressive tendencies when younger; d) All of the above.

Key, Chapter 11

Names

1. William James
2. Walter Cannon
3. Charles Darwin

Vocabulary and Details

1. bodily responses; cognitive events (or cognitions); facial; reactions

1. sympathetic
2. parasympathetic
3. James-Lange

1. cognitive appraisal; belief

1. communication
2. right hemisphere
3. experience; facial feedback hypothesis

1. moderate; high or low

1. aggression
2. psychoanalytic; drive
3. frustration-aggression hypothesis
4. social-learning theory
5. vicarious learning; models
6. catharsis

Sample Quiz 11.1

1. b, 401
2. b, 402
3. b, 405
4. c, 410
5. c, 415
6. c, 417
7. d, 423
8. a, 424
9. d, 425
10. a, 429

Sample Quiz 11.2

1. d, 401
2. c, 402
3. a, 410
4. b, 413
5. d, 413, 416
6. b, 416
7. a, 423
8. b, 423
9. b, 429
10. d, 431

Mental Abilities and Their Measurement

Learning Objectives

1. Be familiar with the range of tests that measure ability and understand the two dimensions (aptitude-achievement, general-specific) that describe such tests.

2. Be able to specify the difference between reliability and validity and why each is necessary for a test to be trustworthy.

3. Be familiar with the development of tests of intellectual ability and the general format of the Stanford-Binet and Wechsler Intelligence Scales. Know how items are selected and how scores are interpreted.

4. Be able to discuss the relationship between ability test scores and academic performance, including the problems of selection and group differences in test scores.

5. Be able to describe how factor-analytic techniques were used by Spearman and Thurstone to separate the different abilities that contribute to intelligence.

6. Be familiar with the information-processing approach to analyzing performance on intelligence test items.

7. Understand the distinction some psychologists make between "academic intelligence" and "practical intelligence," and the significance of the distinction in evaluating current tests of intelligence.

8. Be familiar with the evidence for genetic contributions to intelligence. Understand what a heritability estimate does and does not tell you.

9. Be able to discuss environmental influences on intelligence, including the evidence from Head Start programs and children living in kibbutzim.

10. Know what the public concerns about psychological testing are and what psychologists think about these concerns.

Names

1. The first attempt to develop tests of intellectual ability was by the nineteenth-century naturalist and mathematician _____. (443)

2. The first psychologist to devise what by current standards would be considered a test of "intelligence" was the Frenchman _____. (444)

3. The most familiar revision of Binet's test, the Stanford-Binet Intelligence Test, was first adapted and standardized in the 1930s by the American psychologist _____. (445-446)

4. One of the first intelligence tests designed to measure separate abilities was designed in the 1930's by _____. (447)

5. The originator of factor analysis and the concept of a general intelligence factor was _____. (460)

6. The psychologist _____ objected to Spearman's notion of general intelligence and argued that intelligence consists of a number primary abilities. (460)

Vocabulary and Details

Types of Ability Tests

1. A _____ is a sample of behavior taken at a given point of time. (437)

2. A test designed to measure accomplished skills (or mastery of a specific subject matter) and indicate what a person can do is called an _____. (437)

3. Along the same continuum, a test designed to predict what a person could accomplish with training--and that assumes little in terms of relevant prior experience--is called an _____. (437)

4. An _____ test is an aptitude test that is designed to to predict performance over a general range of abilities. (440)

Requirements for a Good Test

1. Test scores are said to be _____ when they are reproducible or consistent. (441)

2. The degree of correlation between paired scores for a group of individuals on a given test is expressed as a _____. The _____ (lower/higher) the correlation, the higher the reliability. (442)

3. Tests are said to be _____ when they measure what they are intended to measure. (442)

4. To assess validity, scores on a test may be correlated with some other measure of the ability, called a _____; the resulting measure of correlation is termed the

_____. The _____ (lower/higher) the correlation, the more accurate the prediction that can be made from the test. (442)

Tests of Intellectual Ability

1. Intelligence tests are tests that measure _____. (443)

2. Alfred Binet and his colleague, Théophile Simon, distinguished between the age at which the average child could solve problems on their intelligence test, called _____, versus the actual age of a child taking their test, called _____. (444)

3. Terman adopted an index of intelligence called the _____ which expresses intelligence as _____ (cite the formula). (446)

4. Scores on the Stanford-Binet Intelligence Scale, like many other characteristics of people, are distributed in the population in the form of a _____; such a distribution is bell-shaped with _____ (many/few) cases around the midpoint and _____ (many/few) cases at the endpoints. (446)

5. One of the best known intelligence tests that measure separate abilities is the _____, which separates abilities into two divisions, using a _____ scale and a _____ scale. (447)

6. A version of the WAIS for children is called the _____. (448)

Predictive Validity of Tests

1. One of the most important factors in determining the size of a validity coefficient is _____ of the group being measured; the greater the selectivity, the _____ (lower/higher) the coefficient. (453-454)

Nature of Intelligence

1. Spearman designed a mathematical technique called _____ to determine the minimum number of abilities, or _____, required to explain an observed pattern of correlations for an array of tests. (460)

2. Spearman proposed that all individuals possess a factor called _____ or _____, that is the general determinant of performance on intelligence tests. (460)

3. In addition, factors that are specific to particular abilities or tests Spearman called _____ or _____. (460)

4. In contrast, Thurstone argued that intelligence, rather than general in nature, actually consists of a number of _____. (460)

5. In his search for primary abilities, Thurstone used the _____ approach. (461)

6. Since the 1960s, an alternative to the factorial approach is the attempt to understand intelligence in terms of cognitive processes; this is termed the _____ approach. (461)

7. According to Sternberg's _____ model, a person brings to a test a set of mental processes called _____ that produce the test responses. (462)

Genetic and Environmental Influences

1. The proportion of a trait's variation within a specified population that can be attributed to genetics is termed _____ (_____). (466)

2. Heritability is expressed by the formula _____, where V_G is the variability due to _____ factors and V_T is the *total* variability due to genetic plus _____ factors. (466)

Ideas and Concepts

1. a) When were ability tests first devised and for what purpose? (437)

*   b) Summarize a major controversy regarding the use of ability tests. (437)

Types of Ability Tests

1. Cite some examples of ability tests. (437)

* 2. a) What do your authors mean when they say that whether a "test is labeled an aptitude of an achievement test depends more on its purpose than on its content"? Give an example. (438)

*   b) Using the term *specificity of relevant prior experience* and an example, indicate a second way that aptitude and achievement tests can be distinguished from one another. (438)

    c) Describe a test that is somewhere in between ability and achievement tests in terms of its measurement of both aspects of performance. (See also Figure 12-1.) (439)

* 3. a) What is meant by the generality-specificity continuum in regard to ability tests? Give an example of a relatively specific test. (440)

*   b) Conversely, why do intelligence tests fall on the other end of the continuum? Describe some of their characteristics. (440-441)

Requirements for a Good Test

1. Since the many tests we take throughout life play such an important role, what characteristics are essential? (441)

2. a) Cite some of the reasons that a test may be unreliable. (441-442)

*   b) How do we go about evaluating reliability? Indicate three specific ways of accomplishing this task? Why is a statistical measure needed? (442)

*Basic ideas and concepts

176   Chapter 12

*   c)   What would we expect for a reliability coefficient of a well-constructed test? (442)

    3.   a)   Give some examples to distinguish the concept of validity from that of reliability. (442)

*   b) Can a test be reliable but not valid? (Do you think that a test could be valid if it was not reliable?) (442)

*   c)   How do we go about measuring validity? (442)

*   d)   Why is it difficult to use some tests for prediciton, such as the Medical College Admissions Test? (442-443)

*   4.   a)   Upon what aspect of assessment procedures are reliability and validity dependent? Give some examples. (443)

    b)   Can all extraneous variables be accounted for? Explain. (443)

Tests of Intellectual Ability

    1.   Why do many psychologists consider the term "intelligence test" inappropriate? (443)

*   2.   a)   What did Galton believe about differences between families and how did he conceptualize intelligence? (443-444)

*   b)   Outline Galton's methods for supporting his conception and (from his point of view) the "disappointing" results he obtained. (444)

*   3.   a)   What was Binet's task, and how did he go about achieving his aims? (444)

    b)   Discuss the reasoning by which Binet came to develop the notion of mental age. (444)

*   c)   Describe the relationship between mental and chronological age for an "average" child and children above or below the average. (444)

*   4.   a)   What kinds of items should be used in intelligence tests? (444)

*   b)   Distinguish between *novel items* and *familiar items* in conceptualizing this aim. (445)

*   5.   a)   Using Terman's formula for IQ, determine the value for each of the following unknowns. (446)

    —MA = 9, CA = 10, IQ =

    —IQ = 100, CA = 5, MA =

    —IQ = 120, MA = 12, CA =

b) Using appropriate terms, describe the distribution of IQ's in a normal population, as shown in Figure 12-3. (446)

* c) Why have changes in the Stanford-Binet test been made in the most recent revision, and what categories of intellectual abilities have been identified? (446-447)

6. a) Be able to distinguish the kinds of items used on the WAIS. (See also Table 12-4.) (448)

* b) What would a discrepancy between verbal and performance scores on the WAIS or WISC prompt an examiner to look for? (449)

* 7. a) Distinguish between *individual ability tests* and *group ability tests* and cite some advantages of each. (449)

* b) Cite two kinds of group tests of general ability that are familiar to many college-bound students (including their abbreviations). What kinds of changes have been instituted recently in each of these tests and why? (451)

Predictive Validity of Tests

* 1. a) Discuss the relationships (including the size of the related correlations) between elementary teachers' rankings of their students' intelligence and actual IQ. (452)

* b) What variables influence the teachers in their judgments, and when do the tests provide a more accurate assessment? (452)

* 2. a) What happens to the relationship between IQ and school performance as a person progresses up through high school and college levels and what is one of the most important factors in this trend? (453)

* b) What is the relationship between scores on the Scholastic Aptitude Test (SAT) and performance in college? (453-454)

* c) Discuss in detail why these correlations are not higher and the conditions under which they would be. (454)

d) What happens to the level of predictability from SAT scores when a college uses less stringent SAT requirements for entrance? More stringent requirements? (Be able to relate the actual values to levels of predictability of class standing.) (454)

* 3. a) Cite some examples of differences in performance ability attributable to the following population subgroups. (454-455)

—socioeconomic level:

—minority status:

—sex:

178   Chapter 12

*   b)   In general, what has been happening in recent decades to sex differences in intelligence test scores? (455)

*   c)   To what variables do your authors attribute the trends discussed in b)? (455)

*   4.   a)   What is the one area of cognitive ability in which there are consistent sex differences? What is the relationship of this fact to differences in mathematical ability? (456)

*   b)   Discuss two reasons for these differences. (456)

*   5.   a)   Outline the two points your authors raise in connection with group differences in performance on ability tests. (456-457)

     b)   Indicate the interaction between forms of societal discrimination against minority groups and ability test scores. (457)

  6.   What kinds of variables are not assessed by ability tests? Therefore, how can the usefulness of ability tests to predict performance be enhanced? (458)

Nature of Intelligence

*   1.   a)   Discuss the views of intelligence held by Alfred Binet and David Wechsler. (459)

     b)   What is the contrasting view of many other psychologists concerning the nature of intelligence? (460)

*   2.   What is the basic idea behind factor analysis and what does the factor analysis of an array of data tell us? (460)

*   3.   a)   According to Spearman, what determines whether a person is, say, generally bright or generally dull? (460)

     b)   Cite some examples of Spearman's s factors. (460)

*   4.   a)   Discuss in detail the procedures used by Thurstone in his challenge to Spearman's concept of the general intelligence factor. (460)

*   b)   What were the primary mental abilities identified by Thurstone? (See also Table 12-7.) (460)

*   c)   What became of Thurstone's primary mental abilities? Use the term *Test of Primary Mental Abilities* and comment on its predictive power. (460)

     d)   Cite two reasons why Thurstone's hope that he could factor analyze intelligence into its elements was not fulfilled. (460-461)

  5.   What has led to doubt about the factorial approach? Is it still in use? (461)

*   6.   a)   List three questions raised in the information-processing approach to research on intelligence. (461)

*   b) What does the information-processing model assume regarding individual differences on a task? (462)

*   c) Indicate the goal of the information-processing model and the kinds of measures employed in seeking that goal. (462)

7. a) List the five classes of components identified by Sternberg's componential model of intelligence. (462)

*   b) Give an illustration of Sternberg's model in action using the specific components *encoding process* and *comparison process* in your answer. (462)

    c) Discuss in detail the kinds of individual differences that appear in research on skilled and less-skilled performers on analogy problems. (462-463)

8. Discuss the way in which a factorial and an information-processing approach can be used together to yield complementary interpretations of intelligence test performance. (463)

* 9. a) List the four components that Sternberg suggests are relevant to both academic and practical intelligence. (463)

*   b) In light of this list, why are most intelligence tests available today effective in assessing, say, academic achievement, but not in assessing achievement in the nonacademic world at large? (463)

*   c) What classes of variables will have to be assessed in a new generation of intelligence tests and what method may provide the flexibility and depth required? (463)

Genetic and Environmental Influences

* 1. On what do most experts agree and how do they differ when it comes to genetic and environmental influences on intelligence? (464)

* 2. a) How has most evidence on the role of genetics in intelligence been obtained? Summarize the main trends of this area of research. See also Table 12-9. (465-466)

*   b) How is it known from the data in Table 12-9 that environmental factors are also important in determining intelligence? (466)

3. a) What are the numerical limits of heritability? Using the formula for heritability, illustrate conditions under which it would approach its limits. (466)

    b) Why is it important to note that heritability refers to populations rather than to individuals? (466)

*   c) What is the heritability estimate for the data in Table 12-9? Give two reasons why estimates of heritability differ so widely across studies. (466-467)

*   d) State in detail your authors' conclusions regarding the role of heredity in intelligence. (467)

4. List some of the environmental variables that may influence intelligence. (467)

5. a) Describe various approaches used in Project Head Start . (467)

   b) In general, what kinds of results has the Head Start program yielded? In particular, outline three results obtained with follow-up studies on children given special programs in preschool. (468-469)

   c) What variable emerges as the most important in Head Start programs? (469)

6. Describe the differences among two groups of Israeli children and the effects of rearing them in Kibbutzim . (469-470)

Ability Tests in Perspective

1. a) Indicate one area of concern in the use of ability tests with schoolchildren. What must both parents and teachers realize? (470-471)

*   b) Why has the use of tests to classify schoolchildren become a controversial social concern? (471)

*   c) What must be taken into account in making decisions about placement in special classes? (471)

*   d) List three important positive functions of *individual* ability testing. (471)

2. Illustrate by example some of the valuable information that may derive from a comparison of intelligence and achievement test scores. (471)

3. What is a concern that relates to the type of talent measured by ability tests and how may this concern be addressed in selection procedures? (471-472)

* 4. Cite your authors' general conclusion regarding the use of ability tests. (472)

Sample Quiz 12.1

1. If we wish to assess accomplished skills and what a person can do at the time, we would use an: a) achievement test; b) intelligence test; c) ability test; d) WAIS.

2. The statistic used to measure the degree to which a test measures what it is intended to measure is called a(n): a) mean; b) average; c) validity coefficient; d) reliability coefficient.

3. The Stanford-Binet Intelligence Test was developed by: a) Alfred Binet; b) Leland Stanford; c) Lewis Terman; d) Francis Galton.

4. If a person's MA were 20 and CA were 20, their IQ would be: a) 75; b) 100; c) 150; d) cannot tell without more information.

5. In the case of _____, a tester can be certain that questions are understood, can evaluate a person's motivation, and can carefully observe approaches to different tasks for clues as to intellectual strength: a) group ability tests; b) the Professional

and Administrative Career Examination; c) individual ability tests; d) none of the above.

6. The greater the selectivity of a population on which a validity coefficient is determined, the _____ the value of the coefficient: a) higher; b) lower; c) less variable; d) more predictive.

7. Which of the following is *false?* a) The basic idea behind factor analysis is that two tests that correlate very highly with each other are probably measuring the same underlying ability. b) According to Spearman, what determines whether a person is generally bright or dull is the amount of *g* that he or she possesses. c) Binet and Wechsler were in basic agreement that intelligence is a fundamental or global human capacity. d) Thurstone's primary abilities are now recognized as the basic elements of intelligence and appear in most tests of intelligence.

8. Thurstone used the _____ approach in his search for primary abilities: a) information processing; b) heritability; c) componential; d) factorial.

9. Sternberg has shown that individual differences on analogy problems owe to the efficiency of: a) the encoding process; b) the comparison process; c) object assembly abilities; d) both a and b.

10. Individual ability testing in schools helps to: a) determine whether earlier group-administered tests accurately reflect ability; b) determine the best instructional program for improvement of skills; c) improve assessment of a child's particular intellectual strengths and weaknesses; d) all of the above.

Sample Quiz 12.2

1. The term "test" was defined in this chapter as: a) a set of questions assessing achievement and/or aptitude; b) a collection of sub-scales measuring meaningful psychological dimensions; c) a device for determining enduring traits and characteristics of the individual; d) a sample of behavior taken at a given point in time.

2. The Scholastic Aptitude Test (SAT) is: a) primarily an aptitude test; b) primarily an achievement test; c) both an aptitude and an achievement test; d) neither an aptitude nor an achievement test.

3. The _____ the reliability coefficient, the greater the reliability: a) higher; b) lower; c) more stable; d) more variable.

4. The reason that many ability tests have strict time limits is to: a) match the temporal restrictions imposed on comparable tasks in the real world; b) determine how well the individuals being tested can function under stress; c) make the scoring of the test easier; d) minimize the influence of extraneous variables.

5. A verbal scale and a separate performance scale are intelligence test characteristics of: a) Binet's original test; b) the Stanford-Binet; c) the Wechsler Adult Intelligence Scale; d) Thurstone's Test of Primary Mental Abilities.

6. WISC is to WAIS as: a) g factor is to s factors; b) high correlation is to low correlation; c) VT is to VG; d) children are to adults.

7. The area of cognitive ability in which consistent sex differences continue to be found is: a) mathematical reasoning; b) verbal proficiency; c) visual-spatial relations; d) all of the above.

8. Sternberg, from his information-processing perspective, has argued that intelligence tests in use today are poor predictors of achievement outside of the academic world because they are ineffective in assessing: a) the ability to think or reason abstractly; b) motivation and practical problem-solving ability; c) the ability to learn and profit from experience; d) all of the above.

9. Heritability equals: a) VG/VT; b) VT/H; c) VG/H; d) VT/VG.

10. With respect to the role of heredity in intelligence, your authors conclude that: a) heredity is solely responsible for differences in intellectual ability; b) the degree to which heredity affects intelligence can now be accurately determined; c) heredity is probably less influential than some researchers have claimed; d) heredity has no effect on intelligence at all.

Key, Chapter 12

Names

1. Francis Galton
2. Alfred Binet
3. Lewis Terman
4. David Wechsler
5. Charles Spearman
6. Louis Thurstone

Vocabulary and Details

1. test
2. achievement test
3. aptitude test
4. intelligence

1. reliable
2. reliability coefficient; higher
3. valid
4. criterion; validity coefficient; higher

1. general intellectual abililty
2. mental age (MA); chronological age (CA)
3. intelligence quotient (IQ); IQ = MA/CA X 100
4. normal distribution curve; many; few
5. Wechsler Adult Intelligence Scale (WAIS); verbal; performance
6. Wechsler Intelligence Scale for Children (WISC)

1. selection; lower

1. factor analysis; factors
2. general intelligence factor; *g*
3. special factors; *s*
4. primary abilities
5. factorial
6. information-processing
7. componential; components

1. heritability; H
2. $H = V_G/V_T$; genetic; environmental

Sample Quiz 12.1

1. a, 437
2. c, 442
3. c, 445-446
4. b, 446
5. c, 449
6. b, 453-454
7. d, 459-460
8. d, 461
9. d, 462
10. d, 471

Sample Quiz 12.2

1. d, 437
2. c, 439
3. a, 442.
4. d, 443
5. c, 447
6. d, 447-448
7. c, 456
8. b, 463
9. a, 466
10. c, 467

Personality
through the Life Course

Learning Objectives

1. Be able to discuss the evidence concerning genetic influences on personality characteristics, including the results of twin studies.

2. Know the four kinds of parenting patterns that have been the subject of research and what the results indicate concerning their effects on children's development.

3. Describe, with examples, what is meant by a "built-in correlation" between a child's inherited characteristics and his or her environment.

4. Be prepared to define the three dynamic processes of personality-environment interactions (reactive, evocative, and proactive) and to give examples of each.

5. Understand how these three processes can explain the results of studies suggesting that the influence of environment is negligible (for example, the finding that children from the same family seem to be no more alike than children chosen randomly from the general population once their genetic similarities are subtracted out).

6. Be able to describe the cross-cultural studies showing that different lifestyles value different personality traits and that cultures shape these traits in their members through different childrearing practices.

7. Be able to discuss the evidence for continuity of personality provided by the two longitudinal studies described in the text. What characteristics showed the strongest continuity?

8. In the above study, be able to describe the differences between subjects whose personalities remained stable from adolescence to adulthood (nonchangers) and those whose personalities did not (changers). Understand how cultural pressures to conform to sex-role norms may have contributed to the outcome for both sexes.

9. Be prepared to explain, with examples, how the three processes of personality-environment interaction influence the continuity of personality.

10. Be able to distinguish between the cumulative consequences and the contemporary consequences of early personality characteristics and to provide examples of each from the longitudinal studies of ill-tempered or dependent children.

Vocabulary and Details

1. The characteristic patterns of thought, emotion, and behavior that define an individual's personal style and influence interactions with the environment consitute _____. (475)

Shaping of Personality

1. Mood-related personality characteristics, called _____, begin to appear shortly after birth and provide early "building blocks" for later personality. (475)

2. A person's inherited characteristics are called his or her _____. (481)

3. In the interaction between genotype and the environment termed _____, different individuals exposed to the same environment experience it, interpret it, and react to it differently. (481)

4. In the form of interaction termed _____, an individual's personality evokes distinctive responses from others. (481)

5. In the third form of interaction, termed _____, individuals select or create environments of their own. (482)

Continuity of Personality

1. Studies that observe or assess the same persons over time are called _____. (487)

Consequences of Personality

1. The processes of interaction may shape the life course through _____, the consequences that arise when an individual's early personality channels him or her into particular life paths. (494)

2. Alternatively, we speak of _____ when early personality carries forward into adult life in the form of current personality to evoke distinctive responses from the environment. (494)

Ideas and Concepts

Shaping of Personality

* 1. a) What does the early appearance of temperamental characteristics suggest and what is one way this may be investigated? (475)

* b) Discuss the results of some actual studies done in this area that relied on ratings from parents as well as studies employing more objective methods. (475)

c) Outline a study done in Sweden on the heritability of *extraversion* and *neuroticism*. (475-476)

*Basic ideas and concepts

186   Chapter 13

2. a) What is one difficulty in interpreting results of twin studies and how may it be addressed? (476)

* b) Discuss the methods of the *Minnesota Study for Twins Reared Apart*. (476)

* c) What three conclusions can be drawn from this and other research along the following lines. (476-477)

—similarity of personalities in identical twins:

—degree of heritability in a variety of twin studies:

—measures with highest heritabilities:

* 3. a) Summarize some relationships between early forming of secure attachments to primary caregivers and later development. (477)

b) Do the relationships discussed in a) stem from the behavior of the caregiver or of the child? Cite some related evidence. (478)

* 4. a) In the table below, distinguish between: a) four types of parents using the terms *authoritative, authoritarian, indulgent,* and *neglecting,* and b) the characteristics that often appear in their children. Be sure you understand all of the characteristics of the parents cited. (See also Figure 13-1.) (478-480)

	Accepting Responsive Child-centered	Rejecting Unresponsive Parent-centered
Demanding Controlling	*Parent (term):* *Child:*	*Parent (term):* *Child:*
Underdemanding Not controlling	*Parent (term):* *Child:*	*Parent (term):* *Child*

b) Describe the characteristics of the children of parent-centered parents versus child-centered parents observed in a study in Finland. (480)

* c) Discuss the reasons why the classification shown in the table above is only a summary and should not be applied to a particular parent. (480)

d) Generally characterize the results of studies relating child-rearing practices to personality. (480)

* 5. a) Explain and give some illustrations of your authors' contention that there is a "built-in correlation" between genotype and environment. (481)

—positive correlation between environment and genotype:

—negative correlation between environment and genotype:

* b) For each of the forms of environment-genotype interactions, be able to cite some examples. (481-482)

Interaction	Examples
reactive interaction	
evocative interaction	
proactive interaction	

c) How does the relative importance of the three forms of personality-environment interactions change over the course of development? (482)

* 6. a) Indicate three ways in which personality comparisons between identical and fraternal twins are "too good." (483)

b) Give two reasons why the personalities of identical twins may be so similar. (483)

* c) What is an important feature of environmental-genotype processes as they may operate in identical twins? Illustrate and contrast with the case of fraternal twins and siblings. (483)

* 7. a) Discuss a surprising result that has emerged from studies of personality among twins. (483-484)

* b) Outline the explanation offered by your text for this controversial finding. (484)

* 8. a) What is one reason why differences between families in childrearing practices do not seem to produce systematic effects on children's personalities? (485)

b) Distinguish between western and non-western societies in terms of their emphasis upon independence and self-assertiveness and in differing parent-child interactions. (485)

* c) Summarize the results of the Barry et al. study on the traits stressed in childrearing in societies that are high on food-accumulation (agricultural societies) versus those that are low on food-accumulation (hunting societies). (486)

Continuity of Personality

* 1. a) Note the fundamental procedures of two large-scale longitudinal studies begun in California at the Institute of Human Development (IHD) about 60 years ago. (487)

*   b) Outline the results of these and other longitudinal studies indicating especially the features of personality that do and do not show continuities. (488)

   —strongest continuities:

   —weakest continuities:

*   c) How do these results compare with those of heritability studies and what does this suggest? (488)

* 2. In the table below, outline the personality differences between *nonchangers* and *changers* in the two sexes obtained in the IHD studies. (488-489)

	Males	Females
Nonchangers		
Changers		

3. a) Cite a possible biological reason for the differences between changers and nonchangers in the IHD studies. (490-491)

*   b) In contrast, what environmental variable may have strongly influenced participants in the IHD studies and how might it have differentially influenced the outcomes for females? (491)

   c) Cite further evidence for the role of cultural factors in continuities or discontinuities from childhood to adulthood obtained in a Fels Research Institute longitudinal study. Be sure to contrast results obtained for males and females. (491-492)

* 4. Using the example of an adolescent boy with temper tantrums, show how the three classes of personality-environment interactions can influence continuity of personality. (492-493)

5. a) In what ways can proactive interactions exert an influence on continuity via our selection of our companions? (493)

*   b)   Discuss the results of another IHD study that investigated whether spouses who were alike would produce greater continuity in personality in one another than those who were not so alike. (493)

Consequences of Personality

1.   Cite examples of cumulative consequences and contemporary consequences. (494)

*   2.   a)   Outline the procedures for the study of cumulative and contemporary consequences of the personality trait *ill-temperedness*, as traced in the Berkeley Guidance Study. (494)

*   b)   With respect to male subjects in this study, in detail, what were the life course factors studied and what was the "path" that the trait of ill-temperedness took from childhood to adulthood? Use the term *path analysis* in your answer and be able to relate different paths to differential significance of correlation coefficients. (494-495)

*   c)   What variables showed the effects of cumulative consequences and contemporary consequences, respectively, in this study? How do we know? (495)

       d)   What other aspect of these men's lives were influenced by the ill-temperedness factor? (496)

3.   a)   With respect to the women in the Berkeley Guidance Study, why could path analysis not be applied to determine whether the persistence of childhood ill-temperedness into adult life reflected cumulative or contemporary consequences? (496)

*   b)   Was ill-temperedness shown to persist for these women? What features of the women's lives in the Berkeley study appeared to correlate with this personality characteristic? (496)

*   4.   a)   Give some reasons why the consequences of childhood dependency are especially interesting when studied across the life course. (496)

       b)   Briefly indicate the procedures of a Berkeley study of childhood dependency. (496-497)

*   c)   For the case of the male subjects, outline the main results of the Berkeley study noting each of the following effects. (497)

—the relationship between childhood dependency and adult personality:

—the relationship between childhood dependency and adult domestic behaviors:

*   d)   In contrast, describe the results for the female subjects in this study. (498)

—the relationship between childhood dependency and adult personality:

—the relationship between childhood dependency and adult behaviors in the arena of marriage, childbearing, and education:

Sample Quiz 13.1

1. Mood-related personality characteristics: a) are called temperaments; b) begin to appear shortly after birth; c) are the "building blocks" for later personality; d) all of the above.

2. Which of the following is *true?* a) The early appearance of temperaments suggests that they are largely learned at a very young age; b) Whereas studies of identical twins that relied on parents ratings of temperament have shown a significant heritability component, studies using more objective methods have not; c) Correlations between identical twins on temperaments average around .50; d) None of the above.

3. Parents who are accepting, responsive, child-centered, and place few demands on their children are called: a) authoritative; b) neglecting; c) authoritarian; d) indulgent.

4. When your authors say that there is a "built-in correlation" between genotype and environment, they mean that: a) environment determines genotype; b) a child's genotype inevitably determines all features of the environment; c) parental genotype has some effect on the way their children's environment is structured; d) the coefficient of correlation between genotype and environment is always about .80.

5. Which of the following is *not* a form of dynamic interaction between the child's genotype and his or her environment: a) reactive interaction; b) evocative interaction; c) proactive interaction; d) retroactive interaction.

6. In proactive interactions: a) early personality carries forward into adult life and evokes distinctive responses from the environment; b) an individual's personality evokes distinctive responses from others regardless of period of life; c) different individuals exposed to the same environmental experience interpret and react to it differently; d) individuals select or create environments of their own.

7. Two ambitious studies at the Institute of Human Development that dealt with continuities in personality used _____ procedures: a) case history; b) laboratory; c) longitudinal; d) survey.

8. The descriptors "intellectual," "warm," "productive," and "self-satisfied," apply best to the personalities of: a) male nonchangers; b) female nonchangers; c) female changers; d) both a and b.

9. In general, it has been found that spouses who are like one another in personality: a) become more dissimilar across time; b) become more similar across time; c) have more marital conflicts; d) both a and c.

10. Divorce is greater among: a) men with histories of childhood ill-temperedness; b) women who were ill-tempered in childhood; c) both a and b; d) none of the above; there is no relationship between divorce and ill-temperedness.

Personality through the Life Course   191

Sample Quiz 13.2

1. Which of the following is not one of the components of personality as defined in your text: a) patterns of emotion; b) patterns of behavior; c) patterns of thought; d) patterns of physiological reactions.

2. Temperaments begin to appear: a) shortly after birth; b) at about 2 to 3 years of age; c) when the child starts attending school; d) with the onset of puberty.

3. Summarizing across a number of twin studies, it has been concluded that about _____ of the variability among individuals on many personality characteristics can be attributed to genetic differences: a) 50%; b) 10-15%; c) 75-80%; d) 0%.

4. A person's genotype is: a) the collection of mood-related personality characteristics that provide the early building blocks for later personality; b) a person's own inherited characteristics; c) the environmental influences that shape and alter adult personality; d) the brand of designer pants in which he or she feels most comfortable.

5. The fact that we interact with an arrogant individual differently than a humble individual illustrates the personality-environment interaction called: a) reactive interaction; b) the genotype-environment correlation; c) proactive interaction; d) evocative interaction.

6. In an experiment discussed at length in your text, it was found that societies low on food-accumulation stressed _____ in their child-rearing practices: a) achievement, self-reliance, and independence; b) responsibility and obedience; c) both a and b; d) neither a nor b.

7. Studies that observe or assess the same persons over time are called: a) cumulative; b) contemporary; c) longitudinal; d) proactive.

8. When individuals whose personalities remained stable from adolescence to adulthood were compared to those whose personalities changed, better adustment during adolescence was observed for: a) changers if they were male and nonchangers if they were female; b) changers if they were female and nonchangers if they were male; c) nonchangers regardless of gender; d) changers regardless of gender.

9. Early personality is to current personality as: a) reactive is to proactive; b) cumulative consequences are to contemporary consequences; c) environmental influences are to genotype; d) indulgent is to neglecting.

10. Childhood dependency seems to produce: a) sympathetic and nurturant men but constricted and self-pitying women; b) sympathetic and nurturant women but constricted and self-pitying men; c) sympathetic and nurturant individuals of both sexes; d) constricted and self-pitying individuals of both sexes.

Key, Chapter 13

Vocabulary and Details

1. personality

1. temperaments
2. genotype
3. reactive interaction
4. evocative interaction
5. proactive interaction

1. longitudinal studies

1. cumulative consequences
2. contemporary consequences

Sample Quiz 13.1

1. d, 475
2. c, 475
3. d, 479
4. c, 481
5. d, 481
6. d, 482
7. c, 487
8. d, 489
9. b, 493
10. c, 496

Sample Quiz 13.2

1. d, 475
2. a, 475
3. a, 476
4. b, 481
5. d, 481-482
6. a, 485-486
7. c, 487
8. c, 489
9. b, 494
10. a, 498

Personality Theory and Assessment

Learning Objectives

1. Know the difference between type theories and trait theories of personality. Be able to describe the three goals of trait psychologists.

2. Understand Allport's distinction between common traits and personal dispositions. Be able to define and exemplify cardinal, central, and secondary dispositions.

3. Be familiar with factor-analytic methods of determining personality traits, the factors arrived at by Cattell and Eysenck, and the criticisms of the trait approach.

4. Be familiar with the key concepts of Freud's psychoanalytic theory, including his assumptions about personality structure, dynamics, and development. Be able to discuss the theories of later psychoanalysts and to evaluate the psychoanalytic approach in terms of its portrait of human personality and criticisms of the theory.

5. Understand the basic assumptions of the social learning approach to personality, including the role of operant and classical conditioning and the person variables that account for individual diffferences in behavior. Be able to describe the social-learning portrait of personality and to evaluate the contribution of this approach.

6. Understand how the phenomenological approach differs from psychoanalytic and social learning approaches. Be familiar with the basic assumptions underlying the humanistic theories of Carl Rogers and Abraham Maslow, and the more cognitive view of George Kelly. Be able to describe the phenomenological portrait of human personality and to evaluate this approach.

7. Know how the requirements of reliability and validity are applied to personality tests. Be familiar with the tests used to assess personality traits, including use of the method of empirical construction to develop personality inventories.

8. Know what is meant by a projective test and the problems encountered in interpreting the results of the Rorschach and TAT.

9. Be familiar with the methods used by social learning theorists to assess behavior in naturalistic settings and with methods used by phenomenological psychologists.

10. Explain what is meant by the consistency paradox and be prepared to discuss the possible reasons why studies find low correlations between measures of the same trait in two different situations or between personality test scores and situational measures of a trait. Include the solutions offered by the person-centered approach, aggregated measures, and interactionism.

Names

1. An influential trait theorist of personality known for his distinction between common traits and personal dispositions was _____. (505-506)

2. The psychologist who applied factor analysis most extensively to the study of personality traits and distinguished between 16 different factors is _____. (507)

3. Another psychologist who uses factor analysis in the analysis of traits, but who has arrived at fewer dimensions than Cattell, is _____. (508)

4. The creator of the psychoanalytic theory of personality was _____. (511)

5. The individual whose views on "self-actualization" and whose nondirective therapeutic methods grew out of the principles of humanistic psychology was _____. (523)

6. Another important humanistic psychologist who became known for his notion that individuals behave in accordance with a hierarchy of needs was _____. (524-525)

7. A third notable humanistic psychologist, whose "personal construct" approach emphasizes individualistic dimensions for interpreting (or construing) the world, was _____. (527)

Vocabulary and Details

Trait Approach

1. According to William Sheldon's theory, bodily physiques, called _____, correlate with temperament. (504)

2. Theories, like Sheldon's and others, which propose that individuals can be categorized into discrete, qualitiatively different types are called _____ or _____. (504)

3. Closely related, theories that assume that persons vary simultaneously on a number of continuous personality dimensions or scales are termed _____. (505)

4. Allport distinguished between trait dimensions on which individuals can be compared with one another, termed _____, and unique patterning of traits within the individual, termed _____. (506)

5. A statistical method that examines intercorrelations among a number of measures and groups those that are highly correlated is called _____; the groups of measures are independent dimensions called _____. (507)

6. Cattell's questionnaire for measuring basic traits is called the _____. (507)

Psychoanalytic Approach

1. The doctrine (influential in psychoanalytic theory) that all thoughts, emotions, and actions have causes, is known as _____. (511)

2. In the psychoanalytic view, personality is composed of three systems or structures, the most primitive of which is the _____, consisting of the basic biological impulses or drives. (512)

3. The id is said to operate on the _____ principle, striving to immediately obtain pleasure and avoid pain. (512)

4. The second personality system is the _____, which attempts to mediate between the impulses of the id and the demands of society to behave appropriately. (512)

5. The ego obeys the _____ principle, delaying gratification until it can be obtained in socially appropriate ways. (512)

6. The third structure of personality is the _____, the internalized representation of the values of society that prompts a person to adhere to moral standards. (512)

7. In Freud's *personality dynamics*, the psychic energy for personality derives from the _____, primarily sexual in origin. (513)

8. Freud used the term _____ for the ego's strategies by which a person can avoid or reduce the anxiety attendant upon expressions of the id. (514)

9. The most basic of these strategies is termed _____, in which unacceptable thoughts or impulses are pushed by the ego out of consciousness and into the unconscious. (514)

10. Freud referred to the developmental periods in which the impulses of the id focus on different areas of the body as _____. (514)

11. During the phallic psychosexual stage a conflict emerges, called the _____, in which a young child regards the same-sex parent as a rival for the affection of the opposite sex parent. (514)

12. Freud also maintained that an individual could be stopped or _____ at a given stage of psychosexual development, with later consequences for personality. (515)

Social-Learning Approach

1. The approach to personality that assumes that behavior is the result of learning and continuous interactions between personal and environmental variables is termed the _____. (518)

2. Social-learning theorists emphasize three forms of learning in the development of personality: a) _____, in which behavior is a function of its consequences; b) _____, in which people learn by observing the actions and consequences of others' behavior; and c) _____, in which the relationships between conditioned and unconditioned stimuli play a role. (519-520)

Phenomenological Approach

1. The approach to the study of personality that focuses on the individual's personal subjective perception and interpretation of events in the environment is termed the _____; central to this approach is the subdiscipline _____. (522)

2. From the standpoint of Rogers' brand of humanistic psychology, the basic motivating force of the individual is the tendency toward _____. (523, 550)

3. Rogers' method of humanistic therapy assumes that the individual will strive toward growth and has the ability to personally decide on the direction for change; this technique is called _____. (523)

4. The central concept in Rogers' approach, termed the _____, consists of all the ideas, perceptions, and values that characterize the individual. (523)

5. From this perspective, how a person would *like* to be is called that individual's _____ self; thus, how the person actually *is* may be termed the _____ self. (524)

6. Maslow's concept of a _____ proposes that needs are organized so that the more basic ones must be satisfied before increasingly more complex, psychological needs will influence action. (525)

7. Maslow used the term _____ to describe individuals who have made extraordinary use of their potential. (525)

8. Moments of happiness and fulfillment that may accompany self-actualization Maslow termed _____. (526)

9. Kelly's theory emphasizes the dimensions that individuals use to interpret themselves and their social worlds. These dimensions are the individual's own _____, and the approach is called _____. (527)

Personality Assessment

1. A test that gives reproducible and consistent results is said to be _____. (530)

2. A test that measures what it is intended to measure is _____, which is assessed by correlating the test with some external criterion to obtain a _____. (530)

3. In the _____ method for personality trait assessment, a rater (sorter) is given a set of cards containing personality statements and asked to describe an individual by placing the cards into stacks ranging from least to most descriptive. (531)

4. A questionnaire in which a person reports reactions or feelings in certain situations is called a _____. (533)

5. A well-known personality inventory that assesses attitudes, emotional reactions, and various symptoms on 10 "clinical" scales is the _____, or _____. (533)

6. A personality inventory designed to assess more "normal" personality traits than the MMPI, such as dominance and responsibility, is the _____. (535)

7. Tests used in psychoanalytic assessment that present ambiguous stimuli and allow for a broad range of responses are called _____. (536)

8. One projective test is the _____, in which a series of 10 cards depicting complex inkblots are presented; a subject responds by indicating what each stimulus resembles. (537)

9. Another projective test is the _____, or _____, which consists of ambiguous pictures of persons and scenes; a subject responds by telling a story about each picture. (538)

10. A test designed by Kelly to elicit the personal constructs by which subjects interpret their worlds is called the _____. (541)

Ideas and Concepts

*   1. What are the two attempts of personality psychology? (503)

Trait Approach

1. Outline Hippocrates' four "personality types." (503)

*   2. a) Distinguish among Sheldon's three somatotypes in terms of bodily characteristics and temperament. (504)

—*endomorphic:*

—*mesomorphic:*

—*ectomorphic:*

*   b) Outline the objections to Sheldon's theory and the state of the evidence. (504)

3. Have typologies been useful in other sciences? Why have they not been very popular in personality psychology, and what is the current status of thinking in this area? (504)

*   4. Distinguish between *continuous* and *discontinuous* categories of personality and relate these concepts to type theories and trait theories. Cite examples. (504-505)

5. In what three respects do trait psychologists attempt to go beyond our day-to-day conceptions of personality? (505)

6. a) Within the context of Allport's theory, provide examples of the following. (506)

—common traits:

—personal dispositions:

*Basic ideas and concepts

Personality Theory and Assessment   199

*   b)   In the following table, provide definitions in your own words of the forms of personal disposition referred to and an example of each. (506)

	Definition	Example
cardinal dispositions		
central dispositions		
secondary dispositions		

       b)   Upon what kinds of traits do most trait psychologists focus and why? In what application is Allport's concept of personal dispositions especially useful? (506).

*   6.   a)   Describe Allport and Odbert's method for developing a list of common traits. Why is this a reasonable approach? (506-507)

*   b)   What technique did Cattell apply to Allport and Odbert's list of traits, and what was the result? (507)

*   c)   Discuss Eysenck's variation on the application of factor analysis to the problem of personality traits. Be able to distinguish among the various types defined by his dimensions of personality. (508)

       —*introversion-extraversion*:

       —*stable-unstable (neuroticism)*:

*   7.   a)   Identify three reasons why there is such a large discrepancy among the various trait theorists in terms of the numbers of traits they assign to people? (509)

*   b)   What consensus regarding numbers of traits appears to be emerging, and what are the dimensions? (509)

   8.   a)   Is the trait approach a theory of personality? Explain. (510)

       b)   At which of the two tasks of personality psychology--specifying variables or synthesizing personality functions into an integrated account--is the trait approach most successful? (510)

*   c)   What has been the major criticism of the trait approach? What is the alternative to the notion that traits determine personality across a variety of situations? Provide an example. (510-511)

Psychoanalytic Approach

   1.   Describe the early development of Freud's approach using the terms *free association* and the *unconscious* in your answer. (511)

200   Chapter 14

2. According to psychoanalytic theory, what causes most psychological events, and what are some manifestations? (511)

* 3. a) Use examples to ensure that you can distinguish among the id, ego, and superego. (512)

* b) What happens if the moral standards of the superego are violated and how is this anxiety experienced? Describe a case of an overdeveloped superego and of a weak superego. (512-513)

c) Do the three structures of personality coexist peacefully? Discuss. (513)

* 4. a) Discuss the influence of the view of energy conservation on Freud's notions regarding personality dynamics. (513)

* b) By this view, what happens if forbidden impulses are suppressed? Give an example. (513)

* 5. Describe events in each of the following psychosexual stages of personality development and indicate the age at which they occur. (514-515)

	Age	Description
oral stage		
anal stage		
phallic stage		
latency period		
genital stage		

* 6. a) Outline the sequence of events in the development of a male child's Oedipal conflict. Use the term *castration anxiety*. (514)

b) Describe a normal case in which the Oedipal conflict is successfully resolved. What has been formed in the resolution? (514)

* c) Indicate the cross-cultural taboo and its proposed function cited by some as evidence for the universality of the Oedipal conflict. (514)

* 7. Describe the consequences of fixation at a stage of psychosexual development. Illustrate with the personality attributes that would result from fixation at two different stages. (515)

8. a) In what respect was Freud flexible in his thinking? Cite two examples. (515)

Personality Theory and Assessment 201

b) In what respect was Freud not so open to revisions, and on what topic was that especially apparent? (515)

* c) Indicate the result of Freud's rigidity on the field of psychoanalytic theory and name some representative individuals. (515)

* d) On what aspect of Freud's theory have more recent psychoanalytic theorists concentrated their efforts? Cite some instances, including *object relations theory*. (515-516)

9. Similarly, discuss the ways in which Erikson's theory of *psychosocial stages* represents a departure from Freud's views. (516)

10. a) Compare Freud with Copernicus and Darwin in terms of how the views of each have challenged time-honored notions of the preeminence of the earth or of man. (516)

* b) What stand does classic psychoanalytic theory take on each of the following issues? (516-517)

—personality as evil:

—personality as fixed and passive:

—personality and psychological health:

* 11. a) Is psychoanalytic theory true or false? Explain, and indicate three major contributions of Freud's theory to our understanding of human behavior. (517)

* b) In contrast, discuss the shortcomings of psychoanalytic theory in terms of its concepts and the general outcome of empirical tests. Use examples when they are helpful. (517)

c) Describe Malinowski's ingenious test of the Oedipal conflict hypothesis. Of what do Malinowski's results serve as a reminder insofar as Freud's population for study is concerned? Explain. (517-518)

* 12. On what dimensions has Freud's theory survived experimental tests and on what dimensions has it not proved viable? Refer to both the "structural" and the dynamic "psychosexual" aspects of Freud's theory in your response. (518)

Social-Learning Approach

* 1. a) Characterize the social learning approach in terms of its emphases, form of relationship between person and situation, and bases for prediction of behavior. (518)

b) To what approaches in psychology is social-learning theory most related? (518)

* 2. a) What do your authors mean when they say that social-learning theory is a special case of operant conditioning? (518-519)

*   b)   Is reinforcement necessary for learning in this approach? If not, what function does reinforcement serve? Cite an example. (519)

*   3.   a)   Describe the three forms of reinforcement that are said to control the expression of learned behavior. Can you think of an example for each? (519)

      —*direct reinforcement*:

      —*vicarious reinforcement*:

      —*self-administered reinforcement*:

*   b)   Upon what three factors do a person's actions depend in a given situation? (519)

*   c)   Describe the role that *generalization* and *discrimination* play in the consistency or apparent lack of consistency in behavior. (519)

*   d)   Based on your answer to c), what is the position of social-learning theorists on the role of traits in personality? (519)

*   4.   To what kinds of behavior do social-learning theorists view classical conditioning to be relevant? Give an example and use the terms *unconditioned stimulus* , *conditioned stimulus*, and *conditioned response* in your answer. (519-520)

   5.   Contrast trait theories, psychoanalytic theory, and the social-learning approach to personality in terms of their ability to specify the variables on which people differ from one another and the processes of personality functioning. (520)

*   6.   Describe Mischel's social learning approach through an explanation of how each of the following **person variables** is said to operate in person-environment interactions. (520)

Functions in Person-Environment Interactions

competencies	
encoding strategies	
expectancies	
subjective values	
self-regulatory systems and plans	

Personality Theory and Assessment   203

*   7.   Contrast the social-learning approach with other approaches to personality on the following issues. (521)

—determinism:

—human beings as good or evil:

—modifiability of behavior:

—passive/active role of the individual:

*   8.   Summarize some of the contributions and shortcomings of the social-learning approach. (521-522)

Phenomenological Approach

*   1.   In what notable respects does the phenomenonological approach differ from other approaches to personality? (522)

*   2.   Prior to the 1960s, essentially what were the two "forces" in psychology? Be familiar with the principles associated with the so-called "third force" that emerged. (522-523)

*   3.   a)   Discuss the nature of the basic motivating force of the human individual from the perspective of Rogers. (523)

b)   In person-centered therapy, what is the role of the therapist, and how does this differ from the therapist's approach in psychoanalytic therapy? (523)

4.   a)   Does a person's self-concept necessarily reflect what he or she "is" or "does"? Give an example. (523-524)

*   b)   Discuss Rogers' view of the role of the self-concept in relation to how people want to behave and what happens if their reality is not congruent with their potential. Relatedly, what results when this incongruence is too great? (524)

c)   Characterize the well-adjusted person from this perspective. (524)

*   5.   a)   In terms of the "real" and the "ideal" self, how is fulfillment realized and what accounts for unhappiness and dissatisfaction? (524)

*   b)   Therefore, based on your answer to a) and your discussion in 4 b), what are two kinds of incongruence in Rogers' system? (524)

*   6.   a)   Distinguish between the following two fundamental ways in which parents and others may relate to a child and the consequences in terms of the child's self-concept. (524)

204   Chapter 14

—unconditional positive regard:

—conditional positive regard:

b)   Illustrate the experiential effects of conditional positive regard by example, and cite Rogers' suggestion for the best approach in such cases. (524)

*   7.   a)   Be familiar with the relative kinds of motives reflected in the levels of Maslow's hierarchy of needs. (525)

b)   What is the highest motive in this conceptualization? Give some examples of individuals that Maslow believed had attained this level of self-expression. (525)

*   c)   Be able to characterize the self-actualizer and the kinds of activities that permit this level of self-fulfillment. (526)

8.   In what terms do people describe their peak experiences, and during what kinds of activities do they occur? Can you think of peak experiences of your own? (526)

*   9.   a)   From Kelly's standpoint, what is the goal of the psychologist? (527)

*   b)   In this perspective, in what sense may people be considered to be "scientists" and in what ways does this impact on their beliefs? (527)

c)   Relatedly, what is the purpose of therapy from Kelly's approach and what technique, in particular, may be useful in achieving this end? Provide an example. (527)

*   10.   a)   In terms of determinants of behavior and psychological health, what portrait does the phenomenological approach paint of the human personality? Are individuals basically good or bad in this perspective? (527-528)

b)   Discuss the "radical" political implications of the humanistic movement, noting in particular its relationship to feminist views by way of illustration. (528)

*   11.   From your authors' perspective, evaluate the phenomenological approach to personality along each of the following dimensions. (528-529)

—contributions:

—completeness:

—empirical methods and evidence:

—population for study:

—fundamental human values:

Personality Assessment

1.   Cite four reasons why the objective assessment of personality is important. (529-530)

* 2. a) What are the two features of a good test? (530)

* b) Indicate the method used to obtain each of the following forms of reliability. (530)

Type of reliability   Method

test-retest reliablity *(temporal stability)*	
alternate form *reliability*	
internal consistency	
interscorer agreement *(interjudge reliability)*	

3. a) Can a test be reliable but not valid? Give an example. (530)

* b) Indicate how each of the following forms of validity would be obtained and provide an example. (530-531)

Type of validity   Method and Example

criterion validity *(empirical validity)*	
construct validity	

4. What is the "criterion problem" in personality psychology? (531)

5. a) Indicate the most direct way of assessing how much of a particular trait an individual possesses. Give an example. (531)

* b) In what important respect is the Q-sort technique different from asking raters to rate an individual on a set of traits? Use the terms "common traits," "personal dispositions," and "patterning" in your answer. (532)

* c) Discuss how the results of two Q sorts can be used to assess each of the following forms of reliability or validity. (532)

206   Chapter 14

—test-retest reliability:

—interjudge reliability:

—criterion validity:

6. a) In what respects does the personality inventory resemble a structured interview? (533)

   b) Using examples, describe the application of personality inventories to the assessment of a single personality dimension and to multiple dimensions. (533)

*   c) In your own words, distinguish between the *rational* and the *empirical* (or *criterion*) methods of test construction. Cite an example of each method. (533-534, 550)

* 7. a) How are responses on the MMPI scored? (534)

*   b) For what purpose was the MMPI developed? Were specific personality traits assumed in the process of test construction? Discuss in detail the method that was used. (534)

   c) Does it matter whether or not what a person says in response to a question on the MMPI is true? Why or why not? (534-535)

*   d) Indicate both an advantage and a disadvantage in the empirical method of test construction represented by the MMPI. (535)

* 8. How should the MMPI be used in the assessment of nonclinical populations? Why? (535)

9. a) How was the California Personality Inventory constructed? (535-536)

   b) Discuss the relationships obtained between scores on the California Personality Inventory and two forms of achievement. (536)

* 10. Describe three variables that may influence test responses on personality inventories. How have test constructors tried to counteract one of these variables? Are such efforts completely successful? (536)

* 11. a) What is a fundamental need in the area of psychoanalytic assessment, and how is this addressed? (536)

   b) Indicate the assumption of projective tests. (537)

12. a) Along what dimensions is the Rorschach Test scored? (537)

*   b) Have the scoring systems for the Rorschach been shown to have predictive value? On what do many psychologists base their interpretations? (537)

* 13. a) What are stories on the TAT designed to reveal? Use the term "apperception" in your answer. (538)

b) What do psychologists look for when using the TAT? (539)

* 14. a) Indicate the general outcome of reliability and validity assessments of the Rorschach Test. (539)

* b) Similarly, how has the TAT fared in evaluations of reliability? (539)

* c) In terms of validity, what may be a difficulty with using the TAT in assessment? Cite an example. (539-540)

* d) In what terms do users of projective tests such as the Rorschach and TAT defend these instruments? (540)

* 15. a) What type of methods have social-learning psychologists developed for assessment and why? Cite two examples. (540)

b) Illustrate the use of self-observation in behavioral assessment with an example. (540)

c) Indicate two other classes of variables used in assessment by those who take a social-learning approach to personality. (540-541)

* 16. a) What is the one valid source of information in phenomenological assessment and what is the most common means for obtaining it? (541)

* b) What technique did Rogers employ in an attempt to obtain more reliable phenomenological data? Describe his procedure. (541)

c) Discuss the correlations and implications of a large self—ideal discrepancy as reflected by Rogers' Q-sort technique. (541)

* d) Indicate how Rogers used his Q-sort method to reflect the outcome of therapy noting the specific correlations reported. What are two ways in which such results may have been obtained? (541)

17. a) Discuss in detail the procedure used by Kelly in arriving at constructs with the Role Construct Repertory Test. (541-542)

b) In what two applications has the Rep Test proved valuable? (542-543)

Consistency Paradox

1. a) Outline the forms that the assumption of cross-situational consistency takes in type and trait theories, psychoanalytic theory, and phenomenological theory. (543)

* b) Describe the procedures, results, and conclusion of the classic Hartshorne and May investigation of consistency in personality in the 1920s. (543-544)

* c) What similar results and conclusion did Mischel present in the 1960s, based on his review of the related literature? (544)

* 2. a) State the *consistency paradox*. (544)

*   b)   Review the main subsections under the heading, *Consistency Paradox* , then state in your own words what is meant by each of the following terms as they refer to solutions to the paradox. (545-548, 550)

—*person-centered solution:*

—*aggregation solution:*

—*interactional solution:*

3.   a)   Give an example to illustrate Allport's person-centered solution to the consistency paradox. What is the "fallacy of the trait-centered approach to personality"? (545-546)

    b)   Use another example to show that our intuitions appear to follow the person-centered approach to consistency in behavior. (546)

4.   Provide several illustrations of your authors' statement that "a more accurate estimate of cross-situational consistency would be obtained if investigators combined several behavioral measures of the same trait to arrive at an aggregated score." (546-547)

*   5.   Discuss three forms of interactions to show how personal dispositions and situational variables may come together to account for apparent consistency in personality across situations. (548)

—reactive interaction:

—evocative interaction:

—proactive interaction:

Sample Quiz 14.1

1.   Endomorphic is to mesomorphic as: a) soft is to muscular; b) relaxed is to energetic; c) sociable is to assertive; d) all of the above.

2.   The personality psychologist who distinguished between common traits and personality dispositions was: a) Rogers; b) Allport; c) Eysenck; d) Cattell.

3.   Kelly is to the Rep Test as Cattell is to the: a) Rorschach Test; b) TAT; c) 16 PF; d) Q-sort.

4.   Trait theorists differ in terms of the numbers of traits they have identified through factor analysis because: a) different trait scales are put into their analyses initially; b) different kinds of data are analyzed by each theorist; c) different factor analytic techniques are employed; d) all of the above.

5.   With respect to Freud's psychosexual stages of development, children were assumed to observe the difference between males and females and to direct their

awakening sexual impulses toward the parent of the opposite sex during the: a) phallic stage; b) oral stage; c) anal stage; d) genital stage.

6. Psychoanalytic theory regards: a) human nature as essentially evil; b) human personality as relatively fixed by inborn drives and childhood experiences; c) psychological health as a function of firm ego control over the impulses of the id; d) all of the above.

7. Social-learning theory emphasizes _____ in the development of personality: a) classical conditioning; b) vicarious learning; c) operant conditioning; d) all of the above.

8. "Incongruence" in Rogers' system may be: a) between the self and experiences of reality; b) between the real self and the ideal self; c) between safety needs and esteem needs; d) both a and b.

9. People who make exceptional use of their potential have been referred to as: a) self-actualizers; b) ideal selves; c) person-centered types; d) unconditional self-regarders.

10. Projective tests: a) are questionnaires in which a person reports reactions or feelings in certain situations; b) require the person to sort cards containing personality statements into stacks ranging from least to most descriptive; c) involve the presentation of ambiguous stimuli that allow for a broad range of responses; d) are used primarily to assess "normal" personality traits, such as dominance and responsibility.

Sample Quiz 14.2

1. Discrete, qualitatively different categories are to continuous dimensions as: a) types are to traits; b) common traits are to personal dispositions; c) factors are to typologies; d) constructs are to inventories.

2. Factor analysis is: a) a statistical technique that groups together measures that are highly correlated with one another; b) the method employed by Sheldon in the identification of his somatotypes; c) the means by which Q-sorts are interpreted; d) George Kelly's method of identifying subjects' personal constructs.

3. The major criticism of the trait approach to personality has been that: a) most trait theorists over-emphasize the in-depth study of the individual; b) there is too much emphasis on the processes of personality functioning and not enough on the content of personality; c) no consensus can be seen emerging regarding the number of traits needed to describe individuals; d) perhaps traits do not exist at all.

4. Libido is: a) a storehouse of basic needs; b) the same as one's conscience; c) psychic energy; d) strategies by which anxiety is reduced.

5. Freud referred to the stages through which a person passes as he or she grows up as: a) psychosocial stages; b) psychosexual stages; c) psychobiological stages; d) psychoanalytic stages.

6. In Mischel's social-learning approach, the person variables, intellectual abilities and social and physical skills, are examples of: a) self-regulatory systems; b) competencies; c) expectancies; d) subjective values.

7. Another term for George Kelly's theory is: a) personal construct theory; b) self-actualization theory; c) person-centered theory; d) Kelly social-dimension theory.

8. When a researcher uses a theory to construct a test and to make predictions about performance, positive results from several converging studies serves to establish: a) construct validity; b) empirical validity; c) criterion validity; d) all of the above.

9. The MMPI: a) utilizes the rational method of test construction; b) is constructed by assuming specific personality traits and formulating questions to answer them; c) is derived by finding items that discriminate between criterion and control groups; d) both a and b.

10. In terms of reliability: a) the Rorschach Test does poorly, but the TAT is fairly good; b) the TAT does poorly, but the Rorschach fares well; c) both the Rorschach and the TAT do poorly; d) both the Rorschach and the TAT are fairly good.

Key, Chapter 14

Names

1. Gordon Allport
2. Raymond Cattell
3. Hans Eysenck
4. Sigmund Freud
5. Carl Rogers
6. Abraham Maslow
7. George Kelly

8. Rorschach Test
9. Thematic Apperception Test; TAT
10. Role Construct Repertory Test (or Rep Test)

Vocabulary and Details

1. somatotypes
2. type theories; typologies
3. trait theories
4. common traits; personal dispositions
5. factor analysis; factors
6. Sixteen Personality Factor Questionnaire (or 16 PF)

1. psychological determinism
2. id
3. pleasure
4. ego
5. reality
6. superego
7. libido
8. (ego) defense mechanisms
9. repression
10. psychosexual stages
11. Oedipal conflict
12. fixated

1. social-learning approach
2. operant conditioning; observational (or vicarious) learning; classical conditioning

1. phenomenological approach; humanistic psychology
2. self-actualization
3. person-centered therapy
4. self (or self-concept)
5. ideal; real
6. hierarchy of needs
7. self-actualizers
8. peak experiences
9. personal constructs; personal construct theory

1. reliable
2. valid; validity coefficient
3. Q-sort
4. personality inventory
5. Minnesota Multiphasic Personality Inventory; MMPI
6. California Psychological Inventory (or CPI)
7. projective tests

Sample Quiz 14.1

1. d, 504
2. b, 505-506
3. c, 507
4. d, 509
5. a, 514
6. d, 516-517
7. d, 519-520
8. d, 524
9. a, 525
10. c, 536

Sample Quiz 14.2

1. a, 504-505
2. a, 507
3. d, 510
4. c, 513
5. b, 514
6. b, 520
7. a, 527
8. a, 531
9. c, 534
10. a, 539

Stress and Coping

Learning Objectives

1. Be able to give a general definition of stress and to describe how the cognitive appraisal of an event determines the degree of stress experienced.

2. Be familiar with the physiological reactions to a stressful situation, including the complex responses of the two neuroendocrine systems controlled by the hypothalamus.

3. Be familiar with the various psychological reactions to a stressful situation. Be able to discuss Freud's theory of anxiety and the research on learned helplessness.

4. Be able to discuss the sources of stress, including life changes and their relationship to illness.

5. Know how predictability, controllability, and social supports affect the severity of stress. Be able to cite studies (drawn from various sections of the chapter) where the ability to control a stressor influenced the degree of stress experienced.

6. Distinguish between problem-focused coping and emotion-focused coping, giving examples of each.

7. Be able to describe Freud's concept of repression and the defense mechanisms that aid repression. Explain how the defense mechanisms of rationalization and intellectualization differ from rational and intellectual thinking and how reaction formation and projection differ in their defense against an undesirable trait

8. Be able to define psychosomatic disorders and behavioral medicine. Be familiar with the research relating heart disease to Type A behavior and to occupational and social stress.

9. Be familiar with the research showing the effects of stress on the body's immune system.

10. Be able to describe the characteristics of stress-resistant individuals.

Vocabulary and Details

Concept of Stress

1. _____ is a state that occurs when people a) are faced with events they perceive as endangering their physical and psychological well-being, and b) are unsure of their ability to deal with these events. (555)

2. In stress, the events that are perceived as threatening are called _____; the person's reactions to these events are called _____. (555-556)

3. The process of evaluating an event with respect to its significance for a person's well-being is termed _____. (555)

4. During stress, it is theorized that cognitive appraisal takes two forms: a) appraisal of the stressful situation, called _____, and b) appraisal of one's resources for coping with the threat, called _____. (556)

Physiological Reactions to Stress

1. The part of the brain that has been called the "stress center" is the _____. (557)

2. The hypothalamus activates two neuroendocrine systems in response to an emergency. In one case, it activates the _____ system of the autonomic nervous system resulting in the arousal of a wide range of physiological stress responses. (557)

3. In the other case, the hypothalamus signals the _____ as the first step in a complex of events within the _____ system. (557)

4. A critical hormone in the adrenal-cortical system, sometimes called the body's "major stress hormone," is _____. (557)

5. The entire innate complex of internal and external responses to stress prepare an organism to fight or flee and thus has been called the _____. (557)

Psychological Reactions to Stress

1. "Normal" anxiety that motivates a person to deal with threat adaptively is called _____; anxiety that is out of proportion to the danger posed by threat and that reduces the ability to cope is called _____. (561)

2. When aggressive emotional reactions are directed away from a source of frustration we may speak of _____ aggression. (562)

3. When animals are exposed to repeated unavoidable and inescapable aversive events (such as painful shocks), they may fail to respond to avoidable aversive stimuli in later situations; this is the phenomenon termed _____. (563-564)

Sources of Stress

1. Immediately after a traumatic event, survivors may experience disorientation, an inability to initiate tasks, followed later by anxiety and an inability to concentrate; together these symptoms may be termed the _____. (566)

2. More serious, a persisting syndrome called _____, including emotional numbness, intruding memories and dreams of the trauma, and anxiety or guilt may develop immediately or some time after a period of severe stress. (566)

3. One well-known measure of stress in terms of life changes is the _____. (567)

4. When a person must choose between incompatible, or mutually exclusive goals or actions, we speak of _____. (570)

Coping with Stress

1. The process by which a person attempts to manage stress is called _____. (573)

2. If an individual evaluates a stressful situation and does something to change or avoid it, we speak of _____. (573)

3. If, on the other hand, an individual attempts to deal with stress-induced anxiety without dealing directing with the stressor, we speak of _____. (573)

4. Freud called unconscious processes that defend a person against anxiety by distorting reality in some way _____. (574)

5. In Freud's view, the most basic and important of defense mechanisms is _____, the exclusion of painful or frightening impulses from consciousness. (574)

Stress and Illness

1. Physical disorders in which emotions are believed to play a central role are termed _____. (578)

2. Psychology and medicine join forces in the interdisciplinary field of _____, which seeks to relate psychological, social, and biological variables to causes of illness and ways to promote health. (578)

3. The study of the relationship between psychological variables and the body's immune system is called _____. (583)

Ideas and Concepts

Concept of Stress

* 1. a) Do researchers agree on the definition of stress? (555)

   b) Give some examples of stressors. (555)

*Basic ideas and concepts

*   c)   Cite four classes of stress responses. (555)

*   d)   What is a "striking" feature about the experience of stress? Cite some examples. (555)

*   2.   a)   What fundamental question is asked in primary appraisal? Distinguish among three kinds of judgments about events at which we may arrive through primary appraisal. (556)

*   b)   In turn, distinguish among three kinds of judgments regarding the nature of events appraised to be stressful. Include examples. (556)

*   c)   What question is answered by secondary appraisal? Cite examples. (556)

Physiological Reactions to Stress

1.   Describe some of the common physiological responses in emergency situations and their biological advantages. (557)

*   2.   In the table below, indicate the functions of each of the portions of the physiological stress response. Be sure you can trace the relationships between the respective systems, organs, and hormones. See also Figure 15-1. (557-558)

sympathetic system	Functions
adrenal medulla	
epinephrine	
norepinephrine	
adrenal-cortical system	Functions
pituitary gland	
ACTH	
adrenal cortex	

*   3.   Why do stress researchers argue that many activities included within the fight-or-flight response are not very adaptive in the modern-day environment? (557-558)

*   4.   a)   What was the original view of the physiological stress response, and how has that view changed? (558)

*   b) Distinguish between *distress* and *effort* during stress. Discuss Frankenhauser's evidence on the relationship between sympathetic and adrenal-cortical activity indicating which hormones are prevalent in each case. (558-559)

—distress:

—effort:

*   5.   a)   What can be the positive effects of repeated exposure to intermittent stressors? Use the term "physiological toughness," and cite some related data. (559)

      b)   Which aspects of the physiological stress response appear to be correlated with beneficial performance effects and which with negative performance effects? (559)

Psychological Reactions to Stress

*   1.   a)   What is the relationship between stress and cognitive functioning? Use *test anxiety* as an example. (559-560)

      b)   To what behaviors do people resort under stress? Illustrate and see if you can think of a related instance from your own life. (560)

*   2.   What is the primary emotional response to a threatening situation? (560)

*   3.   a)   Discuss Freud's classic view of objective and neurotic anxiety. What is your authors' view of the common distinction between "fear" and "anxiety" that stemmed from Freud's notions? (561)

*   b)   Further develop Freud's views on anxiety using the terms *id impulses, ego, superego,* and *defensive maneuvers*. Include an example. (561)

   4.   Discuss two alternative forms of explanation for a person who reacts with inordinate anxiety to a situation that others may view as mildly stressful. (561-562)

—association approach:

—loss of control (helplessness) approach:

*   5.   Discuss each of the following situations involving aggressive responses to stressors; use examples when they are helpful. (562-563)

—responses to laboratory stressors:

—frustration:

—direct versus displaced aggression:

*   6.   a)   Besides active aggression, what is another common (but opposite) response to stress? (563)

      b)   Discuss one line of explanation for apathy as it may develop in children. (563)

Stress and Coping   217

*   c)   Outline the procedures and results of animal experiments dealing with the kind of apathy called learned helplessness. (563-564)

          d)   To account for human reactions to uncontrollable events, how must the concept of learned helplessness be expanded? (564)

Sources of Stress

    1.   List the first four subheadings for this section to help you to organize categories of stressors. (565-570)

*   2.   a)   Provide some data to show that post-traumatic stress disorder may last a long time after a traumatic event. (566)

*   b)   When was post-traumatic stress disorder recognized as a diagnostic category and why? (566)

          c)   Cite some possible reasons for the high incidence of post-traumatic stress disorder among Vietnam veterans. (567)

*   3.   a)   Describe how Holmes and Rahe put together their Life Events Scale. (567)

          b)   Does everyone assign the same priority to the individual events in the scale? Discuss. (567)

*   c)   How are scores on the Life Events Scale established? What is considered a "high" life-change score and with what does it appear to correlate? (As a personal exercise, you might try to determine your own score from Table 15-1.) (567-568)

*   d)   How did Holmes and Rahe account for the relationship between high life-change scores and disorders? Discuss in detail four reasons why their hypothesis has been challenged by other researchers. (568)

*   4.   How have some psychologists dealt with the issue of whether positive life changes are stressful, and what has been found? (568)

    5.   What *does* appear to be the relationship between life changes and health? (568)

*   6.   a)   In addition to significant life events, what is another possible source of stress and what have researchers found when examining the impact of this variable? (569)

          b)   Does everyone respond to "daily hassles" the same? Cite some data. (569)

*   c)   What personality characteristic appears to correlate with resistance to the effects of hassles and why? (569-570)

*   7.   Discuss the way in which serious conflicts may evolve in each of the following motive clashes. (570-571)

          —independence versus dependence:

          —intimacy versus isolation:

218   Chapter 15

—cooperation versus competition:

—impulse expression versus moral standards:

* 8. a) Among the situational factors that influence stress, show with laboratory examples that both animals and people prefer *predictable* to *unpredictable* aversive events. (571)

   b) In what two ways can the effects of predictability be understood? (571)

   c) Cite some real-life examples of the effects of unpredictability on human health. (571-572)

* 9. a) Discuss two interesting demonstrations of the effects of *controllability* upon human stress reactions. (572)

*   b) What was a difference in the procedures of these studies that enabled the researchers to show that it is the *perception* of controllability that is important? (572)

* 10. Provide examples to show that *social support* can reduce the effects of stress in the case of personal loss or community disasters, but that sometimes families or friends can have the opposite impact. (572-573)

Coping with Stress

1. a) Give some examples of problem-focused and emotion-focused coping. Can you think of any instances from your own life? (573)

*   b) When is emotion-focused coping more likely to occur? What about problem-focused coping? (573-574)

   c) Distinguish by example between behavioral and cognitive strategies for emotion-focused coping. (574)

2. a) What do your authors mean when they say that all defense mechanisms involve some "self-deception"? (574)

* b) Be sure that you can recognize each of the defense mechanisms in the following table by providing a definition for those listed in bold type and examples for all. (574-577)

Defense Mechanism	Definition	Example
repression	(See *Vocabulary and Details*)	
rationalization		
reaction formation		
projection		
intellectualization		
denial		

* 3. a) Distinguish between repression and **suppression** . (575)

*   b) Did Freud think that repression was always effective? Explain, and indicate the relationship between this conclusion and the other defense mechanisms. (575)

   4. a) What two things does rationalization do for us? (575)

      b) Cite a demonstration of rationalization in a hypnotized subject. (575)

   5. When might denial be better than facing facts? Exemplify. (577)

* 6. List some of the strategies employed in problem-focused coping. (577)

      —outward-directed:

      —inward-directed:

   7. a) What kinds of strategies do most people use in dealing with the stresses of everyday life? (577-578)

      b) Cite examples of times when problem- and emotion-focused coping can facilitate each other and impede each other. (578)

Stress and Illness

* 1. a) Are people with psychosomatic disorders really "sick" and in need of medical attention? Explain. (578)

220   Chapter 15

b) What hypothesis was originally advanced with regard to the role of attitudes in certain disorders, and what has been the outcome of efforts to research those relationships? Is there any exception? (578)

* 2. a) What is the leading cause of death and chronic illness in the United States, and what three physical variables promote this type of disease? (579)

* b) Be able to characterize the behavior pattern that also has been positively correlated with coronary heart disease, along with the opposite behavior pattern. (579)

— *Type A* behavior pattern:

— *Type B* behavior pattern:

* 3. a) Outline the methods and results of an early large-scale study of the role of Type A behaviors in heart disease. (579-580)

* b) What characteristics that were said to define the Type A individual were not supported in recent studies of the role of Type A behaviors in heart disease and what variable was implicated? Cite two studies of professional populations that further implicate this variable. (581)

* c) Discuss the possible role of hostility in heart disease from the standpoint of the sympathetic and parasympathetic nervous systems. (581)

* 4. Describe a recent study aimed at determining the beneficial effects of modifying Type A behavior including a) the specific behaviors that were targeted for change and b) the outcome in terms of the critical dependent variable. (581-582)

* 5. a) Indicate the two main psychological factors that contribute to the stressfulness of jobs. Which type of occupations are the most stressful? (582)

b) Cite the results of one study of these factors in the workplace. What additional factor was found to contribute to cardiovascular risk in this study? (582)

c) Outline the relationships for women between cardiovascular health, working, and raising children. (582)

* d) Discuss an animal study that linked disruptions of the social environment to cardiac disease factors. Which animals in particular showed the largest effects in this study, and what conclusion may be drawn from this effect? (582-583)

* 6. a) What is the immune system and what does it do? (583)

* b) Summarize the results of four studies that related the effects of stressful events to immune responses. (584-585)

* 7. a) Indicate a psychological factor that can *reduce* the effect of stress on immune functioning. (586)

* b) Outline the procedures of a series of animal studies designed to study the role of controllability of electric shock in stress responding. See also Figure 15-2, and be sure you understand what is meant by the term *yoked control*. (586)

* c) What are *T-cells*? Discuss the effects of controllability on T-cells found in one study using the yoked control design outlined in b). (586)

   d) Discuss the effects of controllability in another study in which tumors were implanted into rats. (586)

8. Provide some additional evidence to show the role of each of the following independent variables in immune responses. (587)

   —perception of control:

   —loneliness:

* 9. a) Outline the methods of the Kobasa study that identified the role of three cognitive variables in resistance to stress. (588)

   b) What is one issue that was left unanswered by this study, and how was it addressed in subsequent research? Which of the three variables that again emerged as significant was the most important? (587-588)

* c) Discuss how the three characteristics of the stress-resistant individual interrelate with other factors dealt with in this chapter. (588)

   —commitment:

   —control:

   —challenge:

Sample Quiz 15.1

1. Stress occurs when an individual: a) is faced with endangering events; b) is unsure of his or her ability to cope; c) feels anxious; d) both a and b.

2. As a result of primary appraisal we may judge an event as: a) stressful; b) irrelevant; c) benign positive; d) all of the above.

3. The body's "stress center" is the: a) adrenal gland; b) reticular system; c) hypothalamus; d) pituitary gland.

4. Which of the following is *true?* a) The primary emotional response to stress is depression. b) Intermittent stress with recovery periods may lead to stress tolerance. c) Your authors' view is that there are important differences between fear and anxiety, rendering a distinction between them essential. d) All of the above.

5. Aggressive emotional reactions directed away from a source of frustration are called: a) displaced aggression; b) nondirected aggression; c) blind rage; d) indecisive anger.

6. In the Overmier and Seligman study of learned helplessness in dogs: a) the initial training provided unavoidable electric shocks; b) when later opportunities to escape electric shock were available, most animals developed an effective jumping response; c) an excellent model was provided for the effects of uncontrollable events in most research with human subjects; d) both a and c.

7. Post traumatic stress disorder includes: a) intruding memories and dreams of a traumatic event; b) anxiety; c) numbing; d) all of the above.

8. Attempts to deal with stress-induced anxiety without dealing directly with the stressor are called: a) cognitive appraisal; b) emotion-focused coping; c) problem-focused coping; d) psychoimmunology.

9. Freud maintained that the most basic of the defense mechanisms was: a) rationalization; b) repression; c) reaction formation; d) denial.

10. Social support is to commitment as competency is to: a) commitment; b) control; c) challenge; d) helplessness.

Sample Quiz 15.2

1. A stressor is: a) a hormone released by the adrenal-cortical system; b) a general physiological response to stressful situations; c) an event perceived as threatening; d) any event endangering a person's well-being, whether or not it is perceived as such.

2. The innate pattern of physiological responses to stressors has been called the _____ syndrome: a) bite-or-fright; b) frightful-sight; c) might-we-fight; d) fight-or-flight.

3. In stress, the hormones epinephrine and norepinephrine are secreted by the: a) adrenal cortex; b) pituitary gland; c) hypothalamus; d) adrenal medulla.

4. The primary emotional response to a threatening situation is: a) depression; b) anger; c) anxiety; d) discouragement.

5. Anxiety that is out of proportion to the danger posed by a threat and which reduces the ability to cope is called: a) psychotic anxiety; b) neurotic anxiety; c) objective anxiety; d) subjective anxiety.

6. In a study evaluating the importance of daily hassles in producing stress it was found that, compared to major life events, the minor frustrations and annoyances of daily life correlated _____ with emotional and physical health: a) less highly; b) more highly; c) equally highly; d) none of the above; daily hassles did not correlate with health at all.

7. Which of the following is *false?* a) People prefer predictable to unpredictable aversive events. b) Social support can reduce the effects of stress, but sometimes

social interactions have the opposite effect. c) It is clear from research that it is actual lack of controllability over aversive events and not merely the perception of controllability that is important in human stress reactions. d) Emotion-focused coping is more likely to occur when a person is already experiencing stress and has decided that nothing can be done to modify the stressor.

8. A professor who sexually harasses students spends a great deal of time talking about how the females in his class come on to him in provocative ways. This would be an example of the defense mechanism called: a) intellectualization; b) repression; c) reaction formation; d) projection.

9. Behavioral medicine is a(n): a) branch of medicine only; b) branch of psychology only; c) branch of neither medicine nor psychology, but an independent field in its own right; d) interdisciplinary field of both medicine and psychology.

10. Which of the following characteristics of Type A individuals has been found to consistently relate to heart disease, even in studies finding no overall relationship between Type A behavior and coronary illness: a) hostility; b) time urgency; c) competitiveness; d) all of the above.

Key, Chapter 15

Vocabulary and Details

1. stress
2. stressors; stress responses
3. cognitive appraisal
4. primary appraisal; secondary appraisal

1. hypothalamus
2. sympathetic
3. pituitary gland; adrenal-cortical
4. adrenocorticotrophic hormone (or ACTH)
5. fight-or-flight response

1. objective anxiety; neurotic anxiety
2. displaced
3. learned helplessness

1. disaster syndrome
2. post-traumatic stress disorder
3. Life Events Scale
4. conflict

1. coping
2. problem-focused coping
3. emotion-focused coping
4. defense mechanisms
5. repression

1. psychosomatic disorders
2. behavioral medicine
3. psychoimmunology

Sample Quiz 15.1

1. d, 555
2. d, 556
3. c, 557
4. b, 559-561
5. a, 562
6. a, 563-564
7. d, 566
8. b, 573
9. b, 574
10. c, 588

Sample Quiz 15.2

1. c, 555
2. d, 557
3. d, 557
4. c, 560
5. b, 561
6. b, 569
7. c, 573
8. d, 576
9. d, 578
10. a, 581

Stress and Coping   225

16

Abnormal Psychology

Learning Objectives

1. Know the four criteria that may be used in defining abnormality, as well as the characteristics that are considered indicative of normality.

2. Understand the advantages and disadvantages of classifying abnormal behavior into categories. Be familiar with the DSM-III-R system of classification, including the variables covered in an individual diagnosis and some of the major categories.

3. Be able to describe four types of anxiety disorders and show how their symptoms either express anxiety directly or reflect attempts to control anxious feelings.

4. Be able to explain the development of anxiety disorders from the standpoint of psychoanalytic, behavioral, and cognitive theories. Know what research on biological factors has contributed thus far to our understanding of these disorders.

5. Be able to describe the two major mood disorders and to compare psychoanalytic, behavioral, and cognitive theories of depression.

6. Be familiar with the evidence indicating that genetic and biochemical factors play a role in mood disorders.

7. Know the defining characteristics of schizophrenia and give examples of each.

8. Be familiar with the research on the causes of schizophrenia; be able to discuss the probable contributions of genetic, biochemical, social, and psychological factors.

9. Understand the role of vulnerability and stress in the development of mental disorders; describe how studies of children at risk for schizophrenia are investigating these two factors.

10. Be able to define personality disorders; know the defining characteristics and probable causes of antisocial personalities.

227

Names

1. An influential cognitive theory of depression, devised by _____, emphasizes the role of distorted thinking and negative and self-critical attitudes as the cause for the disorder. (612)

2. Another cognitive theorist of depression is _____, whose theory stresses the role of expectations of future *helplessness*. (613)

Vocabulary and Details

Abnormal Behavior

1. Literally, behavior that is "away from the statistical norm" is _____; but a more satisfactory definition must take into account a number of additional criteria, including deviation from social norms, maladapativeness, and personal distress. (591-592)

2. The classification of mental disorders used by most mental health professionals is the _____, more commonly cited by its abbreviation _____. (594)

3. Traditionally, the term _____ referred to a group of disorders characterized by serious anxiety, unhappiness, and maladaptive behaviors, but DSM-III-R separates such disorders into several categories. (596)

4. Traditionally, the term _____ applied to more serious mental disorders characterized by disturbance of thought processes, loss of contact with reality, inability to cope, and requiring hospitalization. (596)

5. Rather than a category of disorders called psychoses, DSM-III-R, recognizes that people with serious disturbances may exhibit _____ during their disorder. (596)

6. Psychotic behaviors may include a) _____, false sensory experiences, such as voices or visions, and b) _____, that is, false beliefs. (596-597)

Anxiety Disorders

1. Disorders in which anxiety is the main symptom or is experienced when the individual attempts to control certain maladaptive behaviors are called _____. (597)

2. _____ is characterized by constant tension and worry, somatic complaints, and difficulty in concentration. (598)

3. Episodes of acute and overwhelming apprehension and terror recur in the disturbance called _____. (598)

4. Intense fear to a stimulus or situation that most people do not consider dangerous is called a _____. (598)

5. When a person feels compelled to think about unwanted things or to carry out unwanted acts, we speak of an _____ disorder. (600)

6. Persistent intrusions of unwelcome thoughts or images are called _____; irresistible urges to carry out certain acts or rituals are called _____. (600)

7. The idea that organisms are biologically predisposed to be more readily classically conditioned to some stimuli than to others is termed _____. (603)

8. The tranquilizers, Valium and Librium, are in the class of antianxiety drugs called the _____. (606)

Mood Disorders

1. When a person is severely depressed or manic (wildly elated), we speak of _____. (607)

2. In one form of mood disorders, called _____, the individual is extremely sad and dejected without mania. (607)

3. In the other form of mood disorders, called _____, periods of severe depression alternate with periods of mania, usually with a return to a normal state in between. (607)

4. The likelihood that two twins will have a characteristic, such as depression, given that one twin does is called the _____. (614)

5. Two neurotransmitters believed to have a role in mood disorders are _____ and _____. (614)

6. Two major classes of antidepressant drugs that influence the effects of norepinephrine and serotonin are _____ and _____. (614)

Schizophrenia

1. The term _____ applies to a group of disorders characterized by severe personality disorganization, distortion of reality, and an inability to function in daily life. (616)

2. Beliefs that society would disagree with or regard as misinterpretations of reality are called _____. (619)

3. When it is falsely believed that one's thoughts are having an undue influence on others or that one's thoughts, feelings, and actions are caused by external forces, we speak of _____. (619)

4. False beliefs that others are threatening or plotting against one are called _____. (619)

5. False beliefs that one is powerful or important are termed _____. (619)

6. A person who has delusions of persecution is said to be _____. (619)

7. The most common kind of hallucinations in schizophrenia are _____ (visual/auditory). (619-620)

8. The extreme absorption in one's own thoughts and fantasies that occurs in schizophrenia is also called _____. (621)

9. The neurotransmitter _____ is active in the limbic system of the brain, an area that is implicated in the regulation of emotion. (624)

10. The _____ proposes that schizophrenia is caused by too much dopamine at certain synapses in the brain. (624)

11. It is believed that the drugs called _____ relieve the symptoms of schizophrenia by affecting the usable dopamine in the brain. (625)

Personality Disorders

1. Long-standing and inflexible patterns of maladaptive behavior that impair the individual's ability to function are called _____. (628)

2. Among the 11 types of personality disorders categorized in DSM-III-R, _____ refers to the type of individual who is preoccupied with fantasies of success, who constantly seeks admiration and attention, and who is insensitive to the needs of others. (628)

3. Another personality disorder is _____, characterized by a passive orientation, indecisiveness, irresponsibility, and requiring continual support from others. (628)

4. The individual classified as having an _____ shows little guilt for misdoings or concern with others' needs, is impulsive, seeks thrills and excitement, and may often be in trouble with the law. (629, 634)

Ideas and Concepts

Abnormal Behavior

* 1. a) Is there general agreement on the meaning of "abnormal behavior"? (591)

* b) Discuss the applications of each of the following four criteria to the definition of abnormal behavior, indicating limitations where possible. Which of these criteria by itself provides a satisfactory description of abnormality? (591-592)

—*deviation from statistical norms* (use the term *statistical frequency*):

—*deviation from social norms*:

—*maladaptiveness of behavior*:

—*personal distress*:

*Basic terms and concepts

*   2. Similarly, describe six criteria for normality. Do these characteristics make sharp distinctions between normal and abnormal behavior? Explain. (592-593)

    3. Are most mentallly ill people also creative? Discuss. (593)

*   4. Discuss three advantages and two disadvantages of classifying abnormal behavior. (593-594)

    5. a) What does DSM-III-R provide for the task of diagnosis of an individual? (595)

*   b) Outline the five axes of DSM-III-R. (Why were axes I and II separated?) (595-596)

*   6. a) Discuss the reasons why DSM-III-R does not include the traditional categories of neuroses and psychoses among the classified disorders. (596)

*   b) Indicate the categories of DSM-III-R that now include the disorders formerly called neuroses and the disorders formerly called psychoses. (596)

    7. a) From Table 16-2, note the prevalence of several serious forms of disorders. Which are the first and second most common disorders in the group, respectively? (596-597)

        b) Cite some additional statistics on the prevalence of serious abnormal behaviors in the population, noting sex and age differences. (597)

Anxiety Disorders

*   1. After reading this section, organize the scrambled terms below into an outline to help you to recall the several forms of anxiety disorders in DSM-III-R. (597-602)

social phobia	obsessive-compulsive disorders
panic disorders	simple phobia
generalized anxiety	phobias
agoraphobia	

    2. When is anxiety considered abnormal? (597)

*   3. a) What is the main symptom of generalized anxiety and panic disorders? (See also 4a below.) (597)

        b) What is the source of the bodily symptoms that occur in panic attacks? (598)

*   c) Why is the anxiety in generalized anxiety and panic attacks called "free-floating"? (598)

*   4. a) When is anxiety experienced in the course of phobic and obsessive-compulsive disorders? (597)

        b) Do persons with phobias realize that their anxiety is irrational? What is the effect of this knowledge? (598)

*   c) Discuss and exemplify the relationship between age and some phobias. (599)

Abnormal Psychology   231

*   5. a) Define and provide an example of each of the following kinds of phobias. After reading this subsection, indicate the treatability of each kind. (599)

—*simple phobia:*

—*social phobia:*

—*agoraphobia:*

b) Describe the history typical of agoraphobia and the variety of related fears. What personality characteristic may accompany this disorder? (599)

6. Compared with people with phobias, what do those with compulsions fear? (600)

*   7. a) Can you think of obsessive thoughts or ritualistic behaviors of your own? What distinguishes between these and the activities that define obsessive-compulsive disorders? Give examples. (600-601)

*   b) Indicate the effect of routines or rituals during "normal" stress and contrast with the effects of obsessive-compulsive behaviors. (601)

c) Is an obsessive-compulsive personality merely a latent form of obsessive-compulsive disorder? Explain, noting the differences between individuals in both categories. (601-602)

*   8. For each of the following perspectives on anxiety, state the general approach in your own words and, where possible, indicate how the view would apply to generalized anxiety, phobias, and obsessive-compulsive disorders. Use examples when they are helpful. (602-606)

	Description	Applications to Disorders
psychoanalytic perspective		
behavioral perspective		
cognitive perspective		
biological perspective		

* 9. a) Using examples, discuss the application of the classical conditioning paradigm in the behavioral perspective on phobias. What problems emerge with this approach? (603)

*   b) How are such problems handled with the notion of prepared conditioning? Illustrate with examples. (603)

*   c) Discuss an experiment that demonstrated prepared classical conditioning of fears in human subjects. (603-604)

       d) How does the notion of prepared conditioning also account for the course of extinction of certain fears? Cite another related experiment. (604)

* 10. From the behavioral perspective, indicate a source of phobias in addition to direct classical conditioning. (604)

* 11. Do anxiety disorders tend to run in families and to what degree? Does this prove that anxiety disorders are hereditary? Explain. (605)

* 12. a) Discuss the role of the brain chemical, *cholecystokinin*, in panic disorder. In what other way can panic attacks be initiated? (605)

       b) Does your answer to a) necessarily imply that panic disorder is strictly biochemical in origin? Discuss. (605)

       c) Cite another finding that suggests a biological basis for obsessive-compulsive disorders. (605-606)

* 13. a) What recent evidence supports the likelihood that generalized and specific anxieties involve the complex interactions of neurotransmitters in the brain? (606)

*   b) Discuss three specific effects at the benzodiazepine receptor site that implicate the role of natural substances in both anxiety and the inhibition of anxiety. (606-607)

Mood Disorders

* 1. a) What are common precipitators of "normal" depression and what two characteristics define abnormal depression? (607)

*   b) Describe the four sets of symptoms of depression. Which set is the most salient? (607-608)

       —emotional (mood) symptoms:

       —cognitive symptoms:

       —motivational symptoms:

       —physiological symptoms:

* 2. Discuss the data on the duration and recurrence of depression. (608)

3. a) What is another term for bipolar disorders? (608)

*   b) Describe the characteristics of the manic individual. (608-609)

*   c) Indicate the prevalence of mania by itself and of bipolar disorders generally. (609)

*   d) How does manic-depression differ from other mood disorders? (609)

* 4. For each of the following perspectives, indicate the theoretical source(s) of depression and illustrate with an example or related observation. (609-614)

	Sources of Depression	Examples or Observations
psychoanalytic perspective		
behavioral perspective		
cognitive perspective		
biological perspective		(See item 9 below.)

* 5. a) In the psychoanalytic approach, what complicates the reaction to loss in people who are prone to depression? Give an example. (609)

       b) Discuss the psychoanalytic view on the role of self-esteem in depression. (609-610)

*   c) Indicate the status of evidence with regard to the psychoanalytic perspective on depression. (610-611)

* 6. Discuss the "vicious cycle" of activities and rewards outlined by the behavioral perspective on depression. (612)

* 7. a) Characterize the cognitions of depressed persons according to Beck's theory. Use examples. (612-613)

* b) On what experiments did Seligman base his cognitive approach to depression? Discuss the three dimensions that contribute to the sense of helplessness in depressed individuals. Give examples. (613)

—*internal-external:*

—*stable-unstable:*

—*global-specific:*

* c) Based on this analysis, what specific kinds of predictions will characterize a depressed person when unfortunate events occur? (613)

* 8. a) Does research clearly show that depressive cognitions cause depression? Discuss the outcomes of studies showing each of the following. (613-614)

—correlations between helpless cognitive style and depression:

—the relationship between depressive cognitions and effects of a depressive event:

—the role of depressive cognitions in recovery from depression:

* b) What is another variable that may account for depression more effectively than the interpretation of negative events? (614)

* 9. a) Cite the concordance rates for manic-depressive disorder and depression. Therefore, which disorder appears to have a stronger genetic component? (614)

* b) Discuss the hypothesis that implicates norepinephrine and serotonin levels in depression and mania. Cite some related observations. (614)

* c) Similarly, discuss the possible mechanisms by which two classes of drugs, the MAO inhibitors and the tricyclics, may exert their antidepressant effects. (614-615)

* d) Do the antidepressant drugs produce their effects by modifying the *levels* of relevant neurotransmitters? Discuss the emerging evidence regarding the long-term effects of antidepressants. (615)

10. On what issue concerning mood disorders is there no doubt and what is one question that remains unresolved in this area? (615)

* 11. a) Discuss the concept of ***vulnerability*** to depression, indicating two classes of variables that may be important. (615)

b) List other factors that may play a role in vulnerability. Which of these may be the most important in women, and how do we know? (615-616)

Schizophrenia

1. a) Describe the patterns of onset of schizophrenia. (617)

*   b) Summarize the characteristics of schizophrenia outlined in each of the following subsections of your chapter. (617-621)

—disturbances of thought and attention (use the term "word salad" and note the general difficulty in schizophrenic thought):

—disturbances of perception:

—disturbances of affect:

—withdrawal from reality:

—decreased ability to function:

*   2. a) What does it mean that schizophrenic patients show disturbances in both the *form of thought* and the *content of thought*? (619)

b) Cite examples to show disturbances in the content of schizophrenic thought in terms of lack of insight and delusions. (619)

*   3. a) Discuss evidence on the genetic risks of developing schizophrenia from studies of related and unrelated persons. What result obtained with identical twins also shows the importance of environmental variables? (622)

*   b) Discuss two studies concerning the way that schizophrenia may be genetically transmitted. Taken together, what do these results suggest about the nature of the disorder, and what is yet another possibility? (622-623)

4. What method has been used to study the possibility of biochemical bases for schizophrenia, and what is one of the major problems in this area? Cite examples. (623)

*   5. a) In line with the dopamine hypothesis, indicate two possible reasons for excess dopamine in certain areas of the brain in schizophrenia. (624)

*   b) Discuss the evidence relative to antipsychotic drug effects that lends support to the dopamine hypothesis. (624)

*   c) Relatedly, how does evidence on the effects of amphetamines favor the dopamine hypothesis? (624)

*   6. a) Indicate a problem with the dopamine hypothesis. Outline new methods by which possible functional or structural problems in the brains of schizophrenia sufferers are studied in the search for alternative explanations for this group of disorders. (624)

*   b) What results have been obtained to date and to what speculations concerning the origins of schizophrenia have these led ? (624-625)

*   7. a) From the social and psychological perspective on schizophrenia, what observation has been consistently made on the incidence of the disorder? Discuss the following three explanations for this fact. Which have been supported? (625)

236   Chapter 16

—differential diagnosis:

—downward drift:

—increased stress:

b) What has been a major problem in the attempt to study the psychological factors in schizophrenia by focusing on relationships within families? (625)

c) Discuss the results of a related study on family communication problems. (626)

8. a) Outline the procedures of another study that attempted to address the problem indicated in 7b). (626)

b) Indicate the results of this research noting in particular the characteristics of parents in those families in which the highest incidence of schizophrenia occurred. (626-627)

c) Why do your authors say that the causal variables for schizophrenia in family interactions are still not clear from this research? Nevertheless, what is known? (627)

* 9. a) How are children who are at high risk for schizophrenia usually defined? Describe the methods of a number of longitudinal studies of such children conducted in efforts to determine the role of vulnerability and stress in the disorder. (627)

* b) Discuss four ways in which the subjects who developed schizophrenic symptoms differed from matched control subjects in these studies. (628)

Personality Disorders

1. In what respects do personality disorders differ in general from mood and anxiety disorders or schizophrenia? (628)

* 2. a) What was the former term for "antisocial personality"? Why is either term somewhat misleading when applied to most people who display antisocial behaviors? (628-629)

* b) Among the features of antisocial personality (or "sociopaths") discussed in your text, what two stand out as the most characteristic? (629)

3. Is the individual with an antisocial personality usually a product of an antisocial family environment? Discuss, and indicate the general status of theory in this area. (629)

* 4. a) Insofar as biological factors in antisocial personality are concerned, discuss an experiment demonstrating evidence of low anxiety in sociopathic subjects. (630-631)

*   b) Cite additional evidence obtained from studies in prisons that lend support to the hypothesis that the antisocial personality is characterized by an underrreactive autonomic nervous system. What other interpretation is possible? (631)

*   c) Outline the explanation for the features of antisocial personality provided in your text. (631)

5. a) In terms of parent-child factors in antisocial personality, discuss the psychoanalytic interpretation of this disorder. Does this view conform to the data? (631)

*   b) Explain the learning theory model by which we might account for antisocial personality. How does this accord with at least two characteristics of sociopaths? (631-632)

    c) Discuss a longitudinal study of individuals, some of whom were later given a diagnosis of antisocial personality. What findings lend support to the learning model for this disorder? (632-633)

Sample Quiz 16.1

1. The criterion for abnormality that takes into account whether or not a behavior has adverse effects on society is: a) deviation from statistical norms; b) deviation from social norms; c) maladaptiveness; d) personal distress.

2. Episodes of acute apprehension and terror are defining features of: a) manic episodes; b) delusions of influence; c) disturbances of perception; d) panic disorders.

3. We would expect phobias related to heights and enclosed places to be most severe in: a) children; b) people in their 20s; c) people in their 40s and 50's; d) the elderly.

4. The approach to anxiety that emphasizes what people *think* about situations and potential dangers is the: a) behavioral perspective; b) psychoanalytic perspective; c) biological perspective; d) cognitive perspective.

5. Bipolar disorder is characterized by: a) periods of severe depression; b) alternation between obsessions and compulsions; c) periods of mania; d) both a and c.

6. The theorist who stresses the role of helplessness in the origins of depression is: a) Beck; b) Freud; c) Seligman; d) Atkinson.

7. We would do best to treat a mood disorder with: a) cholecystokinin; b) an MAO inhibitor; c) an antipsychotic drug; d) a benzodiazepine.

8. The most general difficulty in schizophrenic thought appears to be: a) filtering out irrelevant stimuli; b) downward drift; c) auditory hallucinations; d) repetitive words and phrases.

9. Extreme absorption in one's own thoughts and fantasies in schizophrenia is called: a) narcissism; b) phobic self-involvement; c) autism; d) inward drift.

10. Longitudinal studies of children at risk for schizophrenia have shown that, relative to high-risk children who do develop the disorder, high-risk children who do not become schizophrenic: a) are less likely to have been separated from their mother at an early age; b) are more likely to display inappropriate behavior in school; c) have fathers less likely to have been hospitalized; d) are more likely to have suffered birth complications.

Sample Quiz 16.2

1. Literally, the term "abnormal" means: a) causing of distress; b) away from the norm; c) socially unacceptable; d) maladaptive.

2. The main reason neuroses and psychoses do not occur as major categories in DSM-III-R is that: a) there is no essential difference between neurotic and psychotic behavior; b) the terms are too broad and include a number of mental disorders with quite dissimilar symptoms; c) the terms do not imply enough about origins or treatment; d) none of the above; neuroses and psychoses define the first two axes of the DSM-III-R classification scheme.

3. False beliefs that characterize many psychotics are called: a) delusions; b) obsessions; c) compulsions; d) hallucinations.

4. Irresistable urges to carry out certain acts or rituals are called: a) compulsions; b) obsessions; c) psychotic behaviors; d) drives.

5. According to the _____ perspective, phobias are seen as protecting the individual from recognizing the true source of his or her anxiety by displacing that anxiety onto objects or situations that can be avoided: a) biological; b) psychoanalytic; c) cognitive; d) behavioral.

6. It has been found that injections of the brain chemical cholecystokinin will produce panic attacks in: a) normal individuals; b) phobics; c) individuals who suffer from spontaneous panic attacks; d) all of the above.

7. Which of the following is *not* a major characteristic of schizophrenia: a) the occurrence of hallucinations; b) disturbances of thought and attention; c) exaggerated emotional responses; d) decreased ability to function.

8. The most common kind of hallucinations in schizophrenia are: a) olfactory; b) auditory; c) tactile; d) visual.

9. An individual suffering from a narcissistic personality disorder: a) is overly absorbed in his or her own thoughts and fantasies; b) shows little guilt for misdoings and is often in trouble with the law; c) is preoccupied with fantasies of success and constantly seeks admiration and attention; d) is indecisive, irresponsible, and requires continual support from others.

10. The most characteristic features of antisocial personality are: a) verbal and physical aggressiveness; b) helplessness and anxiety; c) lack of empathy and guilt; d) antisocial acts and low intelligence.

Key, Chapter 16

Names

1. Aaron Beck
2. Martin Seligman

Vocabulary and Details

1. abnormal behavior
2. Diagnostic and Statistical Manual of Mental Disorders, 3rd edition, revised; DSM-III-R
3. neuroses
4. psychoses
5. psychotic behavior
6. hallucinations; delusions

1. anxiety disorders
2. generalized anxiety
3. panic disorders
4. phobia
5. obsessive-compulsive disorder
6. obsessions; compulsions
7. prepared conditioning
8. benzodiazepines

1. mood disorders
2. depressive disorders
3. bipolar disorders
4. concordance rate
5. norepinephrine, serotonin
6. monoamine oxidase (or MAO) inhibitors; tricyclic antidepressants

1. schizophrenia
2. delusions
3. delusions of influence
4. delusions of persecution
5. delusions of grandeur
6. paranoid
7. hallucinations; auditory
8. autism
9. dopamine
10. dopamine hypothesis
11. antipsychotic drugs

1. personality disorders
2. narcissistic personality disorder
3. dependent personality disorder
4. antisocial personality

Sample Quiz 16.1

1. c, 592
2. d, 598
3. b, 599
4. d, 604
5. d, 607
6. c, 613
7. b, 614
8. a, 618
9. c, 621
10. a, 628

Sample Quiz 16.2

1. b, 591-592
2. b, 596
3. a, 596-597
4. a, 600
5. b, 602
6. c, 605
7. c, 617-621
8. b, 620
9. c, 628
10. c, 629

Methods of Therapy

Learning Objectives

1. Be familiar with the historical background and current trends in the treatment of abnormal behavior.

2. Be able to specify the backgrounds and professional roles of the different specialists involved in psychotherapy.

   Be able to describe the following approaches to psychotherapy, including the therapist's techniques and the patient's or client's experiences that are presumed to yield improvement:

3. Psychoanalysis and psychoanalytic therapies.

4. Behavior therapies.

5. Cognitive behavior therapies.

6. Person-centered therapy.

7. Be familiar with the techniques, advantages, and disadvantages of group therapy and family therapy. Understand what is meant by an eclectic approach to therapy.

8. Be able to discuss the difficulties involved in evaluating the success of psychotherapeutic techniques. Know the factors, common to the various psychotherapies, that may be most important for behavior change.

9. Be familiar with the techniques, advantages, and disadvantages of the three forms of biological therapy; be able to describe the major classes of psychotherapeutic drugs.

10. Be familiar with the variety of community resources being explored as ways of enhancing mental health and with the suggestions offered for promoting your own emotional well-being.

Names

1. One individual notable as a more humane approach to mental disorders began to evolve in Europe was the Frenchman _____, who successfully unchained inmates in an asylum in Paris in the late 1700s. (637-638)

2. The individual most closely identified with classical psychoanalysis was _____. (643)

3. The psychologist who emphasizes the role that modeling may play in the course of behavior change, and also the concept of self-efficacy in cognitive behavior therapy is _____. (650, 655)

4. The famous humanistic psychotherapist who was responsible for the development of person-centered therapy was _____. (657)

Vocabulary and Details

Historical Background

1. In the mental health field, the transition from treating mentally disturbed individuals in hospitals to providing treatment in the community is called _____. (639)

Techniques of Psychotherapy

1. The treatment of mental disorders by psychological means is termed _____. (643)

2. Psychoanalysts use the technique of _____ in which a client is encouraged to give free rein to thoughts and feelings without editing or censoring. (644)

3. In Freud's terms, when a client's unconscious exerts control over sensitive material during therapy, a form of blocking or _____ has developed which indicates an area to be explored. (644)

4. Another technique used in psychoanalysis is the exploration of dreams, called _____. (644)

5. The assumption of dream analysis is that the obvious, conscious or _____ content of dreams disguises an unconscious wish or fear, the so-called _____ content. (644)

6. The tendency for a client to make a therapist the object of emotional responses that relate to important people in the client's life is known as _____. (645)

7. A hypothesis that summarizes some portion of a client's behavior and provides an explanation for its motivation in an effort to provide client *insight* is termed an _____. (645)

8. Anxiety may be reduced and realistic problem-solving may be developed in the psychoanalytic process of examining and reexamining conflicts and reexperiencing painful childhood emotions; this is termed _____. (645)

9. Psychotherapies that share Freud's conceptions of the role of unconscious conflicts and fears in mental disorders, but that differ from classical psychoanalysis along a number of dimensions are called _____ or _____. (646)

10. A number of different therapeutic methods based on the principles of learning and conditioning are collectively called _____. (646)

11. One technique of behavior therapy is _____ in which an individual is taught to relax in the presence of stimuli that have previously caused anxiety. (647-648)

12. Another method employed by behavior therapists is _____, in which successive approximations to a desired form of behavior are reinforced. (649)

13. The process by which a person learns new behaviors by observing and imitating others (through observational learning) is called _____. (650)

14. Monitoring one's own behavior and using behavioral techniques such as self-reinforcement or self-punishment to effect change is known as _____. (652)

15. _____ refers to the class of treatment methods that use behavior modification techniques as well as procedures designed to change malaptive cognitive factors, such as erroneous beliefs. (654)

16. Therapies that are based on the phenomenological approach to personality and that emphasize personal growth and self-actualization are termed _____. (656)

17. A form of humanistic psychotherapy that minimizes therapist intervention while helping clients to develop self-awareness and their own solutions to problems is called _____ (formerly _____). (657)

18. When psychotherapists do not adhere strictly to any single method of therapy, but rather select the ones they feel are most appropriate for a given client, they are said to adopt the _____ approach. (659)

19. When clients work out their problems by exploring attitudes and behaviors while interacting with others, we speak of _____. (660)

20. Two variants of group therapy are a) therapy provided to couples, called _____, and b) therapy for parents and/or their children, called _____. (661-662)

Effectiveness of Psychotherapy

1. The phenomenon called _____ refers to the fact that many people with psychological (as well as physical) problems improve without professional treatment. (664)

Biological Therapies

1. The _____ approach to treating abnormal behavior assumes that mental disorders are caused by biochemical or physiological dysfunctions of the brain. (670)

2. The most successful of the three main classes of biological therapies is the use of _____. (670)

3. Drugs that reduce anxiety, or _____ drugs, belong to the family called _____, commonly called _____. (670)

4. Most of the drugs that relieve the symptoms of schizophrenia, or _____ drugs, are in the family called _____. (671)

5. Drugs that elevate the mood of depressed individuals, or _____ drugs, include two major classes: _____ and _____. (672)

6. In the second main class of biological therapies, an electric current may be applied to the brain to produce a seizure and alleviate the symptoms of severe depression; this technique is called _____, also known as _____. (673)

7. In the third main class of biological therapies, called _____, selected areas of the brain are destroyed by cutting nerve fibers or by ultrasonic irradiation. (674)

Ideas and Concepts

Historical Background

1. Trace the views of mental disorders that prevailed in ancient times, through the height of the Greek and Roman period, and into the middle ages. (637)

* 2. a) What was an important result of Pinel's intervention with respect to the inhumane treatment of inmates in an asylum in Paris? (637-638)

* b) Describe the mental deterioration that characterizes **general paresis**. What was the main consequence of the discovery that general paresis had a physical origin for the prevailing view of mental illness? (638)

* c) List the additional contributions to the changing attitudes toward mental illness that came through the efforts of Freud, Pavlov, and Beers. (638-639)

3. a) Describe the range of facilities provided in mental hospitals today. (639)

* b) Describe the impetus for deinstitutionalization in terms of the disadvantages of hospitalization and the advent of psychotherapeutic drugs. (639)

* c) What was the national legislation in 1963 that was so important in the initiation of the dramatic trend toward deinstitutionalization and what were some of the intended results? (639-640)

d) Besides favorable consequences for some mental patients, what have been the less fortunate consequences for others of attempts to provide community-based care? (640)

*Basic ideas and concepts

* 4. a) Discuss some of the legal issues that bear on the question of whether we should revert to more institutionalization of the mentally disturbed. (640-641)

   b) What two areas of care provision are currently in need of greater support in view of evidence of their effectivenss? (641)

* 5. Distinguish among the mental health professionals listed in the following table in terms of their qualifications and usual role in psychotherapy. (641-642)

Qualifications and Activities

psychiatrist	
psychoanalyst	
clinical psychologist	
counseling psychologist	
psychiatric socialworker	
psychiatric nurse	

Techniques of Psychotherapy

* 1. What do most methods of psychotherapy have in common? Discuss how this is accomplished from the viewpoint of the client and the therapist. (643)

* 2. a) What is the assumption of the psychoanalytic theories of personality? Use the terms *id, ego*, and *superego*. (643)

   b) Using an example, illustrate how unconscious conflicts beginning in childhood can persist to cause later maladjustment. (643)

* c) In terms of psychological treatment, what is a key assumption and goal of *psychoanalysis*? (643-644)

  3. a) What kinds of transference are possible during psychoanalysis? (645)

* b) In what period of life did Freud assume that the emotions in transference originate, and what did he attempt to do with the phenomenon when it occurred? (645)

* 4. Beside client *insight*, for what purpose may interpretations be used, and why is the timing of interpretations so critical? (645)

5. How long does psychoanalysis often take and to what kinds of individuals is it generally limited for greatest effectiveness? (645-646)

* 6. a) Use the example of "ego analysis" to illustrate a more recent form of psychoanalytic psychotherapy. Indicate both the goal and strategy of the ego analysts. (646)

* b) Describe a number of ways that the techniques of psychoanalysis are modified in contemporary approaches. (646)

* 7. a) What is the assumption of behavior therapy and how does its focus differ from psychoanalysis? (646)

b) Cite an example to make the point of behavior therapists that insight may not be sufficient in achieving behavior change. (646-647)

* c) Indicate the kinds of goals and concerns of behavior therapy; contrast with those of psychoanalysis. (647)

* d) Outline the steps of behavior therapy, using examples when helpful. (647)

* 8. a) Describe the process of systematic desensitization in detail, indicating the several steps in the technique. (647-648)

b) Illustrate systematic desensitization, using the example of a client with *agoraphobia* discussed in your text. (648)

c) What variation on the method of systematic desensitization may work even better than the one used in the example in b)? (648)

* 9. a) Cite a case study to illustrate the systematic use of *positive reinforcement* in behavior therapy. Be sure to note both the reinforcement procedure and the specific behavioral effects. (648-649)

b) With an example, show how extinction may also be systematically employed in effecting behavior change. (649)

* c) Describe the application of shaping to the case of a mute child who was given behavior therapy to develop speech. (649)

d) Be sure you understand the concept of the "token economy" as it is used in some mental hospitals. (649)

* 10. a) Describe the procedures of Bandura's study comparing various treatments for snake phobia. Distinguish between the groups on the basis of each of the conditions: systematic desensitization, symbolic modeling, modeling with participation, and no training. (650)

* b) What were the outcomes of this study.? (See also Figure 17-4). (650)

11. Why is modeling effective in overcoming fears and anxieties? Exemplify. (651)

* 12. a) What is *behavior rehearsal*? How is modeling often combined with this method? (651)

*   b)   Describe the process of *assertiveness training* and show how behavior rehearsal might be helpful in this technique. (652)

*   13.   a)   When is self-regulation useful, and what is one advantage of these techniques? (652)

           b)   Provide an example of self-regulation as applied to a person with alcohol dependency. (652)

           c)   Can you think of methods of self-reinforcement and self-punishment you could apply to help in the modification of your own study behaviors? (654)

*   14.   a)   What has been the traditional attitude of behavior therapists toward cognition and how has that view been changed at the hands of cognitive behavior therapists? (654)

           b)   Describe the application of cognitive behavior therapy to a case of depression. Specifically, what cognitive behaviors are identified in the depressed individual, and in what direction are these changed? (654)

*   c)   Show how the behavioral component of this type of therapy is utilized, and cite an example. (655)

           d)   Again by example, show how behavior modification may be combined with techniques for modifying negative thoughts. (655)

*   15.   a)   What do most cognitive behavior therapists argue is important in producing enduring changes in behavior? What is considered to be a more powerful way to achieve this effect than verbal methods alone? (655)

*   b)   Using Bandura's concept of *self-efficacy,* discuss the role of performance and success in developing a sense of personal mastery. (655)

*   16.   a)   From the standpoint of humanistic therapies, why do psychological disorders arise, how are they manifested, and what are the goals of therapy? (656-657)

           b)   In what respects are humanistic therapies like psychoanalysis and how do they differ? (657)

*   17.   a)   Describe some of the characteristics of the therapeutic setting and therapist-client interaction in Rogers' person-centered therapy. (657)

           b)   What appears to be the course of client self-evaluation as person-centered therapy proceeds? (658)

*   c)   Define each of the following qualities of an effective person-centered therapist. (658)

—*empathy*:

—*warmth*:

—*genuineness*:

d) Indicate some of the limitations of person-centered therapy. (658-659)

18. a) Provide some examples to illustrate the eclectic approach to psychotherapy. (660)

*   b) What is another approach to psychotherapy, closely identified with the eclectic model, that may be adopted when it is recognized that no single approach deals successfully with all problems? Cite an example. (660)

19. a) In what kinds of settings might group therapy be used? (660)

*   b) Describe the typical group therapy situation and some variations on this theme. (660-661)

*   c) Indicate several of the advantages of group therapy over individual psychotherapy. When is a group especially effective? (661)

    d) Traditionally, who leads groups, and what is an emerging trend in this area? Cite some examples. (661)

* 20. a) Why has marital (or couples) therapy been on the increase and what does the data show with respect to its effectiveness in solving interpersonal problems relative to individual therapy? (662)

*   b) Outline some of the emphases of marital therapy. Use the term *behavioral contracts* in your answer. (662)

* 21. a) Why did family therapy originate, and what is its premise? Use the term *family system* in your answer. (663)

    b) Indicate two typical problems within a family and be able to provide examples. (663)

    c) Describe some of the methods used in family therapy. (663)

Effectiveness of Psychotherapy

* 1. a) Why is it difficult to evaluate the effectiveness of psychotherapy? (664)

*   b) In what respects is the term "spontaneous remission" not altogether appropriate when describing recovery from psychological problems? What are some of the specific resources other than professional help available to a person with psychological disorders? (664)

    c) In view of the possibility of spontaneous remission, how must psychotherapy be evaluated, and when is it judged to be effective? What ethical issue does this create and how is it dealt with? (664)

* 2. a) Besides spontaneous remission, what is a second problem in evaluating psychotherapy? Use the term "hello—goodbye effect" in your response. (664)

*   b) What three independent measures should be included in the assessment of improvement? (665)

c) Cite some examples of other outcome measures that may help in the evaluation of psychotherapy. (665)

* 3. a) Describe the procedure used in a large scale evaluation of psychotherapy evaluation studies. (665)

* b) What outcomes were obtained in this study? In addition, cite the data on improvement with psychotherapy as a function of numbers of sessions. (665)

* 4. a) What is the conclusion of most reviews of studies that have compared different psychotherapies? (665)

* b) Cite one reason for this "dodo bird verdict." Give some examples of which therapies appear to be effective with which disorders. (666-667)

* c) Cite another reason for the apparent absence of differences between different forms of therapy. (667)

* 5. Describe each of the following factors common across different psychotherapies. Use examples when they are helpful. (666-670)

—Interpersonal warmth and trust:

—Reassurance and support:

—Desensitization:

—Reinforcement of adaptive responses:

—Understanding or insight:

6. What is your authors' suggestion for the training of future psychotherapists? (670)

Biological Therapies

* 1. What was the major impact of the discoveries of the drugs that relieved some of the symptoms of schizophrenia and depression? (670)

2. a) List three common tranquilizers by trade name. (670)

b) What is the effect of tranquilizers on the central nervous system and how is this experienced? (670)

* c) Indicate some of the side effects and dangers of tranquilizers. (671)

3. a) Give the trade names of two common antipsychotic drugs. (671)

* b) Why is the term "major tranquilizer" a misnomer when applied to an antipsychotic drug? What are some of their actual side effects? (671)

* c) Discuss in detail an explanation for the effects of the antipsychotic drugs in terms of their impact on the dopamine receptors. Note also where these receptors are concentrated. (671)

* 4. a) What are the benefits of the antipsychotic drugs for treating schizophrenia, including their effects upon symptoms and relapse rate? Does this mean that these drugs "cure" the disorder? (671-672)

* b) Indicate some of the adverse side effects of the antipsychotic drugs. (672)

* 5. Describe the probable mechanisms for neurotransmitter action of the following two classes of antidepressant drugs. (Use the term *reuptake* when appropriate.) (672)

   —MAO inhibitors (e.g., Nardil and Parnate):

   —trycyclic antidepressants (e.g., Tofranil and Elavil):

6. a) Do the antidepressants produce their effects immediately? What is one implication of this fact? (672)

* b) Do the antidepressants help in treating bipolar disorders? What drug has been found to be effective? (672)

* 7. Discuss your authors' view of drug therapy in terms of its benefits and limitations. (672)

8. a) Why is the use of ECT for depression now less common and when might it still be employed? (673)

* b) List several reasons why the ECT procedure has been so controversial. (674)

   c) Describe the current application of ECT. What is one side effect and how is this alleviated? (673)

* d) Cite one possible explanation for how ECT works to relieve depression. (674)

9. a) To what parts of the brain is psychosurgery typically applied? (674)

* b) When might psychosurgery have some benefits? (674)

Enhancing Mental Health

* 1. Describe three forms of community resources that have been developed in efforts to enhance mental health. (674)

* 2. Discuss two forms of *crisis intervention* that may assist people who need immediate help. (675)

3. a) Cite some examples of the involvement of *paraprofessionals* in psychotherapy. (675-676)

b) Describe the Achievement Place residential mental health program, and indicate some of its positive outcomes. (767)

*   4.   List five ways that you can promote your own mental health. (676-678)

Sample Quiz 17.1

1. A psychiatrist: a) can prescribe medication; b) has a Ph.D. degree; c) is usually a psychoanalyst; d) all of the above.

2. Psychotherapy specifically refers to the treatment of mental disorders by: a) biological means; b) psychological means; c) the methods developed by Sigmund Freud; d) any means whatsoever.

3. Freud: a) founded psychoanalysis; b) is the father of the mental hygiene movement; c) was allowed to unchain inmates in a European asylum on an experimental basis; d) all of the above.

4. In psychoanalysis, when a client is encouraged to give free rein to thoughts and feelings without editing or censoring, we speak of: a) free association; b) transference; c) working through; d) breaking down of resistance.

5. Another name for modeling is: a) self-regulation; b) observational learning; c) shaping; d) transference.

6. In Bandura's study evaluating various treatments for snake phobia, the procedure that was most effective was: a) symbolic modeling; b) symbolic modeling combined with guided participation; c) systematic desensitization; d) no training at all.

7. Cognitive behavior therapists generally argue that cognitive processes are best altered by: a) letting clients work through their problems on their own; b) means of verbal procedures; c) means of behavioral procedures; d) none of the above; cognitive behavior therapists argue that beliefs must remain constant in order to bring about an enduring change in behavior.

8. When people with psychological problems improve without professional intervention, the phenomenon is called: a) working through; b) the Dodo bird syndrome; c) spontaneous remission; d) miraculous.

9. Which of the following has been a surprising finding in the studies investigating the effectiveness of psychotherapy: a) improvement rate is independent of number of therapy sessions; b) psychotherapies are most effective in treating schizophrenia and bipolar disorders; c) there are few differences found among the various psychotherapies in terms of effectiveness; d) individuals receiving psychotherapy are no better off than those receiving no treatment at all.

10. Which of the following statements concerning antipsychotic drugs is *false?* a) They shorten the length of time patients must be hospitalized. b) They restore

rational thought processes. c) They prevent relapse. d) They cure schizophrenia in a significant number of patients.

Sample Quiz 17.2

1. The main result of the discovery that general paresis has a physical origin is that: a) it became treatable with antipsychotic drugs; b) many patients with general paresis were eligible for treatment by M.D.'s rather than clinical psychologists; c) the view that mental disorders are biological in origin was supported; d) hospitalization insurance for victims of the disease could be obtained.

2. Most psychotherapies: a) rely on transference; b) involve a helping relationship; c) make use of biological methods; d) aim at self-actualization of the client.

3. Transference refers to: a) the disguising of unconscious wishes or fears in the manifest content of a dream; b) a technique in which a psychoanalyst encourages free expression of thoughts and feelings; c) the tendency for clients to respond emotionally to their therapist as they do to certain important people in their lives; d) the exploration of dreams in psychoanalysis.

4. The *second* step in the process of systematic desensitization is: a) establishing a hierarchy of anxiety-producing situations; b) learning to relax; c) rehearsing experiences of anxiety-arousing situations while relaxing; d) beginning an anti-anxiety drug regimen.

5. The humanistic psychologist who developed person-centered therapy was: a) Helmholtz; b) Rogers; c) Bandura; d) Maslow.

6. A form of group therapy is: a) systematic desensitization; b) marital therapy; c) family therapy; d) both b and c.

7. The term spontaneous remission as applied to psychological disorders is not really appropriate because: a) it very rarely occurs; b) it only pertains to recovery from physical disorders; c) recovery from psychological disorders is seldom "spontaneous" but usually related to some variable; d) none of the above; the term spontaneous remission is used in psychology appropriately and precisely the way it is used in the field of medicine.

8. If we wished to administer a drug that would relieve symptoms of schizophrenia, we would do best to use: a) an MAO inhibitor; b) a tricyclic; c) a tranquilizer; d) one of the phenothiazines.

9. Which of the following is *false*? a) The term "major tranquilizer" is a misnomer when applied to antipsychotic drugs. b) Certain antipsychotic drugs have been found to cure schizophrenia. c) Among the adverse side effects of antipsychotic drugs are difficulty in concentration and a kind of muscular disorder. d) Antipsychotic drugs block dopamine receptors.

10. ECT is: a) a method for destroying brain tissue with ultrasonic irradiation; b) a technique used to alleviate severe depression; c) a drug effective in treating psychoses; d) a treatment method that emphasizes changing beliefs.

Key, Chapter 17

Names

1. Phillipe Pinel
2. Sigmund Freud
3. Albert Bandura
4. Carl Rogers

Vocabulary and Details

1. deinstitutionalization

1. psychotherapy
2. free association
3. resistance
4. dream analysis
5. manifest content; latent content
6. transference
7. interpretation
8. working through
9. psychoanalytic psychotherapies, psychodynamic therapies
10. behavior therapy
11. systematic desensitization
12. shaping
13. modeling
14. self-regulation
15. cognitive-behavior therapy
16. humanistic therapies
17. person-centered therapy; client-centered therapy
18. eclectic (or integrative)
19. group therapy
20. maritial therapy; family therapy

1. spontaneous remission

1. biological
2. drugs
3. antianxiety; benzodiazepines; tranquilizers
4. antipsychotic; phenothiazines
5. antidepressant; monoamine oxidase inhibitors (or MAO inhibitors); tricyclic antidepressants
6. electroconvulsive therapy (or ECT); electroshock therapy
7. psychosurgery

Sample Quiz 17.1

1. a, 642
2. b, 643
3. a, 643
4. a, 644
5. b, 650
6. b, 650
7. c, 655

8. c, 664
9. c, 665-666
10. d, 671-672

Sample Quiz 17.2

1. c, 638
2. b, 643
3. c, 645
4. a, 648
5. b, 657
6. d, 661-662
7. c, 664
8. d, 671
9. b, 671-672
10. b, 673

Methods of Therapy   253

Social Information Processing

Learning Objectives

1. Be able to define social psychology in terms of its two major emphases.

2. Be able to describe the three tasks that we, as informal scientists, perform in constructing our intuitive theories of human behavior. Give example of the kinds of biases that influence our judgments at each stage.

3. Understand schematic processing. Show how it can lead to errors in processing social information, using the primary effect as an example.

4. Understand the function of stereotypes and show how they can be self-perpetuating and self-fulfilling.

5. Be familiar with the three criteria we use to infer causality, the distinction between dispositional and situational attributions, and the fundamental attribution error.

6. Be prepared to discuss self-perception theory, showing how some of the same processes that govern our judgments of others influence the judgments we make about ourselves.

7. Be able to define attitudes as distinct from beliefs and behavior.

8. Be familiar with the research on consistency among beliefs, among attitudes, between beliefs and attitudes, and between attitudes and behavior.

9. Be able to explain the results of induced-compliance experiments in terms of self-perception theory, cognitive dissonance theory, and impression management theory.

10. Be familiar with the four factors that determine interpersonal attraction, and with the process of social penetration through which liking moves toward intimacy.

Names

1. The founder of modern attribution theory was _____. (696)

2. We attribute self-perception theory to the social psychologist _____. (697)

3. The influential psychologist notable, in part, for his important and heuristic theory of cognitive dissonance was _____. (707)

Vocabulary and Details

1. The study of social interactions--of how we think, feel, and act with others and how, in turn, these activities are influenced by others--defines the field of _____. (683)

Intuitive Science of Social Judgments

1. The social information we attend to is influenced by the _____ of the information to which we attend; we are _____ (more/less) influenced by vivid that by pallid information of equal or greater reliability. (684)

2. Simplified representations of perceptions in memory, or memory structures, are called _____. (686)

3. The perceiving and interpreting of incoming information in terms of schemata is called _____. (686)

4. Schemata of classes of persons are called _____. (686)

5. In general, the first information we receive has the greater impact on our overall impressions; this phenomenon is called the _____. (687)

6. Schemata for events and social interactions are called _____. (688)

7. When two things vary in relation to each other, they are said to _____ or _____. (691)

8. In the intuitive science of social judgments, the act of finding such correlations between events may be called _____. (691)

9. Another term for stereotypes is _____, which refers to the fact that a stereotype is a theory about which traits go with other traits. (692)

10. Because our stereotypes lead us to interactions with others that cause them to fulfill our expectations, we speak of _____ stereotypes. (692)

11. The process by which we attempt to interpret and to explain the causes of the behavior of other people is called _____. (694-695, 720)

12. The bias toward dispositional attributions rather than situational attributions regarding the behavior of others has been termed the _____. (696)

13. A set of organized self-concepts stored in memory may be called a _____. (696)

14. According to Bem's _____ theory, we make judgments about ourselves using the same inferential processes (and making the same errors) that we use for making judgments about others. (697)

15. Studies in which pressures are brought to bear on subjects to comply with experimental procedures are called _____ experiments. (697)

Intuitive Logic of Social Attitudes

1. _____ are likes and dislikes for identifiable aspects of the environment--objects, persons, events, or ideas. (702)

2. Social psychologists regard human activities as a three-part system: Attitudes are the _____ component; beliefs are the _____ component; and actions are the _____ component. (702)

3. That we strive to be consistent in these three components of activity is the basic premise of the _____ theories in social psychology. (703)

4. A basic attitude toward modes of conduct or states of existence is termed a _____. (704)

5. According to the approach called _____, when a person's cognitions are mutually inconsistent, the discomfort produced by this dissonance motivates the person to make the cognitions consistent with one another. (707)

Social Personality of Interpersonal Attraction

1. Liking has been shown to be a function of a number of variables; among them are _____, _____, _____, and _____. (711)

2. A theory of decision making that operates in the area of interpersonal attraction is _____, which states that we consider both the value of a reward as well as the expectancy of obtaining the reward when making a choice. (714)

3. Three dimensions that have been used in the assessment of romantic love are _____, _____, and _____. (716)

4. Liking and early infatuation can progress to greater intimacy in a relationship through _____, a process of coming to know and share areas of life both broadly and deeply. (716)

5. The key to social penetration is when two partners reveal themselves to each other in what is referred to as _____. (716)

6. During romance, the state in which emotions are intense and mixed (e.g., elation with pain and anxiety with relief) is called _____. (717)

7. In contrast, attachment to another person characterized by trust, caring, and tolerance, and emotions of affection and warmth is called _____. (717-718)

Ideas and Concepts

* 1. On what two fundamental observations does social psychology base its approach? (683)

Intuitive Science of Social Judgments

* 1. a) What do your authors mean when they say that "we are all psychologists"? In what three basic tasks do we engage that are essentially the same as those of the formal scientist? Cite examples. (683)

     b) What would happen if our intuitive attempts to apply science to everyday life did not work? Does this mean that we never make errors in social judgments? Explain. (683-684)

* 2. Discuss three sources of nonrepresentativeness and nonrandomness that may pervade the everyday collection of social data. (684)

* 3. a) Discuss a study of the effects of vividness of information on selection of psychology courses. What variable in particular influenced the students? (684)

     b) Cite another experiment that compared vivid and nonvivid testimony of attorneys in a mock trial. At what point in the experiment did the effect of vividness become notable? (684-685)

*   c) Summarize the conditions under which the vividness effect has appeared in several studies and what this seems to imply concerning the mechanism involved. (685)

     d) When does the vividness effect pose a special problem? Can you think of an example from your own experience? (685)

* 4. a) What do schemata and schematic processing enable us to do? (686)

     b) Are we actively aware of using schematic processing? (686)

  5. a) Cite an observation to show that schemata help us to process information. (686)

*   b) What is the "price we pay" for efficiency gained through the use of schemata? Give an example, including the term *primacy effect* in your answer. (686-687)

     c) Illustrate the primacy effect as it applies to subjects who observed a student solve problems. (687)

     d) Of what is the primacy effect mainly a consequence? Explain. (687)

  6. Whereas in the primacy effect a preexisting schema can affect how we interpret new data, show by an example how a new schema can affect the recall of old data. (687-688)

*Basic ideas and concepts

258   Chapter 18

*   7.   a)   Give some examples of scripts from the text and from your own experience. What is their function? (688)

*   b)   Discuss a study that shows the power of scripts in influencing the behavior of others at a copy machine and your authors' explanation for the obtained results. (688-690)

*   8.   a)   Describe an experimental demonstration showing that the presentation of data may solidify a person's previous views irrespective of whether the data is supportive or nonsupportive. To what disturbing implication of these findings do your authors point? (690)

          b)   Outline a real-life demonstration of how strongly held beliefs may influence the interpretation of information. (691)

*   9.   a)   Give one or two examples of detecting covariation. In general, does research show that are we good at this task? How does having and not having a theory, respectively, influence our behavior? (691)

*   b)   Discuss a study of clinical assessment to demonstrate the difficulty that may be encountered when a person holds a preexisting theory regarding covariation. (691)

          c)   Outline a follow-up experiment performed with college students that came to the same conclusion as that in the above study. (692)

* 10.   a)   Why do stereotypes have a bad reputation? Does this mean that they are evil in themselves? Discuss, and provide an example. (692)

*   b)   Cite a two-part study to show, first, that stereotypes affect the interactions of interviewers with people of different races and, second, that prejudicial behavior towards others can, in turn, induce stereotyped reactions in them. (692-693)

* 11.   a)   Discuss the impact of the stereotype of the physically attractive person upon judgment by subjects of an attractive person's other characteristics. (693)

*   b)   Describe an experiment that showed that the belief held by one person that another person was attractive may have a self-fulfilling effect upon both parties. (693)

          c)   What is one line of evidence for self-fulfilling stereotypes of physical attractiveness in the real world? Discuss some additional relationships between attractiveness and other characteristics. (693-694)

* 12.   a)   Discuss the use of each of the following criteria in the attempt to infer causality for behavior from covariation. Use an example. (695)

          —*distinctiveness*:

          —*consistency* :

          —*consensus*:

b) Do we use these criteria correctly or sufficiently? Why or why not? (695)

* 13. a) Distinguish between *internal* or *dispositional attributions* and *external* or *situational attributions* in inferences regarding the behavior of others. (696)

* b) With respect to which of these two types of attributions people tend to favor, what did Heider contend and what is the trend of the evidence? (696)

c) Describe the results of several studies demonstrating the power of the fundamental attribution error. (696)

* 14. Discuss each of the following functions of self-schema, using examples when possible. (696-697)

—efficient information processing:

—attending to and recalling information about ourselves:

—interactions with other schemata:

* 15. a) Outline the procedures of a well-known "cognitive dissonance" experiment by Festinger and Carlsmith designed to show the effects of different sizes of incentives on self-perception in a task involving induced compliance. (697-698)

* b) What results were obtained in this study and how would self-perception theory account for them? (698)

c) How did the subjects in this study commit the fundamental attribution error? (698)

16. a) Describe another experiment in which subjects played the role of questioner or contestant in a contrived quiz game. How did both the contestant and an independent observer rate the general knowledge of the players in the game? (699)

b) What kind of judgment error do these results demonstrate? Discuss the implications of these findings for sex-role differences and for maximizing one's apparent knowledgability in daily interactions with others. (699)

* 17. a) What two "selves" are implied by self-perception theory? (699)

b) How does this notion of distinct selves accord with Ernest Hilgard's idea of the "hidden observer"? (700)

* c) Discuss the possibility that the two hemispheres of the brain provide an anatomical basis for the distinction between the intuitive subject-self and the interpretive psychologist-self. (700)

d) Cite some observations of "split-brain" patients that add support to the notion of a left-brain interpreter. (700-701)

18. Cite one additional study to demonstrate that people sometimes identify plausible but inaccurate causes for their emotional states. (702)

Intuitive Logic of Social Attitudes

1. Be sure you understand the concept of attitudes by citing a few examples. (702)

* 2. Explain why this is a section on our adequacy as "intuitive logicians." That is, what is the appropriate (and inappropriate) question to ask about attitudes? (702)

3. a) Describe two examples of apparently disparate political and social attitudes that seem to be bound together by "psycho-logic." (702)

* b) From the standpoint of the cognitive consistency theories, what happens if there is inconsistency among attitudes, cognitions, and behaviors? (703)

* 4. Describe the methods and results of a study that investigated the degree to which beliefs follow the rules of formal logic. Use the term *logical syllogism* in your answer. (703-704)

5. a) What is meant when it is said that values "refer to ends, not means"? (704)

* b) Describe a study of individuals during the time of civil rights demonstrations that illustrates the point that people holding different opinions may share many values but assign different degrees of importance to them. (704)

c) Discuss a follow-up study in which efforts were made to change the subjects' values. (704-705)

6. a) Cite some examples to show that consistency between beliefs and attitudes is quite common. (705)

* b) Distinguish between the processes of *rationalization* and *wishful thinking* in the efforts we make to render our cognitions and attitudes consistent with one another. (705)

* c) What kind of consistency is produced by either rationalization or wishful thinking? (705)

* d) Discuss a demonstration of a form of wishful thinking that helped to produce consistency between attitudes induced during hypnosis and subsequent beliefs outside of hypnosis. (705)

* 7. a) What is a major reason for studying attitudes? Does this view have any support? Illustrate. (706)

* b) By contrast, describe a case in which attitudes and behaviors did not appear to be consistent. (706)

* c) What does the study outlined in b) illustrate, and what are two possible additional factors in attitude-behavior consistency? (706)

* 8. Indicate the three conditions under which attitudes predict behavior best and provide related examples. (706-707)

—*i:*

—*ii:*

—*iii:*

*   9.   a)   In what area has Festinger's cognitive dissonance theory generated especially provocative predictions? (708)

*   b)   Review the Festinger and Carlsmith experiment covered earlier in this *Study Guide* (item 15 in the previous section) for its implications regarding the role of dissonance in motivating attitude change. (708)

*   c)   What general conclusion may be drawn from the Festinger and Carlsmith study? Cite an additional observation on the role of amount of pressure used in inducing compliance in relation to attitude change. (708)

*   10.   a)   Contrast the views of the following theories designed to explain the results of such induced-compliance studies. (708-709)

        —*cognitive dissonance theory:*

        —*self-perception theory:*

        —*impression management theory:*

        b)   What level of support has each of these views received, and what should be the direction of future related research? (709)

  11.   a)   Give some examples of nonconsistency outside the laboratory in the following areas. (709-710)

        —social issues:

        —political issues:

*   b)   What appears to be the norm with respect to consistency of beliefs and attitudes? (710)

*   c)   What is an *opinion molecule*? Provide examples. (710)

*   d)   Cite three important social functions served by opinion molecues. (710)

Social Personality of Interpersonal Attraction

*   1.   a)   How do people rank *physical attractiveness* in surveys of what is important in their liking of other people? Does the evidence support their expressed attitudes? Cite a related study that used a computer dating method to match subjects. (711)

b) Is the importance of physical attractiveness related only to dating and to people of one's own age? Cite the evidence. (711)

* c) Give two reasons why physical attractiveness is so important. Discuss some studies to support the second reason, including a result that shows some limitations on the importance of attractiveness. (711-712)

d) Why is there still "hope for the unbeautiful"? (712)

* 2. a) Summarize the evidence obtained in a study of marriage license applications and in three other studies involving neighbors and roommates that demonstrate the importance of *proximity* in liking. (712)

b) When does the proximity-liking relationship appear to fail and why is this not likely to impact on most encounters between people? (712)

* 3. a) What is a major reason for the relationship between proximity and liking? Use examples to demonstrate the *familiarity breeds liking* phenomenon. (713)

b) Cite a study showing that mere exposure to faces may affect liking. (713)

c) In response to your authors' query, are you able to guess why people prefer reversed prints of themselves whereas others prefer nonreversed prints of the same photos? (713)

* 4. a) While "opposites" may think they attract each other, what does the data show? Cite a number of related observations on the effects of *similarity*. (713)

b) What role does physical attractiveness play in the effects of similarity as determined in a study of independent ratings of the attractiveness of couples? (714)

* 5. a) Apply the expectancy-value theory to why people choose others of similar attractiveness for partners. (714)

b) What other dimensions of similarity may be important in a relationship over the long term? Cite a study that provided some results that favored the importance of similarity in married couples. (714-715)

* c) Give two reasons why similarity produces liking. (715)

* 6. a) Despite the trends in the data discussed in items 4 and 5, under what conditions might opposites attract? Use the term *need-complementarity hypothesis* in your answer. (715)

* b) What is a common limitation and what is a major problem with the need-complementarity hypothesis? (715)

* 7. a) In what ways do investigations by Rubin and other love researchers show that love is more than just intense liking? (716)

* 8. a) Describe the early process of reciprocal self-disclosure in the development of relationships using the expression *norm of reciprocity* . What happens if self-disclosure proceeds too rapidly? (716)

* b) Discuss the pattern of self-disclosure evident in romantic relationships in current times. How does this compare with the social norms on self-disclosure in previous generations? (716)

* 9. a) Cite some statistics to document the trend of attitudes with regard to the importance of romantic love in marriage over the past 25 years. (717)

* b) Despite such attitudes, which form of love, passionate or companionate, appears to be dominant in long-term relationships? Discuss the results of a related study of marriages in two cultures. (718)

Sample Quiz 18.1

1. Social psychology bases its approach to the study of social interactions on the observation that: a) if people define situations as real, the consequences will be real; b) people use different inferential processes to judge themselves than they do to judge others; c) human behavior is a function of both the person and the situation; d) both a and c.

2. With regard to detecting covariation: a) research shows that we are good at the task; b) theories lead us to underestimate covariation; c) when we do not have a theory, we overestimate covariation; d) none of the above.

3. When a person who studies long hours and does well on an examination is said to have gotten a high score simply because he or she is so "intelligent," we have an example of a probable: a) fundamental attribution error; b) self-perpetuating stereotype; c) problem in cognitive consistency; d) none of the above.

4. In the Festinger and Carlsmith study in which some subjects were paid to tell others that a dull task was fun, the subjects who later rated the task as most enjoyable where those who: a) paid the smaller amount; b) paid the larger amount; c) were in the control group who did not have to talk to others; d) actually found the task fun at the start.

5. Likes and dislikes for aspects of the environment are: a) attitudes; b) expectancies; c) attributions; d) schemata.

6. In wishful thinking: a) because we believe that something is desirable, we persuade ourselves that it is true; b) because we believe that something is true, we persuade ourselves that it is desirable; c) because something is real and desirable, we persuade ourselves that we want it; d) because we want something, we persuade ourselves that it is real and desirable.

7. The view in social psychology that the discomfort from mutually inconsistent cognitions motivates behavior to render the cognitions consistent is called: a) cognitive dissonace theory; b) attribution theory; c) primacy theory; d) expectancy value theory.

264   Chapter 18

8. The need-complementarity hypothesis: a) postulates that people with complementary needs may attract and do well together; b) is not well supported by the data; c) works best if there is a basic similarity of attitudes favoring the complementary needs; d) all of the above.

9. Which of the following has *not* been a dimension used in the assessment of romantic love: a) a sense of trust; b) a sense of attachment; c) a sense of caring; d) the degree of sexual attraction.

10. Social penetration refers specifically to: a) gaining entry into a social group; b) the degree to which an external goal motivates a group by "penetrating" the group's value structure; c) the fact that "vivid" social information is more likely to penetrate our attention than "pallid" information; d) coming to know and share areas of life.

Sample Quiz 18.2

1. The vividness effect seems to occur: a) under all circumstances; b) only when the vivid information is presented in the early part of the message; c) only when the vivid information is consistent with preestablished schemata; d) only when both a vivid and a nonvivid presentation compete for our attention simultaneously.

2. Stereotypes are called self-fulfilling because they: a) indicate which traits go with which other traits; b) reduce stress by producing cognitive consistency; c) lead us to interactions with others that cause them to meet our expectations; d) result in feelings of self-satisfaction as we view ourselves as better off than others.

3. Attribution is: a) the process by which we attempt to interpret and explain the causes of the behavior of others; b) the assignment of characteristics to an individual on the basis of preconceived stereotypes; b) the perceiving and interpreting of incoming information in terms of schemata; d) the bias toward dispositional rather than situational explanations regarding the attitudes of others.

4. Which of the following is *not* a criterion employed when attempting to determine if the covariation between two events reflects the fact that one is causing the other: a) consistency; b) vividness of the events; c) consensus; d) distinctiveness of reactions.

5. That we make judgments about ourselves using the same inferential processes we employ when making judgments of others is the basic tenet of: a) self-perception theory; b) cognitive dissonance theory; c) cognitive consistency theory; d) expectancy-value theory.

6. According to your text, the appropriate question to ask about attitudes is: a) are they right or wrong; b) are they held by others; c) are they consistent with one another, associated beliefs, and associated actions; d) are they accurate or inaccurate.

7. Attitudes predict behavior best when they are: a) based upon indirect experience; b) specifically related to the behavior being predicted; c) weak and inconsistent; d) all of the above.

8. Leon Festinger is noted for his theory of: a) self-perception; b) attribution; c) passionate love; d) cognitive dissonance.

9. Which of the following statements concerning reciprocal self disclosure in the development of romantic relationships is true: a) Self disclosure takes place earlier in relationships today than it did in earlier years; b) self disclosure is one of the final stages in the development of a relationship; c) the pacing of self disclosure does not appear to be a very important variable--that it occurs at all is what really matters; d) all of the above.

10. During romance, the state in which emotions are intense and mixed is called: a) companionate love; b) infatuation; c) passionate love; d) puppy love.

Key, Chapter 18

Names

1. Fritz Heider
2. Daryl Bem
3. Leon Festinger

Vocabulary and Details

1. social psychology

1. vividness; more
2. schemata
3. schematic processing
4. stereotypes
5. primacy effect
6. scripts
7. covary; correlate
8. detecting covariation
9. implicit personality theories
10. self-fulfilling
11. attribution
12. fundamental attribution error
13. self-schema
14. self-perception
15. induced compliance

1. attitudes
2. affective; cognitive; behavioral
3. cognitive consistency
4. value
5. cognitive dissonance theory

1. physical attractiveness; proximity;
   familiarity; similarity
2. expectancy-value theory
3. a sense of attachment; a sense of caring; a
   sense of trust
4. social penetration
5. reciprocal self-disclosure
6. passionate love
7. companionate love

Sample Quiz 18.1

1. d, 683
2. d, 691
3. a, 696
4. a, 698
5. a, 702
6. a, 705
7. a, 707
8. d, 715
9. d, 716
10. d, 716

Sample Quiz 18.2

1. d, 685
2. c, 692
3. a, 694-695, 720
4. b, 695
5. a, 697
6. c, 702
7. b, 706
8. d, 707
9. a, 716
10. c, 717

Social Influence

Learning Objectives

1. Be able to distinguish among the three basic processes of social influence.

2. Be able to discuss the research on social facilitation and explain the findings in terms of drive level, mere presence, distraction-conflict theory, and self-presentation theory.

3. Understand how the concept of deindividuation explains mob behavior, including the variables assumed to contribute to and result from this hypothetical state.

4. Be familiar with the factors that determine whether a bystander will intervene in an emergency situation. Be able to differentiate between "pluralistic ignorance" and "diffusion of responsibility."

5. Be able to discuss the Asch studies on social norms and conformity; understand the factors that lead to conformity and those that reduce it.

6. Be able to describe the Milgram studies on obedience to authority and the four factors that contributed to the high obedience rates.

7. Understand the circumstances that can undermine obedience and produce rebellion as identified in the MHRC study.

8. Be able to describe the qualities that a source of influence must have in order to obtain internalization (actual belief or attitude change) and the factors that enable a minority to influence the majority.

9. Be prepared to describe cognitive response theory and show how it explains some of the phenomena of persuasion discussed in the text.

10. Be able to distinguish between the central and peripheral routes that persuasion can take in producing attitude and belief change.

11. Know what is meant by identification with a reference group. Be familiar with the findings of the Bennington study.

Names

1. An important figure in the recent history of social psychology known, in part, for his classic research on conformity was _____. (734)

2. A more recent social psychologist who has contributed to our understanding of the factors that determine obedience to authority is _____. (737)

Vocabulary and Details

1. The way in which an individual's thoughts, feelings, and behaviors are influenced by others is the study of _____. (723)

2. Implicit rules and expectations that dictate what we ought to think and how we ought to behave are called _____. (723)

3. Three processes of social influence have been identified; one is _____, in which the person conforms outwardly to the wishes of the influencing source but does not change private beliefs or attitudes. (723)

4. In the second process of social influence, termed _____, a person changes his or her beliefs, attitudes, or behaviors because of a genuine belief in the validity of the position advocated by the influencing source. (723)

5. The third process of social influence is called _____, in which a person changes his or her beliefs, attitudes, or behaviors in order to identify with or be like a source of influence that is respected or admired. (723)

Presence of Others

1. When a person performs a task faster in the presence of another person who is working on the task we speak of the influence of _____. (724)

2. Even the presence of a positive spectator--an _____ rather than a coactor--will often facilitate performance. (724)

3. This enhancement of performance due to coaction or the presence of an audience is termed _____. (724)

4. A state in which individuals feel that they have lost their personal identities and have merged into the group is called _____. (727)

5. The presence of other people may prevent bystanders from intervening in an emergency in two ways: by _____ as a nonemergency; and by _____ the responsibility for acting. (729)

6. A theory designed to summarize many of the phenomena of social influence, termed the _____, postulates that the social impact of an influence on a target individual a) _____ (increases/decreases) with the number, immediacy, and importance of the sources of influence, and b) _____ (increases/decreases) as the number, immediacy, or importance of targets increase. (732, 760)

270   Chapter 19

Compliance

1. When a source of social influence obtains compliance by setting an example, it is called _____. (734)

2. When a source of influence obtains compliance by wielding authority, it is called _____. (734)

3. A set of beliefs and attitudes is an _____. (741)

Internalization

1. The actual change in beliefs and attitudes obtained through internalization is function of two factors: a) a message that is _____ and b) a persuader who possesses both _____ and _____. (745-746)

2. In the area of persuasion, the theory termed _____ proposes that persuasion induced by communication is actually self-persuasion produced by the thoughts that the person generates while reading or hearing the communication. (747)

3. Beliefs that are so widely held that nobody thinks of questioning them are called _____. (749)

4. Persuasion can take two routes in producing belief and attitude change. In one, called the _____, the individual responds to the substantive arguments of a communication. (750)

5. In the other route to persuasion, called the _____, the individual responds to either a) noncontent cues or b) context cues of a communication. (750)

6. According to the view called the _____ of persuasion, when an issue is of little personal relevance or when people are unwilling or unable to respond to the content of a communication, they will use simple heuristics, or _____, to judge its merits. (751)

Identification

1. Groups with whom we identify are called our _____. (756)

Ideas and Concepts

* 1. a) Provide examples of social influence, including some that are indirect or unintentional, that stem from social norms. Upon what does the success of direct and deliberate social influence often depend? (723)

   b) In what broad sense is social influence dealt with in this chapter? Use the terms *actual, imagined,* and *implied presence* of others. (723)

*Basic ideas and concepts

Presence of Others

* 1. a) Describe Triplett's early observations of social facilitation and several more recent ones. (724)

* b) In what two respects is this effect of social influence more complex than a simple facilitation of performance? (724)

* 2. a) Discuss Zajonc's motivational explanation for these different patterns of effects due to coactors and audiences. (724)

* b) Outline an experiment conducted with cockroaches in support of this interpretation. (724-725)

c) Cite some additional observations on human subjects that also confirm Zajonc's theory of social facilitation. (725)

* 3. a) Discuss some findings that suggest that the variable operating to produce social facilitation at the human level is a cognitive one rather than the mere presence of others. (725-726)

b) What is one problem with the type of studies discussed in a)? What procedures were used to address this difficulty in another experiment, and what results were obtained? (726)

* 4. Distinguish between the two other theories of social facilitation discussed in your text. What is the status of the research on these views? (726)

—*distraction-conflict theory:*

—*self-presentation theory:*

* 5. a) Outline LeBon's dim view of the influence of a mob or crowd on the behavior of the individual member. (727)

* b) Discuss the antecedents and consequents of the more modern concept of deindividuation, as proposed by Diener. In this view, of what is deindividuation the direct result? (727)

* 6. a) Describe an experiment by Zimbardo that showed apparent effects of anonymity on aggression in college women. (727-728)

b) Outline another study that took advantage of the natural anonymity and deindividuation that occurs at Halloween. (728)

* c) Discuss a follow-up to the Zimbardo study in a) that attempted to replicate his findings on anonymity and also explore the effects of the roles that costumes confer on the wearer. Does anonymity necessarily enhance aggression? (728-729)

* 7. Besides deindividuation, what are two other factors that may operate to influence behavior when people are acting within a group? (729)

272   Chapter 19

8. a) What aspects of the Kitty Genovese incident led to the notion of "bystander apathy"? (729)

*   b) What are four reasons why the term "apathy" may not be accurate when applied to bystanders; that is, why it is surprising that "anyone should intervene [in an emergency] at all"? (729)

9. a) What is a common way to deal first with the ambiguity of many emergency situations? (730)

*   b) What is a state of *pluralistic ignorance,* and what two forms may it take? (730)

*   c) Describe an experiment to demonstrate the effects of pluralistic ignorance in leading some subjects to apparently conclude that "where there is smoke there is not necessarily fire." (730)

    d) What may have been another factor operating to produce the results of this study and how was that possibility addressed in a subsequent experiment? (730-731)

* 10. Outline the methods and results of Latané and Darley's ingenious study that investigated the tendency for the presence of others to diffuse responsibility in an emergency. (731)

* 11. What happens to bystander intervention if pluralistic ignorance and diffusion of responsibility are both minimized in an emergency situation? Discuss a study with a more optimistic outcome that took place on a subway train. (731-732)

12. a) Describe a study demonstrating the role of models in enhancing bystander intervention. (733)

    b) Besides actual models, what else may may enhance the likelihood of people helping in an emergency? Again, cite a demonstration. (734)

Compliance

*   1. Why do people "conform" to or "obey" a source of social influence? (734)

*   2. a) Describe the general procedures of the Asch experiments on conformity. (734)

*   b) What startling results did Asch obtain, and what was one line of explanation for why the subjects' confidence in their decision-making ability did not prevail? (735-736)

*   3. a) Discuss the impact of dissension from a majority and why it generates such strong pressures to conform in this type of situation. (736)

*   b) Indicate several additional observations made by Asch and his co-workers when a "dissenter" was added to the influencing group in some conformity studies. (736)

    c) Explain why Asch used a task in which the correct answer was obvious. (736)

* 4. a) Does an analysis of the people and events in Nazi Germany during World War II support a picture of a group of "psychopathic monsters" assembled to commit atrocities? Discuss, and cite Arendt's controversial conclusion. (736-737)

* b) What more recent event appears to provide additional support for this conclusion? (737)

* 5. a) Discuss in detail the procedures and the striking major result of the well-known Milgram experiments on obedience to authority. (737-739)

b) What was Milgram's explanation for the the general phenomenon of obedience? (739)

* c) Discuss the following four factors that influence obedience, providing definitions in your own words, methods by which each factor was manipulated in Milgram's research, and related findings where possible. (739-741)

	Definition	Manipulation and Results (where possible)
social norms		
surveillance		
buffers		
ideological justification		

6. a) Cite a demonstration of obedience to authority in everyday life. (741-743)

* 7. a) What is one reason that compliance experiments yield so much conformity and obedience? Therefore, what alternative procedure should reduce obedience, in accordance with social impact theory. (743)

b) Cite two variations on the Milgram experiments providing some indication of variables that may counter obedience. (743)

* c) Discuss an experiment by Gamson and colleagues that went further in demonstrating substantial rebellion among participants. (743-744)

* d) What variable was probably operating to produce the differences between the results obtained in this study and those that were characteristic of Milgram's obedience studies? (744)

8. Discuss the meaning of your authors' contention that many of the subjects in the Gamson et al. study "were not choosing between obedience and autonomy but between obedience and conformity." (745)

Internalization

* 1. a) What has been a criticism by European investigators of American research on conformity? (746)

* b) In terms of experimental procedures, how have these researchers gone about making their point that minorities can influence majorities? (746)

* c) What has been the general finding of these studies and others on minority influence? What characteristics of the minorities enhance these effects? (746)

* d) Discuss an even more interesting outcome of this research, and cite one related demonstration. (746-747)

2. Cite your authors' general conclusions from these findings. (747)

* 3. a) What does cognitive response theory predict with respect to the process of persuasion under these two conditions? (748)

—the communication evokes supportive thoughts:

—the communication evokes unsupportive thoughts:

b) Cite some observations relative to this theory. (748)

* 4. Show how the cognitive response theory helps to integrate the findings relative to each of the following phenomena of persuasion. (748-749)

	Findings	Explanation
one-sided versus two-sided communication		
inoculation against persuasion		
forewarning		

5. Describe a practical application of cognitive response theory to behaviors of seventh- and eighth-graders. (750)

6. Distinguish by example between noncontent cues and context cues in communication. (750)

* 7. a) When is the central route to persuasion available and when is the peripheral route available? (750)

*	b)	What is one factor that can influence which route to persuasion will be available? Outline the procedures of a study by Petty and Cacciopo demonstrating the effects of high personal involvement in a communication. (Be sure you can explain the differential effects upon attitudes owing to strong as opposed to weak arguments.) See also Figure 19-7. (750-751)

*	c)	Apply the heuristic theory of persuasion to the pattern of effects obtained in the Petty and Cacciopo study when the subjects had low personal involvement in the communication. See also Figure 19-8. (751-752)

*	8.	a)	Illustrate with the example of pharmaceutical advertising that the mass media can have a persuasive effect. What is your authors' account of why this kind of persuasion works? (752-753)

	b)	In contrast, cite some observations that support the contention that, in general, "the effectiveness of media persuasion looks unimpressive." (753)

*	c)	Be sure you understand how each of the following limiting factors in the effectiveness of media persuasion operate. Provide examples. (753-754)

	—"nobody is watching":

	—selective exposure:

	—selective attention:

	—selective interpretation:

*	9.	a)	Discuss the methods and results of the Stanford Heart Disease Prevention Program as a demonstration of the effectiveness of mass media persuasion in reducing risk of heart disease. (755)

*	b)	What were the results of a related study in which a group of individuals at high risk for heart disease were given additional sessions of individual counseling? (755-756)

*	c)	To what factor do your authors' attribute the success of this application of the media to social persuasion, that is, what is the key to internalization? (756)

Identification

*	1.	a)	Why are some groups called reference groups? What additional function may they serve? (756)

	b)	Give an example of the impact that a reference group may have on beliefs. (756-757)

	c)	Does an individual have to be a member of a reference group in order to influenced by it? Cite examples. (757)

*	2.	a)	Indicate a consequence of the fact that most of us have more than one reference group. Cite an example. (757)

    *   b) Discuss in detail the classic Bennington study of the impact of a reference group on political attitudes, noting especially the impact of duration of exposure to the reference group. (757-758)

3. a) On what initial process are our most important beliefs and attitudes probably based? Illustrate the transition from this process to internalization that takes place in college. (758-759)

    *   b) What is an advantage of internalization over compliance? Cite a follow-up to the Bennington study to demonstrate this advantage in a real social context. (759)

    *   c) Besides internalization, note the way in which the particular reference groups of the Bennington women were also important in determining their political attitudes. (759)

Sample Quiz 19.1

1. Implicit rules and expectations that dictate how we ought to think and behave are called: a) heuristics; b) ideologies; c) social norms; d) cultural truisms.

2. In a social facilitation experiment employing cockroaches, it was found that cockroaches took longer to run a simple maze if they were: a) alone; b) joined by another cockroach; c) watched by other cockroaches enclosed in plexiglass boxes; d) verbally encouraged to run faster by the experimenter.

3. A state in which individuals feel they have lost their personal identities and have merged into the group is known as: a) identification; b) deindividuation; c) social diffusion; d) internalization.

4. When diffusion of responsibility is operating in an emergency situation, the greater the number of bystanders: a) the more people are likely to help; b) the faster help is likely to be forthcoming; c) the less likely help is to be offered; d) both a and b.

5. Wielding authority is to setting an example as: a) central routes are to peripheral routes; b) coaction is to audience; b) social influence is to social norms; d) obedience is to conformity.

6. Which of the following statements concerning the Milgram experiments on obedience is *false?* a) The percentage of individuals following orders decreased when the experimenter was out of the room. b) The more direct the subject's experience with the victim, the less likely the subject was to obey. c) The ideology which legitimized the orders given was "the importance of science." d) Only a small minority of subjects continued to obey throughout the entire experiment.

7. Beliefs so widely held that no one thinks of questioning them are called: a) delusions; b) cultural truisms; c) doctrines; d) ideologies.

8. Under what circumstances is the central route to persuasion most likely to be available: a) when the individual has low personal involvement in the issue; b) when the individual has the ability to generate thoughts in response to the substantive aspects of the communication; c) when the individual employs heuristics to infer the validity of the argument; d) both b and c.

9. Groups with which we identify are our: a) coaction groups; b) compliance groups; c) reference groups; d) deindividuated groups.

10. Which of the following findings of the Bennington study on college-student attitudes illustrates that internalization was taking place, not simply compliance: a) some women attributed their attitude change to the seeking of approval from faculty and advanced students; b) the longer students remained at Bennington, the more their attitudes resembled those of the college community; c) attitudes developed in college were found to be maintained 25 years later; d) women's attitudes tended to be similar to those of their husbands when they later married.

Sample Quiz 19.2

1. In the process of social influence termed _____, a person changes their beliefs, attitudes, or actions because of a genuine belief in the validity of another person's position: a) internalization; b) identification; c) compliance; d) conformity.

2. Deindividuation refers specifically to: a) conforming outwardly but not inwardly to the wishes of an influencing source; b) changing beliefs because of a genuine conviction that the position of an influencing source is valid; c) loss of personal identity in a group; d) facilitation of performance due to coaction.

3. The theory of social facilitation that states that the presence of others enhances a person's desire to present a favorable image is termed the: a) self-presentation theory; b) narcissism theory; c) distraction-conflict theory; d) social desirability theory.

4. The term "apathy" may not be appropriate when applied to bystanders in emergencies because: a) we are often unprepared for emergencies; b) we tend to assess deterrents unrealistically; c) "getting involved" usually does not entail significant commitments in terms of time or other entanglements; d) none of the above; the term "apathy" is probably the best descriptor of the reason for failure to respond in an emergency.

5. According to social impact theory, the impact of an influencing source on a target increases as the _____ of the target increases: a) number; b) immediacy; c) importance; d) none of the above; these features of the target will *reduce* the social impact of an influencing source.

6. An analysis of events in Nazi Germany by a social philosopher supports the view that those who committed the concentration camp atrocities were: a) a group of psychopaths; b) a select group of individuals who were very susceptible to the reinforcing effects of suffering in others; c) ordinary people following orders; d) a group of individuals distinguished primarily by abnormal profiles on a personality inventory.

7. The social psychologist who has contributed significantly to our understanding of the factors controlling conformity is: a) Milgram; b) Festinger; c) Heider; d) Bem.

8. Cognitive response theory predicts that when communications evoke unsupportive thoughts, the individual to whom they are directed: a) will shift away from the

278   Chapter 19

position being advocated; b) will shift toward the position being advocated; c) will remain unconvinced; d) either a or c.

9. Research has shown that counterarguments against persuasion can be fostered by: a) two-sided communication; b) forewarning that a communication is about to be received; c) writing an "inoculating" essay refuting the counterargument; d) all of the above.

10. People are observed to use rules-of-thumb (heuristics) when: a) a source of social influence sets an example; b) they are unwilling or unable to respond to the content of a message; c) a persuader wields authority; d) in the presence of an coactor or audience.

Key, Chapter 19

Names

1. Solomon Asch
2. Stanley Milgram

Vocabulary and Details

1. social influence
2. social norms
3. compliance
4. internalization
5. identification

1. coaction
2. audience
3. social facilitation
4. deindividuation
5. defining the situation; diffusing
6. social impact theory; increases; decreases

1. conformity
2. obedience
3. ideology

1. compelling (or persuasive); expertise; trustworthiness
2. cognitive response theory
3. cultural truisms
4. central route
5. peripheral route
6. heuristic theory; rules of thumb

1. reference groups

8. d, 748
9. d, 748-749
10. b, 751

Sample Quiz 19.1

1. c, 723
2. a, 724-725
3. b, 727
4. c, 731
5. d, 734
6. d, 739-741
7. b, 749
8. b, 750-751
9. c, 756
10. c, 759

Sample Quiz 19.2

1. a, 723
2. c, 727
3. a, 726
4. a, 729
5. d, 732
6. c, 737
7. a, 737

280   Chapter 19